CONTRACT LAW OF QATAR

As Qatar's aspirations of becoming a key location for international dispute settlement and international trade grow, so too does the importance of understanding private law in Qatar and the Gulf states. In this innovative book, Ilias Bantekas and Ahmed Al-Ahmed provide an original, English-language treatise on the contract law of Qatar. Using an abundance of case law, the authors combine scholarly and practice-oriented expertise to develop a comprehensive treatment of Qatari contract law. The analysis is drawn from a wealth of judgements from the Qatari Court of Cassation and Court of Appeal, much of which was previously inaccessible to readers. Bringing sophisticated, detailed insights on Qatari law to an English-speaking legal audience, this is a vital text for academics, practitioners and students who wish to comprehend this increasingly influential global player. This title is available as Open Access on Cambridge Core.

Ilias Bantekas is Professor of Transnational Law at Hamad bin Khalifa University (Qatar Foundation) and an Adjunct Professor of Law at Georgetown University. He has authored more than 200 articles in leading peer-reviewed journals, as well as 20 books, including *Islamic Contract Law* (co-author, 2023), *Introduction to International Arbitration* (2015), and *Commentary on the UNCITRAL Model Law on International Commercial Arbitration* (2020).

Ahmed Al-Ahmed is a Former Legal Counsel at Qatar Energy and Former Senior Marketer at Qatar Petroleum for the Sale of Petroleum Products Company Limited. He has 15 years of experience in the Oil & Gas industry in commercial operations and trading of crude oil and its by-products. He provided legal advice on Qatar Energy's new business development activities and was responsible for drafting relevant agreements, regulatory approvals and venture setups.

Contract Law of Qatar

ILIAS BANTEKAS
Hamad bin Khalifa University (Qatar Foundation)

AHMED AL-AHMED
Formerly at Qatar Energy

Shaftesbury Road, Cambridge CB2 8EA, United Kingdom

One Liberty Plaza, 20th Floor, New York, NY 10006, USA

477 Williamstown Road, Port Melbourne, VIC 3207, Australia

314–321, 3rd Floor, Plot 3, Splendor Forum, Jasola District Centre, New Delhi – 110025, India

103 Penang Road, #05–06/07, Visioncrest Commercial, Singapore 238467

Cambridge University Press is part of Cambridge University Press & Assessment, a department of the University of Cambridge.

We share the University's mission to contribute to society through the pursuit of education, learning and research at the highest international levels of excellence.

www.cambridge.org
Information on this title: www.cambridge.org/9781316511510

DOI: 10.1017/9781009052009

First published 2023

A catalogue record for this publication is available from the British Library

A Cataloging-in-Publication data record for this book is available from the Library of Congress

ISBN 978-1-316-51151-0 Hardback
ISBN 978-1-009-05599-4 Paperback

Contents

Figures

Preface

The regulation of contracts is nowadays a matter of transnational concern. Countries in the Gulf have made great efforts to diversify their economies by, among others, enhancing and transnationalising their legal systems. Qatari contract regulation has gone through several phases of development and modernisation in its relatively short history, starting from its first civil code in the early 1970s that was inspired by the Egyptian civil code of 1948. Although this book focuses on Qatar's current civil code, as well as related legislation, the authors are not oblivious to the fact that a big part of the economy is cross-border in nature and by implication, most of the pertinent contracts are governed by foreign laws or (soft law) principles, such as the UNIDROIT Principles of International Commercial Contracts. There is equally an interplay between the influence, or the remnants, of Egyptian private law and the infusion of Anglo-American law as a result of the influx of foreign law firms in Qatar and their dominance in the market. Still, the regulation of contracts by Qatari law is substantial and most contracts entered by state entities are governed, to one degree or another, by this law. What is more, the sustained growth and investment in Gulf legal systems by GCC nations is slowly contributing to a diverse, pluralistic, rich and user-friendly body of private and commercial law that is attractive for global end-users.

For all these reasons, the authors believed it was compelling that a short, albeit comprehensive, exposition of Qatari contract law in the English language would be an important contribution to the global contract law literature. Practice suggests that foreign courts and arbitral tribunals encountering disputes governed wholly or partially by Qatari private law resort to expert opinions of dubious quality and utility. It is hoped that this book will not only change perceptions about the presumed exotic or esoteric nature of Qatari contract law, showing in the process that it is both transnational and modern in its outlook, but that courts, tribunals and non-Qatari legal experts will no

longer be operating in the dark. Because this book was written as a comprehensive guide for the professional legal market, we assumed that fundamental
concepts of contract law were familiar to our audience and so at times we dive
in from the deep end. The book is structured in a manner emulating contract
law textbooks in the common law and civil law tradition. In order to make the
work comprehensive, the first chapter deals with the history and influences
of Qatari contract law, whereas the last chapter addresses the very particular
circumstances of the regulation of contracts in the Qatar Financial Center
(QFC), the country's special economic zone. Although as will become evident Islamic law plays a minuscule role in the regulation of private law in
Qatar, the authors nonetheless desired to provide the reader with some Islamic
law background to key notions and concepts, even if the courts or litigants no
longer refer to such historical background. We do so sparingly and only for the
purpose of providing useful insights.

This work would not have been possible without the belief from our com-
missioning editors that Qatar's private law was worthy of global exposure. Our
wholehearted appreciation, therefore, is extended to Finola O'Sullivan and
Marianne Nield who were the backbone of the book. We express our grati-
tude to Safaa Jaber who provided invaluable research tracking down judgments that were inaccessible. Finally, many thanks to colleagues and friends
who read and commented on the chapters. They are too many to mention.
The authors would like to thank Hamad bin Khalifa University (HBKU) and
particularly Susan Karamanian, Dean of the College of Law, who generously
agreed to cover all expenses associated with the publication of this book.
Despite its relatively short existence, HBKU College of Law has proven to be
a leader in legal education not just in Qatar and the GCC, but also one of
the top law schools in Asia. The authors welcome comments and suggestions
from our readers. Ilias Bantekas wrote Chapters 1, 3, 4, 6–8 and 11–13. Ahmed
Al-Ahmed wrote Chapters 2, 5 and 9–10.

Table of Cases

KUWAIT

Court of Cassation

QATAR

Court of Cassation

Court of Appeal

Doha Court of First Instance

QFC COURT

UNITED ARAB EMIRATES

Abbreviations

AC	Appeal Court [Reports, Eng]
AHRLJ	*African Human Rights Law Journal*
All ER	All England Reports
Arab LQ	*Arab Law Quarterly*
Art	Article
BGB	Bürgerliches Gesetzbuch (German Civil Code)
BIT	Bilateral Investment Treaty
CA	Court of Appeal (England)
CC	Civil Code
CCP	Code of Civil Procedure
CFI	Court of First Instance
chp	chapter
CL	Commercial Law
Colum L Rev	*Columbia Law Review*
Comm.	Commercial
Comm L World Rev	*Common Law World Review*
CLR	Commercial Registry Law
CRPD	Convention on the Right of Persons with Disability
Doc	Document
EC	European Communities
ed	editor
EIA	Environmental Impact Assessment
EU	European Union
EWCA	*England and Wales Court of Appeal*
EWHC	*England and Wales High Court*
FIDIC	International Federation of Consulting Engineers
FL	Family Law
GCC	Gulf Cooperation Council

H	Hajira
HKLJ	*Honk Kong Law Journal*
Int'l Surv. Fam. L	*International Survey of Family Law*
JIDS	*Journal of International Dispute Settlement*
KB	King's Bench (Eng)
LL	Labour Law
LLC	limited liability company
Louisiana L Rev	*Louisiana Law Review*
LPL	Lease Property Law
LQR	*Law Quarterly Review*
LR	*Law Reports* (1865–1950, Eng)
MENA	Middle East and North Africa
MENA Bus L Rev	*MENA Business Law Review*
MoCI	Ministry of Commerce and Industry
n.d.	no date
NY Intl L Rev	*New York International Law Review*
OUP	Oxford University Press
PICC	Principles of International Commercial Contracts
POE	Power of Attorney
QAR	Qatari riyals
QB	Queen's Bench (QB)
QCL	Qatar Companies Law
QFC	Qatar Financial Center
QIC	Qatar International Court [Reports]
SEZ	Special Economic Zone
UAE	United Arab Emirates
UKHL	United Kingdom House of Lords [Reports]
Uniform LR	*Uniform Law Review*
WLR	*Weekly Law Reports*

1

The Sources of Qatari Contract Law

1.1 INTRODUCTION

There are several reasons why an exposition of the contract law of Gulf states, and particularly Qatar, is important to the Western professional legal audience. Firstly, Qatar is the biggest liquefied natural gas (LNG) producer and along with its Gulf neighbours accounts for most of the globe's upstream carbon-based energy.[1] A big part of the contractual framework of such energy production is governed by local law, even if the financing and other elements are governed by a variety of other laws.[2] Secondly, Qatar and its Gulf Cooperation Council (GCC) allies own some of the largest sovereign wealth funds (in terms of dispensable assets), all of which engage in outward investment, both portfolio and otherwise.[3] Again, several components of such agreements are governed by local private law. Thirdly, Qatar, as well as all GCC states, have set up special economic zones (SEZs) with a view to attracting high-end financial services, multinationals and high-technology innovators.[4] These sophisticated SEZs, as analysed elsewhere,[5]

---

[1] See R Al-Gamal, 'Qatar Petroleum Signs Deal for Mega-LNG Expansion' Reuters (8 February 2021), available at: www.reuters.com/article/qatar-petroleum-lng-int-idUSKBN2A81ST

[2] See M Ruchdi, 'International LNG Contracts' (2018) 3 OGEL, available at: www.ogel.org/article.asp?key=3767

[3] For Qatar its investment vehicle is the Qatar Investment Authority (QIA). Although financial data is missing from its website, its estimated assets are 300 billion USD, which ranks it 11th among all sovereign wealth funds according to the Sovereign Wealth Fund Institute, available at: www.swfinstitute.org/profile/598cdaa60124e9fd2d05bc5a

[4] See D Z Zeng, 'The Past, Present and Future of Special Economic Zones and Their Impact' (2021) 24 Journal of International Economic Law 1; L Cao, 'Charter Cities' (2018–19) 27 William and Mary Bill of Rights Journal 717.

[5] See I Bantekas, 'Transplanting English Law in Asian Special Economic Zones: Law as Commodity' (2022) 17 Asian Journal of Comparative Law 1.

are equipped with impressive transnational commercial courts and are even viewed as better alternatives to arbitration.[6] Although the private law of the mother state is less significant there, its general principles, including public policy, are mandatory in the SEZ, and in any event, the Qatar Financial Centre (QFC) has enacted its own distinct contract law, which is analysed more fully in Chapter 13. Fourthly, Qatar and other Gulf countries have generated a considerable volume of trade and commerce, as well as mega-construction projects,[7] in addition to being the leaders in the emerging field of Islamic finance. These activities are very much governed by local private law in tandem with other foreign laws[8] and local courts have generated a significant amount of world-acclaimed case law becoming legal hubs in their own right.[9] Finally, as a result of the above considerations, it is no accident that a consistent body of private law peculiar to the GCC – Qatar as a major player in the region with an investment in education that overshadows all its GGC neighbours – seeks to become the law of choice in transnational commercial contracts.[10]

This chapter is meant to serve as an introduction to the book, particularly to that part of its audience that is unaccustomed to the history and

---

[6]   See Z Al Abdin Sharar, M Al Khulaifi, 'The Courts in Qatar Financial Center and Dubai International Financial Center: A Comparative Analysis' (2016) 46 Hong Kong Law Journal 529; I Bantekas, 'The Rise of International Commercial Courts: The Astana International Financial Center Court' (2020) 33 Pace International Law Review 1.

[7]   It is estimated that construction contracts in the Gulf in 2021 and 2022 are set to be worth 115 billion USD and 112 billion USD, respectively, available at: www.arabianbusiness .com/industries-construction/468768-gulf-construction-sector-tipped-to-rebound-following-covid-impact

[8]   See I Bantekas, 'Transnational Islamic Finance Disputes: Towards a Convergence with English Contract Law and International Arbitration' (2021) 12 Journal of International Dispute Settlement 1. In *The Investment Dar Co. KSSC v Blom Development Bank S.A.L.* [2009] All ER (D) 145, the English High Court was able to override the designation of English law as the governing law of a *Wakala* agreement, on the ground that it was not *Sharia*-compliant with the underlying investment, which the parties had expressly agreed should be so compliant. In similar manner, the English High Court in *Sanghi Polyesters Ltd India v The International Investor KCFC (Kuwait)* [2000] 1 Lloyd's Rep 480, had no trouble finding in the event of a conflict between English and Islamic law that the more pressing law to the issue at hand (in the present instance an Islamic finance transaction) would prevail.

[9]   This is true for the DIFC, which is the leader among its rivals in the Gulf. See R Reed, T Montagu-Smith (eds), *DIFC Courts Practice* (Edward Elgar 2020).

[10]   At present, this can only be achieved through GCC courts. See J K Krishnan, P Purohit, 'A Common Law Court in an Uncommon Environment: The DIFC Judiciary and Global Commercial Dispute Resolution' (2014) 25 American Review of International Arbitration 497.

sources of Qatari contract law, as well as the institutions and forces that shape and develop it.

1.2 BRIEF HISTORICAL ACCOUNT OF THE DEVELOPMENT OF QATARI PRIVATE LAW

The history of Qatari private law should be distinguished from the perspective of at least two historical periods (namely before and after independence in 1971). The first roughly begins with the prevalence of Ottoman private law following the occupation of Qatar by the Ottoman Empire in the early nineteenth century. Just like elsewhere in the Empire, the Ottomans imposed the Hanafi tradition of Islamic law, but their short-lived rule entailed that the codification of the private dimension of Islamic law in the form of the *Majalla*[11] was not bequeathed to Qatar. Very little is known about the administration of private law by the Ottomans in Qatar, but one must assume that this was no different to other Muslim territories under Ottoman rule.[12] Following the Ottoman demise in the Gulf region in the latter part of the nineteenth century, the Al-Thani family assumed political and military power. Under the influence of Saudi Arabia, Hanafi teachings were soon replaced by the Hanbali tradition, which is still prevalent in the Qatari legal system. In 1916, Britain and the rulers of Qatar entered into an agreement whereby Qatar became a British protectorate. Consequently, the British authorities established two parallel systems of justice. Colonial/civil courts administered English and colonial laws, whereas local courts were entrusted with the administration of Islamic law.[13] What is clear from the few transnational cases of that era is that the colonial powers and the West considered Islamic private/contract law as either 'primitive' or simply inadequate to meet the needs of modern commerce. In the *Sheikh of Abu Dhabi* arbitration, the sole arbitrator, Lord

[11] The Majalla (*Medjelle-yi Aḥkām-î ʿAdliyye*) was effectively the civil code in force in the Ottoman Empire, as well as briefly during the very early part of the Turkish republic, from 1285 to 1926, although it was only codified in the latter part of the nineteenth century (1869–1877). It covered contracts, torts, and some principles of civil procedure and is still widely influential concerning the content and scope of classical Islamic private law. See A Cevdet Pasha, *Al-Majalla: The Civil Code of the Ottoman Empire* (CreateSpace Publishing, 2017).
[12] See M Masud et al (eds), *Dispensing Justice in Islam: Qadis and Their Judgments* (Brill 2006); C Muller, 'Judging with God's Law on Earth: Judicial Powers of the Qadi al-Jamaʾa at Cordoba in the Fifth/Eleventh Century' (2000) 7 Islamic Law & Society 159.
[13] See A. Nizar Hamzeh, 'Qatar: The Duality of the Legal System' (1994) 30 Middle Eastern Studies 79. This state of affairs persisted a few years following independence but is no longer the case.

Asquith, although finding that national law was applicable (i.e. Abu-Dhabi law as grounded in the Quran),[14] famously noted that:

> No such law can reasonably be said to exist...... [The Sheikh administers] a purely discretionary justice with the assistance of the Koran; and it would be fanciful to suggest that in this very primitive region there is any settled body of legal principles applicable to the construction of modern commercial instruments.[15]

The most important historical period in the development of Qatari civil/contract law is associated (but does not effectively begin) with the country's independence in September 1971. One of the first laws enacted by the country's legislature was Law No 16 of 1971 on 'The Civil and Commercial Law'. This Law remained intact for more than a decade and was amended by Law No 10 of 1982. The grand reform of the Civil and Commercial Law took place in 2004 with the promulgation of Law No 22, Regarding the Promulgation of the Civil Code (CC). This Civil Code remains in place to the present day, as complemented and supplemented by other specialised laws.

The second historical period cannot be examined in isolation of the development of private law in Egypt, which commenced following the end of World War II at a time when Qatar was a British protectorate. Just like all Arab private law codifications, so too the Qatari CC was influenced by the 1948 Egyptian CC, which was drafted by the great Egyptian scholar Abd al Razzaq Al-Sanhuri.[16] His thinking influenced his students and associates who went on to draft the newer generation of civil codes in the Gulf Cooperation Council (GCC) and the Middle East and North Africa (MENA).[17] As a result, it is more accurate to say that the seeds of the Qatari CC codification commenced in the Sanhuri era, later to be transplanted and fertilised in Qatar and the Gulf

---

[14] _Petroleum Development (Trucial Coasts) Ltd v Sheikh of Abu Dhabi_ (1951) 18 ILR 144, per Lord Asquith at 149; equally, _Ruler of Qatar v Int'l Marine Oil Co. Ltd_ (1953) 20 ILR 534, per Bucknill J at 545, who stated that: 'I have no reason to suppose that Islamic law is not administered [in Qatar] strictly, but I am satisfied that the law does not contain any principles which would be sufficient to interpret this particular contract'.

[15] _Sheikh of Abu Dhabi_, id.

[16] Sanhuri's students later drafted other MENA and GCC civil codes on the basis of his philosophy and ideals. See N Saleh, 'Civil Laws of Arab Countries: The Sanhuri Codes' (1993) 8 Arab LQ 165.

[17] See particularly Abd al-Razzaq Al-Sanhuri, _Mas}âdir al-haqq fî al-Fiqh al-Islâmî, Dirâsah Muqâranah bi al-Fiqh al-Gharbî_ (Cairo University Press 1954–59); See G Benchor, _The Sanhuri Code and the Emergence of Modern Arab Civil Law (1932–1949)_ (Brill, 2007) 177–78; also P N Kourides, 'The Influence of Islamic Law on Contemporary Middle Eastern Legal Systems: The Formation and Binding Force of Contracts' (1970) 9 Columbia Journal of Transnational Law 384.

as a whole, save for Saudi Arabia.[18] This further explains why Egyptian lawyers dominate the Qatari professional landscape, whether as legal consultants,
judges or academics (the latter chiefly at Qatar University).

1.3 REGULATION OF CONTRACT LAW IN THE CIVIL CODE

As already stated, Law No. 22 of 2004 is Qatar's Civil Code. Just like its counterparts in Europe and elsewhere, contracts comprise part of the law of obligations and are found in articles 64–198 and 241–268 CC. The CC is replete
with provisions dealing with contractual matters, such as leases, employment
relationships and others. As the reader will come to appreciate upon reading the various chapters in this book, the Qatari law of contracts as set out
in the CC is similar, if not identical, in scope and content with civil codes
in Europe. Despite a sixty-year British rule in the country, it is poignant that
none of the peculiarities of English contract law (e.g. no general obligation
of good faith; consideration as a quintessential element for the formation of
contracts), which is predominantly the product of common law, have found a
place in the Qatari CC.

1.4 OTHER RELEVANT LEGISLATION

In addition to the CC, contractual matters are further regulated in almost
all statutes dealing with private relationships, chiefly Law No. 8 of 2002 on
Organization of Business of Commercial Agents and Law and Law No. 27
of 2006, Promulgating the Trading Regulation Law (Commercial Law). It
is beyond the scope of this narrow treatise to enumerate all of the applicable
specialised laws, albeit many will be encountered throughout the book. It
should be pointed out that some areas of contract law, such as consumer law,
are not at all as well regulated as their counterparts in European and North
American jurisdictions.[19]

1.5 THE ROLE OF ENGLISH CONTRACT LAW

There exists an exaggeration about the role and significance of English law,
and particularly its common law manifestation, in the Qatari legal order.

---

[18] Although slightly outdated, this is still an excellent exposition of the basis of substantive private
laws in the Kingdom of Saudi Arabia. N Saleh, 'The Law Governing Contracts in Arabia'
(1989) 38 International and Comparative Law Quarterly 761.
[19] See eg Qatari Law No. 8 of 2008 on Consumer Protection.

There are three reasons underlying or explaining this exaggeration. The first stems from the obvious application of English law during Qatar's protectorate status (1916–1971). There are no visible remnants of English law from this period as already explained. The second reason is generally grounded on the assumption that the Qatar Financial Centre (QFC) and its court are mandated to apply and enforce English common law, including the law of contracts. As explained elsewhere, this is a fallacy, even if indeed the QFC Court applies a great deal of English law. The third reason is more plausible but is equally problematic. There is anecdotal evidence that English law is prevalent in transnational commercial transactions, particularly (but by no means exclusively) where the contract's dispute resolution clause provides for foreign-seated arbitration or a foreign court.[20] This has given rise to a popular sentiment among lawyers, mostly foreign, that Qatar's private law is common law based, or certainly mixed.[21] This in fact is not the case.[22] English law, including the common law, merely appears as the governing law in contracts, but in no way constitutes part of the country's legal system. The view of this author is that the Qatari legal system is not at all a mixed legal order, despite the existence of the many foreign and multifaceted elements that help shape it.

1.6 THE LIMITED ROLE OF ISLAMIC LAW

Islamic law has a very limited application, if any, in the Qatari private legal order.[23] This may appear odd to non-experts given the overriding importance of Islam in the very existence of Qatar. Islamic law regulates family and inheritance law,[24] as well as some elements of criminal law. It is perhaps instructive to set out, in brief, a basic outline, as well as an equally brief overview of the

---

[20] I Bantekas, 'The Globalisation of English Contract Law: Three Salient Illustrations' (2021) 137 Law Quarterly Review 130.

[21] Foreign law firms operating in Qatar regularly refer to it as 'mixed'. See M Walker, L van der Merwe, 'Qatar Court of Cassation Confirms Conditions for the Enforcement of ICC Awards in Qatar', available at: www.klconstructionlawblog.com/tag/qatari-court-of-cassation/

[22] There are few truly mixed systems, in the sense of overlapping and mutually binding systems applicable in a single jurisdiction, other than states where Islam constitutes the grundnorm. See N Hatzimihail, 'Cyprus as a Mixed Legal System' (2013) 6 Journal of Civil Law Studies 37; I Castellucci, 'Legal Hybridity in Hong Kong and Macau' (2012) 57 McGill Law Journal 665.

[23] The truth is that this body of law is scattered and disparate and is mostly used nowadays as a means of construing Islamic finance instruments. See I Bantekas, J Ercanbrack, U Oseni, I Ullah, *Islamic Contract Law* (Oxford University Press 2023).

[24] Law No 22 of 2006, Promulgating the Family Law [Family Code], stipulates Art 3 thereof that it is predicated on the Hanbali school of Islam.

sources and key principles of Islamic law. The *Sharia* consists of the *Quran* and those portions of the *sunna* (which itself consists of the deeds and sayings of Prophet Mohamed) that are not only deemed authoritative but also interpretative of the *Quran*. The *Sharia* is the primary source (*asl*), but there are several secondary sources,[25] which, however, cannot under any circumstances fall foul of the *Sharia*. Islamic law is distinct, albeit complementary to the *Sharia*. Out of the 6,239 verses of the *Quran*, only 190 specifically address what we might call legal issues.[26] It is these legal verses that comprise Islamic law, although these cannot artificially be divorced from the other religious verses in the *Quran*. Islamic scholarship has developed methodologies of *Quranic* interpretation known as *ilm usūl al-fiqh* (methodology of theological science) and *fiqh* (theological science), on the basis of which Islamic jurists aim to achieve *maqāsid al-sharia* (goals of the *Sharia*) as well as *siyāsat al-sharia* (policy of the *Sharia*). The development of *fiqh* has allowed a non-static and contextual interpretation of the *Sharia*, even in respect of otherwise controversial issues.[27]

We have already discussed the authority of Sanhuri in generating a species of Pan-Arab private law that straddled along the French (Napoleonic) civil code codifications and private Islamic law teachings. Although one can certainly identify some (albeit limited) traces of the Islamic legal tradition in the Qatari CC, its influence and application are inconsequential. By way of illustration, in order to explain the 'correspondence of offer and acceptance to form a binding contract', the CC makes reference to the concept of 'contract session'. The Qatari legislator derived this principle from the Islamic law tradition, which uses the Arabic term *majlis ala'aquid*. A contract session is defined as a session where the parties meet in person to negotiate the terms and conditions of the contract at the same (i) location and (ii) time.[28]

Ordinary Qatari courts are bound to construe a contract in accordance with the *Sharia* where the particular subject matter is not regulated by statute.[29]

---

[25] For example, *qiyas* (human reasoning by analogy, but only if adopted by a large enough majority of Muslim scholars) and; *ijma*, which represents the actual consensus of the Muslim scholarly community. There are also controversial methods, such as *ijtihad*. See B G Weiss, 'Interpretation of Islamic Law: The Theory of Ijtihad' (1978) 26 American Journal of Comparative Law 199, 198–201.

[26] See C M Bassiouni, *The Sharia and Islamic Criminal Justice in Time of War and Peace* (Cambridge University Press 2014) 23.

[27] See E Polymenopoulou, 'Caliphs, Jinns and Sufi Shrines: The Protection of Cultural Heritage and Cultural Rights under Islamic Law' (2022) 36 Emory International Law Review 743.

[28] N Saleh, 'Definition and Formation of Contract under Islamic and Arab Laws' (1990) 5 Arab LQ 101, at 115; see also Chapter 5, Section 5.1.

[29] Art 1(2) Qatari CC. See Court of Cassation Judgment 323/2014.

The parties may not exclude the *Sharia* where their contract is governed by Qatari law and the latter lacks a statutory provision regulating a particular issue under the contract.[30] This is neither an easy venture nor is it free from contention. Article 1(2) of the Qatari CC provides a hierarchy, with statutes at the apex, followed by the *Sharia* ('if any'), customary practices and finally 'rules of justice'.[31] This is in contrast to article 169(2) Qatari CC, which allows the courts to infer the parties' common intention by reference to commercial custom. While it seems that the two provisions serve distinct purposes, namely that: article 1(2) CC merely attempts to posit the *Sharia* as a secondary source of law, whereas article 169(2) CC refers to commercial custom as an interpretative tool[32]; article 1(2) CC is effectively transformed into an interpretative tool where a statutory provision is deemed to be lacking.

Despite the limited role of Islamic contract law at the time of writing in Qatar, the growth of this field could certainly change the existing volume of Islamic finance, both at the QFC and in Qatar proper.[33]

1.7 THE QATAR FINANCIAL CENTRE CONTRACT REGULATIONS

As will be explained more fully in Chapter 13, the Qatar Financial Centre (QFC) is an SEZ within the State of Qatar, which is endowed with a legal

---

[30] In practice, it seems that several issues in the Qatari CC are regulated by the *Sharia* and the CC in tandem, especially where it is deemed that the *Sharia* is more elaborate. The Court of Cassation in Judgment 21/2008 accepted the applicability of the *Sharia* concerning the acquisition of property by prescription, despite the existence of a relevant provision in the CC (Art 404). While ultimately the Court did not agree with the lower court's interpretation of Islamic law, neither the Court nor the parties expressed any concern about the use of *Sharia* despite the existence of express provisions in the CC. Hence, it is evident that the courts will apply the *Sharia* not only where the CC is silent on a particular issue, but also where the *Sharia* is more elaborate.

[31] See Court of Cassation Judgment 122/2013 on the limitations of justice as a rule that is trumped by the mutual intention of the parties; see equally Court of Cassation Judgment 26/2015.

[32] The Court of Cassation does not shy away from identifying business custom through standard phraseology. Eg in Court of Cassation Judgment 148/2010, it was held that the bank's exposure to the lender is significant and hence compensation for late payments (delay interest) is justified by reference to banking custom, which is moreover 'common knowledge' that does not require proof; equally Court of Cassation Judgment 220/2011; to the same effect see also Court of Cassation Judgment 40/2013; equally Court of Cassation Judgment 107/2013, arguing that where a special commercial/trade law is silent commercial custom shall be applied, with the special custom or local custom being given precedence over the general custom. If there is no commercial custom, the provisions of the civil law shall apply. This was also reiterated in Court of Cassation Judgment 66/2014; see equally Court of Cassation Judgment 371/2014; Court of Cassation Judgment 208/2014.

[33] See I Bantekas, 'The Qatar Financial Centre and How It Can Attract Islamic Finance Arbitration' (16 March 2021) Transnational Dispute Management, available at: www .transnational-dispute-management.com/journal-advance-publication-article.asp?key=1877

system and institutions distinct from those generally applicable in Qatar proper. The QFC promulgated its own contract laws through Regulation No. 4 (2005), known as the QFC Contract Regulations. As will become evident, the Contract Regulations were predicated (almost verbatim) in large part on the UNIDROIT Principles of International Commercial Contracts (PICC).[34]

1.8 THE ROLE OF JUDICIAL PRECEDENT

It is instructive to begin this section by examining the anatomy of judgments in Qatar. Unlike other civil and common law jurisdictions whereby judgments from senior courts (at appellate and cassation level) are relatively elaborate and contain extensive references to existing case law and even scholarly works, Qatari judgments lack such detail and sophistication. The majority are no more than two or three pages long and generally desist from referring to existing case law. Judgments typically pinpoint the pertinent statutory provision and go on to offer an analysis of that provision in a Spartan manner that serves the particular purposes of the dispute at hand. Hence, when reading a Qatari senior court judgment dealing with contract law, one is uncertain as to the underlying rationale and origins of the legal arguments. For those versed in Egyptian private law and particularly the key judgments of that country's courts of appeal and cassation, certain vestiges may be noticeable. This is because the vast majority of senior judges will have either studied in Egyptian law schools or Qatar University's law school under the guidance of academics derived from Egypt or coming from the Egyptian private law tradition (all in Arabic). Even so, there are at least two cogent reasons why the Egyptian influence on the development of Qatari private law is slowly shifting, although certainly not diminishing. The first is associated with the (at times) erratic and unpredictable stance of senior Egyptian courts,[35] which is precisely what all GCC courts are at pains to unshackle themselves and their reputation from.

---

[34] See I Bantekas, 'Transplanting the UNIDROIT Contract Principles in the Qatar Financial Centre: A Fresh Paradigm for Wholesale Legal Transplants?' (2021) 26 Uniform Law Review 1.

[35] It is clear that reliance on the case law of Egypt for any progressive legal system is far from an ideal choice, not only because of the difference in culture (broadly understood) but also because of the erratic nature of the Egyptian higher courts. By way of illustration, the Cairo Court of Appeal ruled in 1997 that an arbitral tribunal was allowed to apply interest above the maximum rate set by statute because the parties had come to a mutual agreement and thus the award did not contravene Egyptian public policy. Case No 41/114, judgment (2 October 1997). In 2020, however, the Egyptian Court of Cassation in *Legal Representative of Interfood Co. v The Legal Representative of RCMA Asia Pte Ltd Singapore*, Ruling 282/89 (9 January 2020), overturned the long-standing practice of the Court of Appeal.

The second reason suggests that Qatari and GCC courts produce an ample amount of jurisprudence, such that there is no real need to rely excessively on foreign judgments. This outcome is further coupled by the expanding legal education in Qatar and the influx of foreign law firms largely practicing in the English language and applying foreign and Qatari law.

Unlike other civil law jurisdictions, and very much in the tradition of the English Precedent Act, the judgments of the Qatari Court of Cassation constitute *stare decisis* (binding precedent) on lower courts.[36] This endows Qatari private law with an aura of consistency and continuity that is typically missing from most Arab jurisdictions. However, this author is not aware of any cases challenging judgments deviating from the precedent set down by the Court of Cassation, let alone how effective Qatari Law No. 12 of 2005 has been in enforcing precedent. It is equally problematic that Qatar's law reporting system, Al-Meezan, is at best inadequate given that only a few cases are available, even in Arabic. The same is true of its English-language counterpart, Lexis Nexis Middle East, which despite best efforts only covers a minuscule of cases. In this manner, it is very difficult to engrain a sense of precedent and reliance on cases in the professional legal community. In practice, however, law firms, both local and domestic, endeavour to cite judgments by the senior Qatari courts, and many of these cases are frequently reported on the firms' websites. Hence, at the very least, reliance on Qatari case law by the legal profession is extensive even if the courts themselves do not accurately, if at all, refer to such case law in their own judgments.

1.9 THE DEVELOPMENT OF CONTRACT LAW BY THE LEGAL PROFESSION

The legal profession certainly shapes the practice and direction of private law in Qatar in several ways. The legal profession is inextricably linked to a country's legal education. Qatar University (QU) was the first academic institution to launch a law-related degree in 1990, albeit this was administered by a department of *Sharia* and Islamic Studies, where naturally Islamic law was the dominant discipline. This changed in 2004 when an independent college of law was formed in the style of mainly Western law schools. Education there is chiefly modelled on the tenets of Egyptian law in the context of Qatari legislation. The College offers English-language modules in international and transnational commercial law. Hamad bin Khalifa University, a member of

---

[36] Art 22(3) of Law 12 of 2005 pertaining to Procedures in Non-Penal Cassation Appeals.

the Qatar Foundation, established a Juris Doctor (JD) programme in 2015, initially under the direction of Northwestern University's Pritzker School of Law. This JD programme is taught exclusively in English by academics educated in the Western legal tradition, comprising courses that embody transnational legal elements and content. More recently, in 2021, Lusail University set up an undergraduate law programme in French, in collaboration with Paris 1 University (Pantheon Sorbonne).[37] Before the establishment of QU's law programme, Qataris chiefly ventured to Egyptian law schools to study law, while in the last decade it is not uncommon for Qataris to undertake LLB and LLM degrees in English universities, as well as LLM degrees in US law schools.

The right of appearance before the courts is only available to Qatari citizens. The number is relatively small, chiefly because bar accreditation is not possible for those employed in the public or private sector, save for academics. Public sector employment is generally well paid and opening up a law firm is beset with financial risks. Many qualified Qataris hence work as in-house counsel in public entities without a bar license. A large number of Arabic-speaking lawyers, mainly from Egypt, Sudan and Jordan, are employed as legal consultants to assist Qatari lawyers and law firms. Foreign law firms are allowed to establish their presence in the country subject to pertinent approval and their interest generally revolves around transnational practice and public procurement. The majority of the lawyers in such firms are trained in the Western legal tradition and naturally rely on Arabic-speaking lawyers in respect of local transactions. There is a clear tendency among foreign law firms to steer their clients towards foreign law – to the degree possible – and international arbitration, without however losing sight or ignoring the mandatory provisions of Qatari private law. On the other hand, Arabic-speaking lawyers generally strive for the opposite outcome. Given the positive stance of the Qatari judiciary to international arbitration, especially after the adoption of the country's Arbitration Law in 2017, foreign law firms are now more able to recommend English law governing clauses and international arbitration. Where this is not possible, as in the case of construction contracts, English precedent and good practice are suggested in relevant briefs. It is thus fair to say that Qatari private law is in the process of detaching itself from its deep Egyptian influences and being led by the mixed transnational paradigm of some of its GCC neighbours.

---

[37] The Qatar Police College operates a four-year Law and Police degree in Arabic, but it is not clear that graduates are eligible to join the Qatari bar, let alone that they would be allowed to do so.

2

Contract Formation

2.1 INTRODUCTION

Among Arab legal scholars, the Latin principle 'pacta sunt servanda' plays a fundamental role in dealing with contracts. The English translation is 'agreements must be kept'. The Arabic equivalent of the same principle is (العقد شريعة المتعاقدين) and is pronounced 'al-aa'quid sharee'aat al-mota'aquideen'. Qatari legislators did not deviate from the civil law tradition, which Qatari laws are derived from. Thus, contracts are considered as the main source of obligation under private law, which regulates the relationship between natural and legal persons. As a rule of thumb, whenever an obligation arises, rights appear on the other side of the 'fence'; therefore, when one private party is obligated to perform a promise under a binding contract, the other party(ies) will have a right that such obligation be fulfilled. Contractual rights vested in natural and/or legal persons are characterised as economic rights.[1] Under the civil law tradition, economic rights comprise: (i) rights *in personam* and (ii) rights *in rem*. Rights *in personam* (otherwise known as 'personal rights') are positive rights against specific person(s), which are derived from statutory obligations or contractual obligations, such as the right to receive a rent from the lessee under the lease agreement or the right to receive compensation in tort for false imprisonment. Conversely, rights *in rem* (otherwise known as 'real rights') are negative rights against unspecified persons and are equally derived from statutory or contractual obligations, such as the right to possess and utilise property to its full potential without interference. Thus, a right *in rem* can be exercisable against society at large.

---

[1] There is a consistent line of Islamic scholarship whereby contracts are deemed agreements for the mutual exchange of property. Kasani, *Bada'i', Al-Sana'i' fi Tartif al-Shara'i'* (Dar Al-Kotob al-Ilmiyah, Cairo, 1990), vol 5, at 133; Ibn Qudama, *Al-Mughni* (Dar al Kutub al Ilmiya, Beirut) vol 3, at 560.

The Qatari Civil Code (CC) is detailed but not comprehensive. Specialised legislation has been enacted to complement the CC and regulate additional issues affecting contractual relations. Qatari courts have entertained an extensive array of civil and commercial disputes and have interpreted the relevant statutes where there was ambiguity.[2]

2.2 OBLIGATIONS IN GENERAL

The main source of obligations under Qatari contract law arises from the following: (i) the contract itself; (ii) the intention of the parties at the time of forming the contract; and lastly (iii) the relevant laws enacted by the legislators to regulate contractual matters. Although the terms 'contract' and 'agreement' are used interchangeably to refer to the same legal instrument, it is very important to note that 'every contact is an agreement but not every agreement constitutes a legally binding contract'.

2.2.1 *Definition of Contract*

Article 64 CC elucidates the necessary elements that are required for a contract to be validly formed. It goes on to say that

> Without prejudice to any special formalities that may be required by law for the conclusion of certain contracts, a contract shall be concluded from the moment an offer and its subsequent acceptance have been exchanged if the subject-matter and cause of such contract are deemed legal.

The CC defines the contract as an exchange of promises between an offeror (the party who makes an offer) and an offeree (the party who declares acceptance) for a subject-matter that is deemed legal in its substance and cause. The Qatari legislator emphasised the importance of both substance and cause of the subject-matter of an agreement on the basis of which offer and acceptance are transformed into a legally binding agreement.[3] Thus, the parties'

---

[2] Qatari legislators adopted the Latin concept of *stare decisis*, which means 'to stand by things decided'. According to Art 22(3) of Law 12 of 2005 pertaining to Procedures in Non-Penal Cassation Appeals, lower courts (i.e. the Court of First Instance and the Court of Appeal) are obliged to comply with the judgments of the Court of Cassation as mandatory authority (i.e. precedents). The Court of Cassation is not obligated to uphold its previous judgments; thus, it can overrule itself. Thus, the concept of *stare decisis* works vertically but not horizontally. The Court of Cassation has the role of establishing legal principles in the Qatari legal system.

[3] This is consistent with the emphasis on the subject-matter of contracts under classic Islamic law, known as *mahal al-aqd*. According to Islamic jurists (*fuqaha*), the determinants of the 'thing' allowed to become a subject-matter of a valid contract are the following: (i) it should

agreement may not encompass an illegal act, or conduct that violates public policy. These include, among others: labour rights, particularly the restricted right to termination by the employer;[4] commercial activities in violation of the requirement that a Qatari partner hold at least 51% of shares;[5] exercising a profession without proper licence and registration;[6] rental value and eviction from leased properties;[7] and not bypassing the proper jurisdiction of Qatari courts.[8] Agreements encompassing illegal subject-matters are considered null and void and are not enforceable by the courts.

2.2.2 *Expression of Intention*

It is crucial that the law recognises in advance in what manner the offer or acceptance are to be manifested and expressed in order that they become binding. Article 65 CC states that

1. An intention shall be expressed orally or in writing, by a commonly used sign, by actual consensual exchange, and also by conduct that, in the circumstances, leaves no doubt as to its true meaning.
2. A declaration of intention may be implied when neither the law, nor the agreement, nor the nature of the transaction requires that such declaration be expressed.

Qatari legislators did not deviate from the civil law tradition. The parties may express their intention to enter into a legally binding contract under a variety of methods as long as the chosen means of expression reflect their true intention without ambiguity.[9] These expressions could be verbal, written or

---

be mal *mutaqawam* (legal); (ii) existent; (iii) owned by the seller; (iv) in the possession of the seller; (v) able to be delivered; and (vi) precisely determined (*malom*). See Ibn Abideen, *Radd ul Muhtar Sharah Tanveer al Absar* (Dar ul Fikr, Beirut, 1979) vol 4, at 505. See also E Rayner, *The Theory of Contracts in Islamic Law: A Comparative Analysis with Particular Reference to the Modern Legislation in Kuwait, Bahrain and the United Arab Emirates* (Graham & Trotman, 1991) 157; *Al Mughni* (n 1) vol 4, at 260; Kasani (n 1) vol 5, at 138–140.

4   Court of Cassation Judgments 44/2010 and 73/2010.
5   Court of Cassation Judgments 74/2010 and 102/2010; see also Court of Cassation Judgment 73/2016 on a similar employment issue.
6   Court of Cassation Judgment 226/2011.
7   Court of Cassation Judgment 19/2011; Court of Cassation Judgment 32/2015.
8   Court of Cassation Judgment 62/2011.
9   This is consistent with classic Islamic law, whereby the communication of an offer may typically be achieved in five forms (*namat*): verbally, written, through a messenger, signs or gestures, and conduct that 'is evidence of an offer'. See Majalla, Arts 173–175; see also I. Abdur Rahman Doi, *Shari'ah: The Islamic Law*, (A.S. Noordeen Publisher, Kuala Lumpur, 1992) 356.

predicated on the conduct of the parties pursuant to a commonly accepted industry practice (custom),[10] or a pattern of consistent past commercial transactions. Furthermore, the expression of intention could be explicit or implicit as long as the law or the nature of the commercial transaction does not prohibit a certain form of expression. No doubt, some transactions will require a particular form of expressing intention and this must be followed.[11] However, given that many transactions are concluded by way of email exchanges, the mere payment of the requested fee by the buyer to the seller,[12] or by conduct,[13] intention is clearly presumed upon crucial moments in the lifecycle of the exchange. The buyer is deemed to have agreed to the seller's offer, as well as its terms and conditions, upon emailing his acceptance to the offer, or upon receipt of the goods at his premises, and in more trivial transactions, the offeree's intention is presumed upon payment of the agreed fee. It is equally taken for granted that neither party may unilaterally alter or amend the conditions in the agreement, as this requires the mutual will of all parties.[14] The Court of Cassation, relying on article 4(1) of the Electronic Commerce Law,[15] has emphasised that an offer or acceptance of an offer may be expressed, in whole or in part, by means of electronic communications.[16]

---

[10] Art 169(2) CC allows the courts to infer the parties' common intention by reference to prevailing commercial custom. Art 172(2) CC expands the good faith requirement by stating that obligations arising from a contract encompass, in addition to what the parties have agreed, whatever 'is required by law, customary practice and justice'. By way of illustration, the Court of Cassation has consistently held that interest rates shall be upheld in accordance with prevailing business custom. See Court of Cassation Judgments 66/2014 and 40/2013; equally Court of Cassation Judgment 208/2014. Ibn Taymiyya, a Hanbali scholar, emphasised the importance of customary conduct in contractual transactions. Ibn Taymiyya, *Al-Fatawa al-Kubra* (Dar al Kotob al-Ilmiyah, Beiruit, 1966), vol 3, at 411.

[11] See, for example, Court of Cassation Judgment 123/2010, concerning the registration of real estate transactions.

[12] See Court of Cassation Judgment 76/2011, where it was held that unless otherwise agreed payment of the deposit means confirmation of continuation of the contract.

[13] For example, Arts 588 and 626 CC specify that if the lease contract expires and the lessee continues to benefit from the leased property with the knowledge of the lessor and without objection, the contract shall be deemed to have been renewed with its first conditions. See Court of Cassation Judgment 134/2013.

[14] Court of Cassation Judgment 35/2014. By extension, neither party may unilaterally terminate the contract. The Court of Cassation refers to the contract as 'the law of the parties' and developed its 'two wills' theory. See Court of Cassation Judgment 67/2014; equally, Court of Cassation Judgment 109/2015.

[15] Law No. 16 of 2010 Promulgation of the Electronic Commerce and Transactions Law (Electronic Commerce Law).

[16] Contracting through electronic means is recognised in the case law of the Court of Cassation. See Judgment 275/2016; equally Court of Appeal Judgments 483/2018 and 526/2018.

2.2.3 *Expression and Manifestation of the Offer*

In Chapter 3 we go on to demonstrate that an intention to be bound to one's offer or acceptance is *a sine qua non* condition for the formation of a contract. Article 66 CC exemplifies in what manner such intention to make an offer is expressed and manifested, as follows:

1. An expression of intention shall become effective once uttered. However, the expression shall have no effect unless it comes to the notice of the intended recipient.
2. Subject to proof to the contrary, the intended recipient shall be deemed to have notice of the declaration of intention from the time that it reaches him.

As a result, revocation is possible until such time as the offer or acceptance has not yet reached the intended recipient. Paragraph 2 of article 66 CC introduces a rebuttable presumption concerning the precise point in time at which the addressee received its counterparty's intent. It stipulates that 'the intended recipient shall be deemed to have notice of the declaration of intention from the time that it reaches him'. Consequently, secure methods of receipt, such as email correspondence[17] and recorded delivery, will constitute significant evidence of receipt.

Article 67 CC goes on to say that

> 'The expression of intention shall have no effect if a retraction thereof reaches the intended recipient before or at the same time as the expression reaches him'.

The expression of intention is legally valid when the offeror expresses his/her intent to enter into a binding contract. However, this valid expression of intention does not become binding until the offeree becomes aware of it. Thus, the sole expression of intention by the offeror is not sufficient to make it legally binding for bilateral and multilateral agreements. The only exception here applies to unilateral agreements, which are known under the civil law tradition as 'unilateral dispositions'. Unilateral dispositions will be discussed at a later stage of this chapter. As a general rule, two factors are required for a valid expression of an offer: (i) the expression of intention by the offeror and (ii) the receipt of the expression of intention by the offeree.

---

[17]　In order for electronic evidence to be admissible before the court, it must take the form of a data message which, according to Art 1(4) of the Electronic Commerce Law, is any type of information that was sent, received, displayed or stored by any means of electronic communications, and moreover comply with the requirements of Art 26 of the Electronic Commerce Law. Article 26 generally demands certainty of the origin of the data message and the identity of its receiver to ensure that the data message was not manipulated by the parties or that it was not a counterfeit.

Furthermore, the law stipulates that when the expression of intention reaches the offeree, it is deemed as proof of his or her knowledge of such intention. That is the reason why offerors in practice require a receipt of delivery (time stamped) either through registered mail or electronic receipt by the email server. The exception here applies to face-to-face or telephone negotiations where the expression of intention and the receipt of such intention is instantaneous. We will discuss this matter in more detail when we go on to examine the concept of 'contract session' at a later stage of this chapter. It suffices to say, however, that the Qatari CCP does not ascribe to the so-called parole evidence rule, whereby evidence that is extrinsic to the contract, such as draft contracts, statements and emails exchanged during the negotiation of the contract, travaux or witness statements are inadmissible.[18] The CCP implicitly allows all such evidence in order to allow the judge to ascertain the parties' common intention and excludes nothing that has probative value, subject to the requirements demanded of each evidence.[19]

Moreover, the law allows the offeror to revoke his or her expression of intention if the notice of such revocation reaches the offeree on, or before, the time the original expression of intention reaches the offeree. If this event materialises, then the original expression of intention becomes null and void. The law here provides flexibility to the offeror in case there is a change of heart about the transaction, or where the transaction itself is no longer deemed worthwhile before the expression of intention reaches the offeree.

2.3 OFFER

Article 69 CC aptly captures the fine line between an offer[20] and an invitation to treat or negotiate that is central to the discussion on the formation of contracts and the deference typically afforded to businesses as being offerees to offers made by their clients. It stipulates that

1. An offer may be addressed to unidentified persons, as long as the identity of the desired offeree is not deemed essential to the contract.

---

[18] See Art 4.3 UNIDROIT PICC, which refers to a list of five extrinsic factors as relevant circumstances in interpretating a contract. This is consistent with the Qatari CC, save for the fact that extrinsic factors are expressly permitted in the PICC but not the CC.

[19] It is established that photocopies of originals, whether written documents or photographs have no probative effect except to the extent they lead to the signed originals, if any. See Court of Cassation Judgment 9/2010.

[20] Art 101 of the Majalla defines an offer (*ijab*) as a proposal or 'the first word spoken for making a disposition of property and the disposition is proved by it'.

2. The offer of goods accompanied by an indication of their prices shall be regarded as an offer subject to the rules of trade.

3. Save where the conditions of the situation show otherwise, publications, advertisements, sending or distributing price lists used in current trading, as well as any other statement connected with offers or orders addressed to the public or particular individuals, shall not be regarded as an offer.

The first paragraph of article 69 CC states that where the identity of the offeree is not essential to the offeror, the offer may be addressed to persons not identified in any meaningful way. Even so, it is important that an offer is made in such a way that where an unidentified person fulfils the criteria of the offer, a contract is deemed to have been formed. For example, an employment offer advertisement in a local newspaper for recruitment of manpower does not constitute a legally binding offer on the offeror because the identity of the potential employee is an essential element to a contract of employment. Unilateral disposition is the best means of illustrating a legally binding offer made to the general public, as a supplement to paragraphs 2 and 3 of article 69 CC. Article 193 CC reads as follows:

> Any person who makes a promise to the public of a reward in consideration for the performance of a job, such party shall be bound to deliver the reward to the person who performs such job according to the agreed conditions, even where such person performed the job prior to receiving the promise, or without thought of the promise of reward, or without knowledge thereof.

Where an offeror makes a promise to the public through an advertisement by which he or she promises to pay a sum of money or grant an economic reward in exchange for a specific performance, the offeror will be obligated to fulfil such promise to the offeree performing such act irrespective of its identity. In the case at hand, the identity of the offeree is not essential to the contract. The CC does not require that the offeree had prior knowledge of the offeror's promise in order to be entitled to the reward; mere performance suffices.

The second paragraph of Article 69 CC sheds light on another type of legally binding offer that is made to the public, that is, public display of products with their price tags in retail stores. This type of offer is very common in business practice. Here the law does not obligate the offeror to sell the exact good or service that is displayed; yet, the offeror is bound to sell identical or similar goods from its available stock or equivalent services for the same displayed price.

The last paragraph of article 69 CC makes it clear that mere advertisements for goods and services in publications, in addition to the distribution of price lists to the public as part of customary business practice, do not amount to legally binding offers. Such advertisements to the general public constitute invitations to negotiate, or treat, as long as they do not fall within the ambit of the first paragraph of article 69 CC.

2.3.1 *Retraction of Offer*

Article 70 CC deals with the point in time at which the offeror may validly retract its offer from the offeree. It goes on to say that

1. The offeror shall have the option to retract his offer as long as it is not accepted.
2. Where, however, the offeror has fixed a time limit for acceptance, or such time limit is required by the circumstances or the nature of the transaction, the offer shall remain open throughout such time limit and lapse upon its expiry.

The key in these circumstances is reasonableness. The CC does not provide any indication what constitutes reasonable time for acceptance of an offer, absent stipulation in the offer itself. Readers should consult Chapters 3 and 6, which discuss the various principles enunciated by the Court of Cassation in ascertaining the parties' intention and the construction of contracts. In addition to the expiration of an offer's time limit, or its non-acceptance by the offeree, the validity of the offer is deemed expired and thus retractable, where under article 71 CC the offeror dies or loses its legal capacity.[21]

Qatari law permits the offeror to revoke its offer as long as this was not accepted by the offeree. This is in alignment with article 67 CC. Moreover, the offeror is free to express the time period within which the offer remains valid, following which the offer expires. Thus, if the offeree does not accept the offer within the specified time, the offeror is not bound by its offer. However, if the offeree accepts the offer after its expiration, such 'after-the-expiration' acceptance will be deemed a new binding offer or 'counter-offer' by the offeree to the offeror. The offeror in this case is free to accept or reject the counter-offer.[22] The practice of assigning specified time limits for accepting offers is very common in Qatari commercial transactions, such as tender bids and auctions. Under classic Islamic law an offer may validly be revoked

---

[21] See chapter 12.5 concerning termination on account of a party's death.
[22] Equally an intrinsic part of classic Islamic law, as reflected in Arts 184–185 Majalla.

if it is not subject to a fixed time limit (*khiyarat syarat*) and provided it is not met with acceptance. The Malikis object to this argument.[23] All scholars are in general agreement that an offer may be terminated by revocation, lapse of time, failure of condition subject to which the offer was made, or death of the offeror.[24]

2.4 ACCEPTANCE

The Qatari CC follows well established principles concerning the requirements for the valid acceptance of an offer. Article 72 CC states that

> The acceptance must be in conformity with the offer for concluding the contract.
>
> An acceptance that goes beyond the offer, or that is accompanied by a restriction or modification, shall be deemed to be a rejection comprising a new offer.

Article 72 CC expresses the notion that in order for a contract to be formed the acceptance must be a mirror image of the offer. Any amendment to the offer will be considered a counter-offer. Unlike other civil codes which fail to address the issue of silence, article 73(1) CC makes it clear that although no statement shall be attributed to a person remaining silent, silence in circumstances requiring a statement shall be deemed as expressing acceptance. This rebuttable presumption will no doubt arise in the context of very particular contractual relationships governed by business custom or past and uniform conduct. Paragraphs 2 and 3 of article 73 CC make the point that

> 2. Silence in particular shall be deemed an acceptance where there have been previous dealings between the two contracting parties and the offer is related to such dealings or if it appears to benefit the offeree.
> 3. A buyer's silence after receiving purchased goods shall be regarded as acceptance of the terms of a sale.

Article 73 CC sheds light on a very important legal principle under the civil law tradition, which is that 'silence may not be deemed as acceptance'. This general rule is derived from the Arabic phrase in article 73 CC which reads: 'لا ينسب لساكت قول'. The English translation of the above phrase is 'No statement shall be attributed to a person who remains silent'. Thus, the law here

[23] Abd al-Razzaq al-Sanhuri, *Masadir al-Haqq fil-Fiqh al-Islami* (Cairo University 1954–59) vol 2, at 18.
[24] L A Khan Niazi, *Islamic Law of Contract* (Research Cell Dyal Singh Trust Library 1990) 71.

wants to draw a distinction between (i) silence as a negative response to an offer and (ii) silence as a *positive response* to an offer in the shape of an implicit expression of intention by the offeree. As discussed earlier, the true (common) intent prevails over the expressed intention.[25] So, if the true intent of the offeree matches the implicit expression of intention, then silence in this particular scenario may be deemed as acceptance.[26] Furthermore, the law makes it a crystal clear that if the circumstances of a commercial transaction dictate that the offeree must explicitly express its intent (the norms) but the offeree remains silent, then silence shall be deemed as acceptance. This approach is influenced by the Islamic legal tradition,[27] whereby the Al-Hanafi school of thought opined that silence in situations where a person is expected to declare its rejection shall be deemed an acceptance because such person had the opportunity to say so but did not.[28] Article 73 CC provides a real life example about a pattern of commercial transactions between an offeror and an offeree where silence by the offeree shall be deemed an acceptance because (i) the conduct of the parties is consistent with past transactions; or (ii) the transaction benefits the offeree who did not object to the offer in the first place; or (iii) the collection of the promised goods/ service by the offeree is deemed as acceptance to the offeror's terms and conditions.

Just like the situation with offers, an acceptance is terminated by the death or loss of capacity by the offeree, if this occurs before the acceptance reaches the notice of the offeror.[29] Thus, the knowledge of the offeror of the acceptance plays a crucial role for the validity of a binding acceptance.

2.5 CORRESPONDENCE OF OFFER AND ACCEPTANCE

2.5.1 *Contract Session*

In order to explain how the 'correspondence of offer and acceptance forms a binding contract', it is imperative to discuss the legal concept of the so-called 'contract session'. The Qatari legislator derived this legal principle from the Islamic legal tradition, which uses the Arabic term (مجلس العقد) pronounced

---

[25] See Chapter 3.
[26] A Faraj Yousef, *Restatement and Commentary of the Kuwaiti Civil Code: Comparative Law Study with the Egyptian Civil Code, supported by case law and jurisprudence* (Modern Academic Office 2014) vol 1, at 219.
[27] See Arts 175 and 177 Majalla.
[28] Yousef (n 26) at 219.
[29] Art 74 CC.

as (*majlis ala'aquid*). A contract session is defined as the session where the parties meet in person to negotiate the terms and conditions of the contract at the same (i) location and (ii) time.[30] The parties shall use their *best endeavour* to *negotiate directly* without being occupied with any other matter alongside this potential agreement. Their responses to any potential offer or acceptance shall take place within the contract session. The contract session expires when the parties either: (i) make a valid offer and a matching acceptance that result in a binding contract; or (ii) the offeree explicitly rejects an offer made by the offeror without making a counter-offer, and then walks away; or (iii) when one or all of the parties become occupied with a matter other than the subject-matter of the contract.[31] The accepted structure of a sale or any other contract or unilateral obligation should be considered 'simple'. Therefore, the creation of a contract cannot be supposed through a gradual period of time. The structure of a contract is either created immediately or not formed at all.[32]

According to the narration by Hakim bin Hizam, Allah's Apostle said: 'The seller and buyer have the right to keep or return goods as long as they have not parted or till they part and if both parties spoke the truth and described the defects and qualities (of the goods), then they would be blessed in their trans-action, and if they told lies or hid something, then the blessings of their trans-action would be lost'.[33] 'The *majilis* therefore begins when the parties so come together and ends only when they separate physically or constructively'.[34]

The Hanbali school of thought, which the State of Qatar has adopted, expands the duration of the contract session until the expiration of the validity of an offer made by one of the parties, even if they physically leave the contract session. The response to this timely valid offer can be made either directly or through post. This approach is more flexible and reflects a practical scenario of commercial transactions compared with the rigid approach adopted by the Hanafi school of thought. Moreover, the Hanbalis adopt the rule that the offeree is not obligated to accept an offer instantaneously during the contract session, as long as the offeror did not revoke the offer. This is done in order for the offeree to respond at the time it suits him or her. Once the contract session expires without forming a binding contract, the parties can move away without any legal obligations towards each other.

---

[30] TP Hughes, *Dictionary of Islam*, (W. H. Allen & Co 1885) 32.
[31] Yousef (n 26) at 223.
[32] M Khansary, *Monieyat-al-taleb fe Sharhe-el-Makaseb* (Nashre Eslami Publ. 1418 H) 240.
[33] Bukhari, Hadith 293.
[34] N Saleh, 'Definition and Formation of Contract under Islamic and Arab Laws' (1990) 5 Arab LQ 101, at 115.

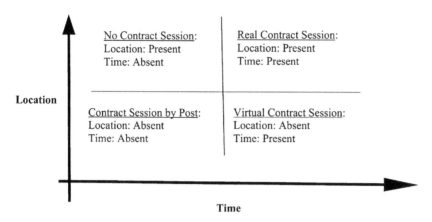

FIGURE 2.1 Contract sessions matrix

2.5.2 *Types of Contract Sessions*

The contract session adopted by the Islamic tradition is known by scholars as the 'real contact session' because the parties to the negotiation are present at the same place and time as explained above.[35] However, the Qatari legislator adopted other types/forms of contract sessions to accommodate real life scenarios, which the law must regulate. If we pay attention to the matrix illustrated in Figure 2.1, one comes to the conclusion that there exist two additional types of contract sessions, namely, (i) 'virtual' contract sessions whereby the parties engaging into contract negotiations are present in time but absent in location; for example, when the parties negotiate using a video teleconference platform, such as Microsoft Teams, Zoom, or through a conventional telephone; (ii) contract sessions by post whereby the parties engaging into contract negotiations are absent in both time and location, as is the case with communication by email or registered mail. Last, but not least, there is no valid contract session if the parties that intend to negotiate a contract are present in a location but absent in time because they cannot communicate during the session.

It is now pertinent to examine the relevant articles of the Civil Code in order to determine how the law regulates each type of contract session. Article 75 CC states that

---

[35] Without wishing to simplify the issue, Islamic scholars, such as Ibn al-Jawzī, speak of the option of meeting session (*khiyar al-majilis*). He establishes the legal elements of a binding sale according to the principle of *khiyār al-majlis* (option of the meeting), which dictates that a sale can be revoked at will until the parties decide to end the session. Abū al-Faraj Ibn al-Jawzī, *Sayd al-khāṭir*, (eds.) Abd al-Qādir Aḥmad ʿAṭā (Dār al-Kutub al-ʿIlmīya 1992) 228–29.

Where the offer is made during the contract session without containing a time limit for acceptance, both parties shall retain the option until the session ends. Where the offeror retracts its offer or the session ends without acceptance, the offer shall be considered terminated.

Article 76 CC goes on to say that

Notwithstanding anything to the contrary, (i) an agreement between the parties; (ii) [or subject to any] requirements by law or customary usage, the contract shall be deemed to have been concluded if the offer is accepted.

It is clear that articles 75 and 76 CC allow both the offeror and offeree to retain their decision until the end of the contract session. If an offer is made by the offeror during the session without time limit, then the offeree can accept or reject the offer on, or before, the end of the session. Moreover, the offeror may revoke or retract its offer, if the offeree does not make an unconditional acceptance before the revocation reaches him or her. If the contract session expires naturally as per the rules governing the real contract session as explained above, the offer becomes invalid and non-binding. If the offer meets the unconditional acceptance during the contract session, then the contract is binding by virtue of the law and customary usage.

Article 77 CC addresses promises made by the offeror and offeree concluded by correspondence. Contracts concluded in this manner 'shall be deemed to have been made at the time and place when and where acceptance reaches the offeror's notice, unless otherwise agreed or required by law or usage'. The law here regulates the contract session by post under article 77 CC, where the contract formed by this type of contract session is concluded when the acceptance made by the offeree reaches the offeror's notice; that is, requiring knowledge and awareness.[36] It is worth mentioning that the above approach adopted by the Qatari legislator is much simpler than the postal rule of acceptance under the common law tradition.

Article 78 CC effectively renders contracts made by telephone and over the internet,[37] or by any other similar means as being made in real contract sessions. Article 78 CC stipulates that 'such contract shall, in respect of place, be regarded as having been concluded between absent contracting parties'. While the law regulates the 'virtual' contract session under article 78 CC,

---

[36] See Court of Cassation Judgment 4/2008, where the claimant argued that while he had sent a signed copy of a contract to the Ministry of Municipalities, the Ministry's counter-signature which arrived a month later was no longer valid because of a time lapse. The Court of Cassation held that the original offer by the claimant was still effective, arguing that the meeting of offer and acceptance is a factual situation dependent on context. An offer can only be revoked if it reaches the offeree before the latter dispatched its acceptance.

[37] Not explicitly mentioned in the Arabic original text of Art 77 CC.

the contract between the offeror and offeree is formed when the offer meets acceptance and as long as the parties are negotiating over a video teleconference platform or the telephone. The parties are considered present in respect of time but absent in respect of place.

2.5.3 *Essential and Non-essential Elements*

It is common practice in all legal systems to exclude non-essential elements from the factors inhibiting the formation of contract. Article 79 CC emulates this approach, stating that

1. Where the contracting parties have agreed on all the essential terms of the contract and have left certain details to be agreed at a later date without stipulating that, failing agreement on these details, the contract shall not be concluded, the contract shall be deemed to have been concluded.
2. In the event of a dispute regarding those details not yet agreed upon, the court shall resolve the dispute according to the nature of the transaction, the provisions of the law and custom, and the rules of justice.

Article 79 CC stipulates that a binding contract is formed where the parties reach an agreement concerning all essential terms and conditions. The law grants the parties some latitude to postpone discussions on marginal or auxiliary terms and conditions to a later stage (effectively after the contract has been formed), instead of forcing the parties either to accept all terms and conditions. This approach respects the true intent of the parties and facilitates the conclusion of commercial transactions, which are necessary to keep the economy going. If a dispute arises between the parties before all pertinent terms and conditions are settled, then the court will have the discretion to adjudicate the matter by (i) construing the true intent of the parties and (ii) filling the gaps in the agreement as necessary.[38] If the parties during the contact session mutually agree, explicitly or implicitly, to withhold the conclusion of the commercial transaction until all elements, including the marginal/auxiliary elements, are settled, then the law will respect the will of the parties and the contract will be deemed as not having been formed until that condition is met.

2.5.4 *Contracting by Standard Terms*

Standard terms and conditions are common in Qatari contract law, whether adhesive or commercial in nature. An offer may be made in such a manner

---

[38] See Chapter 6.

that incorporates standard terms. This is aptly recognised in article 80(1) CC, save where 'a party proves that they had no notice of such provisions or had no opportunity to discover them at the time of the agreement'.[39] Article 105 CC underscores the inherent imbalance of power in adhesion contracts, acknowledging in the process that the absence of negotiations as a result of the stronger party's (effective imposition of) standard terms does not entail that the other party has not expressed its acceptance of the offer.[40] An arbitrary term may be expunged under article 106 CC even where the adhering party was aware that the term was arbitrary. Arbitrary contractual terms in adhesion contracts are prohibited as a matter of public policy and the adhering party's knowledge is not considered an abuse of right.[41] Article 80(2) CC goes on to say that

> Where such provisions of which no notice has been taken are essential, the contract shall be invalid. If the provisions are auxiliary, the judge shall resolve any dispute arising therefrom in accordance with the nature of the transaction, current usage and the rules of justice.

This provision aims to regulate a common practice within the commercial and financial sectors, in situations where the parties entering into a contract use an industry-developed 'contract model' as a template for the agreement. Standard terms are useful tools to facilitate negotiations in commercial transactions because they contain detailed provisions regulating matters that the law itself does not regulate in the same level of depth. However, standard terms may pose a risk on the parties' autonomy to draft their contract. The biggest risk here is that the parties most likely accept terms and conditions they do not understand fully. Any adopted provisions from contract models should be redrafted for the specific transaction to avoid overlooking matters that may arise in a potential dispute. Article 80 CC regulates the use of contract models, subject to the full knowledge of the parties during the contract session. If a party challenges these terms before the courts and proves 'no notice of such provisions or no opportunity to discover them at the time of the agreement', then the disputed provisions produce no legal effect. Furthermore, if the disputed standard terms are considered 'essential' to the agreement, then the court will deem the contract null and void. However, if the disputed provisions are considered 'secondary'/'supplemental'/'auxiliary', the contract is deemed to have been formed.

---

[39] See also Art 106 CC.
[40] See Court of Appeal Judgment 241/2010; Court of Cassation Judgment 74/2011.
[41] See Court of Cassation Judgment 17/2012, where it was held that a guarantee for a future obligation under Art 1812 CC is invalid, unless the two parties specify in advance in the guarantee contract the amount of the debt guaranteed by the guarantor.

2.6 OBLIGATIONS IN SPECIFIC CONTRACTUAL TYPES

In addition to the general rules prescribed by the Civil Code for generic contracts, Qatari law has set out special rules for a number of specific contracts outlined in the Civil Code and other special laws. These specific contractual types are commonly used by the public and their regulation is a matter of public interest. The elements required to form such contracts are mandatory, in addition to offer, acceptance and intention to be bound. If there is an overlap between certain elements between the CC and the special laws, then the elements prescribed by special laws supersede. Even so, the courts have discretion to decide which law applies to a specific contract. For example, a lease contract could be regulated by either the Civil Code or the Property Leasing Law.[42] According to the Court of Cassation, if leased premises are transformed into a hotel, then the lease contract falls outside the ambit of the Property Leasing Law and is encompassed under the Civil Code.[43] This is an interpretation of the exemption list as stipulated in article 2 of the Property Leasing Law.

2.6.1 *Sales Contracts*

As stipulated in article 88 of the Commercial Law, two elements are required to form a sales contract, namely, (i) the sale item and (ii) the price. The Qatari legislator emphasised that the buyer must exercise due diligence over the sale item; however, if the seller provides a statement and basic description of the sale item in the sale contract, then the buyer's due diligence is deemed sufficient. Furthermore, article 89 of the Commercial Law echoes the general rule in article 69 CC, which states that the seller's announced sale prices for goods and services to the public shall not be deemed as constituting a binding offer. The announcement is a non-binding invitation to negotiate.

If the sale contract is made conditional to the buyer's acceptance of a trial sample of goods or services, the seller shall facilitate the trial for the buyer as stipulated in article 91 of the Commercial Law. The buyer has the right to either accept or reject the sale within a specified period of time as agreed between the parties. If the sale contract does not specify the trial period for the goods or services, then the buyer shall inform the seller of its decision within a 'reasonable time' decided by the seller. It is worth noting that the law deems the buyer's silence after the expiry of the trial period as acceptance of the sale transaction, thus binding the buyer to the sale contract. Another type of trial condition is mentioned in the law due to its importance in the sale of food

---

[42] Law No. 10 of 2008, as amended by Law No. 20 of 2009.
[43] Court of Cassation Judgment 113/2012.

merchandise; this is the so-called 'taste trial'. Here, the buyer has the right to accept or reject a taste sample within a trial period specified in the sale contract, or in accordance with 'customary tradition'. The sale contract is formed only after the buyer announces its acceptance of the taste sample according to article 92 of the Commercial Law.

Moreover, articles 97, 98 and 99 of the Commercial Law provide the general rule for setting the price of the sale item. The price in sale contracts shall be based on the market price for such commodity at the time and place in which the sale item must be delivered to the buyer. If no market price is available, then the market price shall be determined by 'customary tradition'. If the sale contract does not specify a sale price, then the sale transaction shall be concluded on the basis of the price at which the parties are used to doing business. If there is no previous commercial transaction between the parties, then the sale will be held at the market price unless it becomes clear from the circumstances or from business customary practice that another price should be adopted. The law also allows a third party in the form of a 'referee' or 'market expert' to determine the price of the sale item in question, where the market price shall be adopted on the 'day' of occurrence of the sale transaction.[44] As a last resort, if the third party fails to determine the market price for the sale item, then the competent court will have the discretion to determine the price.

2.6.2 *Lease Contracts*

Pursuant to article 3 of the Property Leasing Law, lease contracts must be written, and thus, oral agreements for leasing property are not acceptable. The law here obligates the lessee to register the lease contract with the Real Estate Lease Registration Office (the 'Office') that is part of the Ministry of Municipality and Urban Planning.[45] In the case of a dispute between lessor and lessee, the competent court will only admit as evidence lease contracts registered at the Office.[46] The Property Leasing Law is applicable to all lease contracts, save for those listed in article 2 thereof, namely, public property, agricultural land, vacant land, industrial service areas, apartments, hotels and tourist accommodation and residential units reserved by the state or the private sector for their employees.

---

[44] See Court of Cassation Judgment 8/2016, where it held that although the price in a sale contract is a cornerstone of the contract, Arts 425 and 426 CC allow for this to be later inserted and/or decided by a third party.

[45] See Court of Cassation Judgment 123/2010, concerning the registration of real estate transactions; equally, Court of Cassation Judgment 221/2014.

[46] Exceptionally, there is an exemption for lease contracts entered into on or before 15 December 2008.

Other general elements for lease contracts are regulated by articles 582 to 589 of the Civil Code. However, unlike offer, acceptance and intention, which are *sine qua non* elements of contracts, the existence of these other elements does not inhibit the formation of the contract. In summary, lease contracts must include details concerning (i) the leased premise(s); (ii) the amount of rent for a specified period; and (iii) the duration of the lease agreement in its entirety.[47] The lessee may pay the rent to the lessor in the form of cash or other financial considerations. If the parties fail to fix the rent amount in the lease contract, then the competent court will assess and determine the rent on the basis of a comparative rent of similar properties. Furthermore, if the parties fail to agree on the actual commencement date of the lease, then the commencement date that is written in the lease contract shall be deemed as the effective date. Moreover, if the parties fail to agree on the duration of the lease contract, then the lease is deemed expired when either party notifies the other of its intention to vacate the premises. The notification must be served to the other party prior to the commencement of the second half of such period, provided that such notice shall not exceed three months.

2.6.3 *Employment/Labour Contracts*

One of the distinct elements of employment/labour contracts is that they must be 'bilateral'. The identity of both the employer and employee must be clear from the outset. Thus, unilateral agreements as described earlier in this chapter cannot be used to create binding employment/labour contracts. Other required elements include (i) the scope of work; (ii) the duration of the contract, that is, definite or indefinite;[48] and (iii) the wage or payment in exchange of the work performed. Employment/labour contracts are regulated by the Civil Code in addition to special laws, such as Law No. 15 of 2016 (the 'Human Resources Law'), Law No. 14 of 2004 ('Labour Law') as amended by Law No. 3 of 2014 and Law No. 15 of 2017 ('Domestic Workers Law'). It is worth highlighting that the Human Resources Law regulates employment in the government sector, whereas the Labour Law was enacted to regulate employment in the private sector. The Domestic Workers Law is self-explanatory as it is meant to regulate employment between individuals and their domestic workers.

---

[47] See Court of Cassation Judgment 159/2012.

[48] Arts 40 and 41 of Labour Law No. 14 of 2004 indicate that the extension of the work relationship, even with successive contracts, is in fact a single employment contract, and its continuity requires that the worker not be deprived of any advantage or benefit derived from the employer for any period during the related service. Hence, offer and acceptance are presumed unless specifically rejected. See Court of Cassation Judgment 98/2014.

2.6.4 *Public or Administrative Contracts*

Contracts between a public and a private entity are known as administrative contracts[49] and are typically regulated by administrative law, with jurisdiction conferred to the administrative circuit of the court of first instance.[50] Qatari law has endowed public contracts with a special consideration compared to civil and commercial contracts due to their overriding public interest. Public contracts require the following additional elements in order to be validly formed, namely, (ii) a public authority (i.e. governmental entity) must be a party to the contract; (ii) the contract must serve a public interest; and (iii) the contract must operate or facilitate a public facility, where the public will have free access to it, such as streets and petrol stations.

---

[49] Administrative contracts are regulated by Law No 24/2015 on the Regulation of Tenders and Auctions, known as the Procurement Law.

The Court of Cassation in Judgment 49/2008 defined administrative contracts as 'contracts concluded between a legal person of public law and which relate to the operation of a public service and which include exceptional and unusual conditions [clause *exorbitante*] that are distinct from the ambit of private law', iterated in Court of Cassation Judgment 118/2008. See also Court of Cassation Judgment 100/2016, which further stipulated that a contract is not of an administrative nature, unless related to the management or organisation of a public facility, and the administration has demonstrated its intention to adopt public law by including in the contract exceptional and unusual conditions.

[50] Disputes arising from administrative contracts confer jurisdiction upon the administrative circuit, in accordance with Art 3(5) of Law No 7/2007 on the Settlement of Administrative Disputes; public housing disputes are not considered administrative disputes. See Court of Cassation Judgment 28/2010.

3

Intention to Be Bound and Cause

3.1 INTRODUCTION

This chapter attempts to build on Chapter 2, which dealt with the two building blocks necessary for the formation of contracts, namely, offer and acceptance. Here, we examine the remaining two requirements: the intention (*nīyya*) to be bound and the existence of good cause or *causa*. Unlike English law where the so-called consideration is additionally required, this is not entertained in the CC, even if in places the language seems to suggest consideration.[1] This is in fact not true.[2] The chapter goes on to show how the parties' intention to be bound may be expressed and how the courts can make sense of such intent when the parties disagree about what it is they had offered or accepted. Intent has been a significant aspect of Islamic law.[3] A significant part of this chapter will deal with the legal nature of promises, as unilateral acts, and whether they are enforceable under any circumstances. As will be demonstrated, Qatari law is generally reluctant to enforce promises.

3.2 EXPRESSION OF INTENTION

In the civil law tradition, the existence of offer and acceptance thereto are insufficient for the conclusion of a contract. The glue that transforms offer and acceptance into a *binding* contract is the parties' intention to be bound.[4]

---

[1] For example, Art 77 CL; Art 193 CC.
[2] It should be mentioned that despite the fact that the QFC hails itself as a common law jurisdiction, Art 31(2) of QFC Regulation No 4 of 2005 (QFC Contracts Regulations) expressly states that 'consideration is not required for a contract to be binding'.
[3] P R Powers, *Intent in Islamic Law: Motive and Meaning in Medieval Sunni Fiqh* (Brill 2015); equally, O Arabi, 'Intention and Method in Sanhuri's Fiqh: Cause as Ulterior Motive' (1997) 4 *Islamic Law and Society* 200.
[4] Court of Cassation Judgment 124/2011; Court of Cassation Judgment 124/2012.

It is not uncommon for the offeree to either a) avoid any desire of being bound to an offer or, b) if he or she desires to be bound, to possess a different understanding of the offer from that intended by the offeror. In both cases there is clearly an offer and (something that resembles an) acceptance, but what is missing is a) an intention to be bound (in the first case) and b) a *dissensus* as to what was actually agreed (in the second case). Where a common intention to be bound[5] is missing there is ultimately no contract to speak of. In most cases acceptance is also a reflection of an intention to be bound, but there may well be cases where acceptance and intention should not be conflated.[6]

In the spirit of the civil law tradition, article 65(1) of the CC emphasises the centrality of intention, further stipulating that

> An intention shall be expressed orally or in writing, by a commonly used sign, by actual consensual exchange, and also by conduct that, in the circumstances, leaves no doubt as to its true meaning.

Article 65(1) CC discourages any reliance on form or formalities concerning the manner of ascertaining or expressing the parties' intention to be bound. This is further enhanced by paragraph 2 of article 65 CC, according to which 'a declaration of intention may be implied when neither the law, nor the agreement, nor the nature of the transaction requires that such declaration be expressed'. No doubt, some transactions will require a particular form of expressing intention and this must be followed.[7] However, given that many transactions are concluded by way of email exchanges, the mere payment of the requested fee by the buyer to the seller,[8] or by conduct,[9] intention is

---

[5] Intention to be bound, as a necessary element in the formation of contracts, should be distinguished from the parties' 'common intention' under Art 169 CC. In the latter case, the parties have already agreed to be bound by their offer and acceptance but are unsure as to the common goal of the contract. See Chapter 6 concerning interpretation.

[6] Art 167 CL. for example, stipulates that passenger embarkation on means of transport represents acceptance, 'unless it is proven that the passenger's intention was not to conclude a contract for transportation'; equally, the Court of Cassation, Judgment 236/2011, held that in order for possession to be considered as a title deed according to Art 970 CC it must be actual and accompanied by the intent of ownership, free of any ambiguity; similarly, Court of Cassation Judgment 60/2012; the intent in the mortgage contract requires official form under Arts 1058 and 1080 CC. See to this effect, Court of Cassation Judgments 62/2013 and 167/2016.

[7] See, for example, Court of Cassation Judgment 123/2010, concerning the registration of real estate transactions.

[8] See Court of Cassation Judgment 76/2011, where it was held that unless otherwise agreed payment of the deposit means confirmation of continuation of the contract.

[9] For example, Arts 588 and 626 CC specify that if the lease contract expires and the lessee continues to benefit from the leased property with the knowledge of the lessor and without objection from him, the contract shall be deemed to have been renewed with its first conditions. See Court of Cassation Judgment 134/2013.

clearly presumed in certain crucial moments in the lifecycle of the exchange. The buyer is deemed to have agreed to the seller's offer, as well as its terms and conditions, upon emailing its acceptance to the offer, or upon receipt of the goods at its premises, and in more trivial transactions, the offeree's intention is presumed upon payment of the fee. It is equally taken for granted that neither party may unilaterally alter or amend the conditions in the agreement, as this requires the mutual will of all parties.[10]

In one case decided by the Court of Cassation, the respondent refused to pay the claimant by arguing there was no contract between them. The claimant relied on email exchanges and photocopies of bank transactions showing that the respondent had indeed intended to contract with him.[11] The Court of Cassation relied on article 4(1) of the Electronic Commerce Law[12] which states that 'An offer or acceptance of an offer may be expressed, in whole or in part, by means of electronic communications'. The Court of Cassation emphasised that the corresponding emails clearly demonstrated that the parties intended to enter into an agreement without the need for written documents.[13]

3.2.1 *Dissensus*

Dissensus, in the sense explained above, is a particularly vexing issue in the law of contract. As neither the law nor the courts can accurately predict the parties' desire when making their offer or acceptance, some sensible principles must be applied in order to, at least, presume or deduce the parties' individual intention. A necessary distinction should be made at this point to avoid confusion. The parties' intention to be bound under article 65 CC is wholly different from the parties' common intention, which refers to the parties' common contractual goal. The parties' 'common intention' is meaningful only where the parties have actually formed an undisputable common intention, in which case the existence of a contract is not in doubt. In such

[10] Court of Cassation Judgment 35/2014. By extension, neither party may unilaterally terminate the contract. The Court of Cassation refers to the contract as 'the law of the parties' and developed its 'two wills' theory. See Court of Cassation Judgment 67/2014; equally, Court of Cassation Judgment 109/2015.
[11] Contracting through electronic means is recognised in the case law of the Court of Cassation. See Judgment 275/2016; equally Court of Appeal Judgments 483/2018 and 526/2018.
[12] Law No. 16 of 2010 on the Promulgation of the Electronic Commerce and Transactions Law (Electronic Commerce Law).
[13] See above (n 10). See commentary in A Al-Amoury, 'Admissibility and Reliability of Electronic Evidence before Qatari Courts', available at: www.tamimi.com/law-update-articles/admissibility-and-reliability-of-electronic-evidence-before-qatari-courts/

cases it makes sense to assess defects of consent[14] as well as provide an objective interpretation of the parties' mutual obligations on the basis of their common intention.[15] Prior to an indisputable intention to be bound there does not exist a 'common intention'.

Paragraph 1 of article 68 CC distinguishes between 'intention' and 'actual intention'. Although the translation is inaccurate, 'actual intention' refers to a hidden intention of the offeror that was not fully expressed. 'Intent' is tantamount to the will expressed and understood by the offeree. Article 68(1) CC goes on to say that where actual intent differs from (expressed and objectively understood) intent, the latter prevails. This is clearly an objective test for intent and earnestness. As true as this usually is, it does not always reflect the parties' reality. It is not uncommon for the offer to be conveyed in such a manner that not only is it unclear and ambiguous in and of itself but also the offeree's understanding of what has actually been offered may be coloured by its, cultural, linguistic or other underpinnings. It is for this reason that paragraph 2 of article 68 CC qualifies the subjective test set out in paragraph 1 thereto. It states that

> However, the offeree may rely on such expression even though it contradicts the intent of the offeror if he proves that he believed the expression conformed, without ambiguity, with the true intent of the offeror.

Paragraph 2 goes on to cement what is otherwise the standard test in the civil law tradition, which is effectively objective in nature, despite language suggesting subjective qualities (e.g. 'he proves', 'he believes'). Because it is next to impossible for the offeree to prove 'without ambiguity' (effectively beyond reasonable doubt) that its personal belief was consistent with what it thought the offeror actually intended, save in limited circumstances, such commonality of intention can only be assessed objectively.[16] That is, the offeree must demonstrate more than simply on a balance of probabilities, that a reasonable person in the circumstances of the parties in question would have understood the offer in the manner argued by the offeree.[17]

---

[14] See Chapter 8 concerning defects of consent.
[15] See Chapter 7.
[16] This objective dimension may also be borne out of the Court of Cassation's Judgment 63/2008. Although in that case the Court dealt with an existing contract (a lease) its rationale may be applied by analogy to ascertain the parties' intention prior to the formation of the contract. The Court postulated that the courts must construe the parties' intention on the basis of relevant facts and circumstances, which belies objective outcomes.
[17] See J Smits, *Contract Law: A Comparative Introduction* (Edward Elgar, 2nd ed, 2017) 65–70.

3.2.2 *The Parties' Common Intention*

In Chapter 6, we explain how the courts interpret the parties' contract in order to determine the existence of their common intent, when this is not abundantly clear from the text of the agreement. That process assumes the formation of a contract, whereas the identification of a common intention in this chapter is a necessary condition for the formation of a contract to be. Even so, the discussion on interpretation is important because the principles on common intention apply mutatis mutandis in the present context. Although the CC is not predicated on classic Islamic contract law, it is important to highlight the centrality of the meeting of the minds (*rida*) in transforming offer and acceptance into a valid contract. This is reflected in the Majalla, which clearly stipulates that intention constitutes 'the connection between offer and acceptance (*ijab wa qabūl*)'.[18]

Article 169(2) CC demands that construction must be predicated on the 'common intention' of the parties:

> … without restriction to the literal meaning of the words, taking into account the nature of the transaction as well as the honesty and confidence that should prevail between the parties in accordance with commercial custom.

In line with transnational practice, the parties' common intention is imputed by the courts and is generally demonstrated by reference to objective standards under the particular circumstances of the parties. There is no indication that the situation is any different in the Qatari CC.[19] The parties' common intention may just as well be demonstrated by what the contract aims to achieve, in which case the individualistic pursuits of one of the parties, contrary to the expressed common pursuit, will not prevail over the common intention. Where the parties' common subjective intention is not susceptible to accurate verification then such common intention will be inferred on the basis of the average person under the circumstances of the parties.[20] Article 169(2) CC makes the task a lot easier for the courts by adding another possible inference as to the parties' common intention, namely, prevailing commercial custom.[21] The courts' pursuit of

---

[18] Majalla, Arts 103–4.
[19] In its Judgment 86/2008, the Court of Cassation was asked to determine whether the parties to a contract providing for arbitration held the same intention following two addenda to their initial contract, one of which clearly opted for litigation. The Court of Cassation held that the lower court was entitled to infer the parties' intention in a manner that it is more fulfilling to their purpose, on the basis of tolerable grounds and without transcending the apparent meaning of words.
[20] Art 4.1(2) UNIDROIT PICC.
[21] This is common to all legal systems, for example, s 346 of the German Commercial Code states that 'due consideration shall be given to prevailing commercial custom and usages

the parties' common intention must not deviate from the apparent meaning of the terms of the contract and associated documents, without, however, being restricted to what is indicated by a specific phrase or words.[22]

Qatari courts employ standard language to emphasise the 'complete' authority of the trial court to interpret both the contract and related documents in order to ascertain the common intention of the parties.[23] The courts are under an obligation 'not to deviate from the apparent meaning of the terms of the contract or other written documents and should consider what a particular expression or phrase therein truly indicates. The courts must be guided by the nature of the transaction and the degree of trust expected, in accordance with the current custom in transactions'.[24] Where the courts in ascertaining the parties' common intention determine that the apparent meaning of contractual terms is different to the parties' common intention they are bound to fully justify how the non-apparent meaning best reflects the parties' common intention.[25] Hence, the overall context of the parties' contractual relationship is central to the construction of the parties' common intention.[26] Under no circumstances should the courts exceed the explicit statement or words in the parties' contract.[27] The Court of Cassation has emphasised that the courts should not put too much emphasis on the meaning of a specific sentence, but on the overall meaning of all its sentences and conditions, guided by the nature of the transaction and the honesty and trust that should guide the parties in the fulfilment of their transaction.[28]

3.2.3 *Timing of Intent*

The precise time of utterance of intent is crucial. As article 66(1) CC stipulates, 'an expression of intention shall become effective once uttered'. Hence,

---

concerning the meaning and effect of acts and omissions among merchants' and Art 1511(2) of the French CCP, which states that tribunals 'shall take into account trade usages'.

[22] Court of Cassation Judgment 5/2012.

[23] Court of Cassation Judgment 44/2010; Court of Cassation Judgment 87/2010; Court of Cassation Judgment 113/2012; Court of Cassation Judgment 53/2012; Court of Cassation Judgment 40/2013; Court of Cassation Judgment 394/2015.

[24] Court of Cassation Judgment 219/2011.

[25] Court of Cassation Judgment 23/2012; Court of Cassation Judgment 323/2014; Court of Cassation Judgment 18/2015.

[26] See Court of Cassation Judgment 126/2013, where it was held that the courts must be led by what is stated in the contract as a whole and the circumstances of its issuance; see also Court of Cassation Judgment 120/2014; equally Court of Cassation Judgment 80/2015; Court of Cassation Judgment 437/2018.

[27] Court of Cassation Judgment 82/2011; Court of Cassation Judgment 84/2011.

[28] Court of Cassation Judgment 219/2012.

once uttered, whether by the offeror or offeree such intent becomes binding and cannot be rescinded, subject to the following discussion. If the intention to be bound could be rescinded at any time, then the existence of contracts would come into doubt. As a general rule, article 66(1) CC, following long-established tradition, iterates that an expression of intention shall have no effect until it comes to the notice of the intended recipient. It may well be that because of the particular method, or underlying exigencies, of the dispatch the intended offer or acceptance does not reach the other party immediately. As a result, revocation is possible until such time as the offer or acceptance has not yet reached the intended recipient. Paragraph 2 of article 66 CC introduces a rebuttable presumption concerning the precise point in time at which the addressee received its counterparty's intent. It stipulates that 'the intended recipient shall be deemed to have notice of the declaration of intention from the time that it reaches him'. Consequently, secure methods of receipt, such as email correspondence[29] and recorded delivery, will constitute significant evidence of receipt.

By implication, if the retraction of intent reaches the addressee prior, or at the same time, as the original expression of intent, then the latter expression of intent is superseded by the retraction, and hence, the contract does not come into existence.[30] Again, this is based on long-standing practice in both the civil law and common law traditions.[31] In line with this tradition, although the CC is silent, an offer may not be retracted if it contains a fixed time for acceptance or is otherwise declared as irrevocable.[32] The same *mutatis mutandis* applies to the revocation of the acceptance by the offeree.

3.2.4 *Evidence to Prove Intent and Common Intent*

The Qatari CCP does not ascribe to the so-called parole evidence rule, whereby evidence that is extrinsic to the contract, such as draft contracts, statements and emails exchanged during the negotiation of the contract,

---

[29] In order for electronic evidence to be admissible before the court, it must take the form of a data message which, according to Art 1(4) of the Electronic Commerce Law, is any type of information that was sent, received, displayed or stored by any means of electronic communications. It must moreover comply with the requirements of Art 26 of the Electronic Commerce Law. Article 26 generally demands certainty of the origin of the data message and the identity of its receiver to ensure that the data message was not manipulated by the parties or that it was not a counterfeit.

[30] Art 167 CC.

[31] Art 2.1.4 UNIDROIT PICC.

[32] Art 2.1.4(2), ibid.

travaux or witness statements are inadmissible.[33] The CCP implicitly allows all such evidence in order to allow the judge to ascertain the parties' common intention and excludes nothing that has probative value, subject to the requirements demanded of each evidence as discussed.[34] This is evident in the language and practice of the Court of Cassation, though which it has supported the authority of trial courts to examine and interpret all relevant evidence pertaining to contracts, so long 'as judgments are reasoned and based on reasonable grounds'.[35] The existence of an employment relationship (which by extension evinces an employment contract) has been viewed as a question of fact by the Court of Cassation[36] and the same is true with the renewal of a lease.[37] As a result, all evidence with a probative value is admissible.[38] This may include the appointment of an expert, which is at the discretion of the courts.[39] The Court of Cassation has made it clear that probative value is tantamount to the 'truth'.[40] In several instances, the Court of Cassation has ordered that the parties provide oral evidence in court where the material presented, including the underlying contract, did not provide sufficient clarity.[41] This rationale is aided by specialist legislation. Article 38 of Labor Law No. 14 of 2004 indicates that if the contract was not in writing, the employee may prove the work relationship by all means of proof.[42] No doubt, such instances are exceptional and the general rule remains whereby it is not permissible to disprove a written document except by another written document.[43]

---

[33] See Art 4.3 UNIDROIT PICC, which refers to a list of five extrinsic factors as relevant circumstances in interpreting a contract. This is consistent with the Qatari CC, save for the fact that extrinsic factors are expressly permitted in the PICC but not the CC.

[34] It is established that photocopies of originals, whether written documents or photographs have no probative effect except to the extent they lead to the signed originals, if any. See Court of Cassation Judgment 9/2010.

[35] Court of Cassation Judgment 161/2010; Court of Cassation Judgment 45/2011; Court of Cassation Judgment 74/2011; Court of Cassation Judgment 22/2012; Court of Cassation Judgment 113/2012.

[36] Court of Cassation Judgment 89/2011.

[37] Court of Cassation Judgment 33/2012; equally, Court of Cassation Judgment 158/2012.

[38] Court of Cassation Judgment 89/2011.

[39] Court of Cassation Judgment 93/2012; equally Court of Cassation Judgment 191/2012.

[40] Court of Cassation Judgment 90/2011; equally Court of Cassation Judgment 154/2012; Court of Cassation Judgment 22/2013; Court of Cassation Judgment 369/2014; Court of Cassation Judgment 139/2014; Court of Cassation Judgment 258/2016.

[41] See Court of Cassation Judgment 10/2011. This was viewed by the Court as a valid exception to the principle of material evidence only as articulated in Arts 261 and 262 CCP; see equally Court of Cassation Judgment 47/2011.

[42] See Court of Cassation Judgment 98/2014.

[43] Court of Cassation Judgment 115/2012.

3.3 INTENTION IN UNILATERAL CONTRACTS AND PROMISES

The following two subsections will examine unilateral contracts and promises. Despite the admonition in article 1 CC, which reserves a supplementary role for Islamic law, there are several unilateral dispositions under Islamic law that are not regulated by the CC. These include: gifts (*hadiyah*), loans (*qard*), wills (*wasiya*) and endowments (*waqf*), as well as promises more generally (*wa'ad*).[44] Qatari law regulates several of these in statute,[45] but an analysis of these is beyond the ambit of this book. A brief analysis should be helpful in order for the uninitiated reader to appreciate the complexities of Islamic law in this field and its potential application to contracts with a *Sharia*-based component.

3.3.1 *The Position in Islamic Law: In Brief*

The term *wa'ād* which is translated as promise is defined by Badr al-Dīn al-'Ainī as notifying someone of conveying something good to him in the future.[46] Ibn Arafah, a proponent of the Maliki School, defined it as notification in which the notifier creates an obligation along with fulfilment in the future.[47] The qualifier 'who is meant to fulfil in the future' is explained by al-Raṣṣā' in his commentary as a promisor who does not intend to fulfil the obligation in the future and as a result the subject of the promise does not qualify as a *wa'ād*.[48] In other words, because it is not recognised as an enforceable promise (*wa'ād*) it is assumed that there is no intention to fulfil the obligation at the time it was made.

With this in mind, a promise is generally lawful in Islam. This is based on several authorities. From the Qur'an, we have the saying of Allah Ta'ālā:

> Also mention in the Book (the story of) Isma'il: He was (strictly) true to what he promised, and he was an apostle (and) a prophet.[49]

---

[44] See I Bantekas, J Ercanbrack, U Oseni, I Ullah, *Islamic Contract Law* (OUP 2023), chp 12.

[45] By way of illustration, Art 5 of Law No 22 of 2006, Promulgating the Family Law [Family Code], stipulates that an 'engagement is a request of marriage and/or the expressed promise of marriage as the consequences of marriage [as] determined by custom'. It goes on to say that it does not have the consequences arising from the contract of marriage. The Family Code, as stressed in Art 3 thereof, is predicated on the Hanbali school of Islam.

[46] A M M bin Ahmad al-Ghaitābī Badr al-Dīn al-'Ainī, *Umdat al-Qārī fī Sharḥ Ṣaḥīḥ al-Bukharī* (Al-Munīriyyah, Cairo, n.d.), 1:220.

[47] M bin Qāsim al-Anṣārī, *Sharḥ Ḥudūd ibn Arafah – al-Hidāyah al-Kāfiyah al-Shāfiyah li Bayāni Haqā'iq al-Imam ibn Arafah al-Wāfiyah* (Al-Maktabah al-'Ilmiyyah, Beirut, 1350H), 428.

[48] Ibid, 429.

[49] Qur'an 19:54.

Here, Allah Ta'ālā has praised his messenger, Sayyiduna Isma'il, and described him as true to his promise. This suggests that fulfilling a promise is a virtuous act; and as a result, it shall be said that making a promise is lawful.[50] The Hanafis as well as the Malikis opined that a promise attached to a condition precedent is binding, provided that such a promise is predicated on good cause.[51] In other words, a promise that is not based on any cause shall not be binding.

Jurists are generally in agreement that where a person promises to perform a prohibited conduct, it is not lawful for such person to fulfil such a promise.[52] This may be gleaned from the saying of the Prophet, as narrated by 'Imrān bin al-Ḥusain, as follows: 'there shall be no (fulfilment of) vowing (*nadhr*) in sinful act'.[53] Similarly, jurists have agreed that where an individual promised to perform an obligatory action, such as taking care of parents or maintaining one's wife, or payment of debt, the promise shall be obligatory upon said promisor. There is also agreement that where one promises to perform a lawful action he or she should fulfil this on the basis of Islamic ethics. According to Ibn AbdulBarr, 'I do not know of any disagreement that fulfilment of promise is recommended. Allah has praised those who fulfil their promises and vows'.[54] There is also consensus that it is lawful to make a promise regarding that which is lawful and with the determination that it shall be fulfilled.[55]

There is some divergence, however, as to whether a promise is binding on the promisor. The majority view is that fulfilment of a promise is not obligatory both in law and religion. The reason is that fulfilment of a promise is supererogatory (*sunnah*), its performance of fulfilment attracts reward and there is no sin for failure to fulfil it. This opinion is held by Shafi'is, Hanbalis as well as a weak minority among the Malikis, given that it contradicts that which was narrated by Malik.[56]

---

[50] Bukhari, Hadith 2296 and Muslim, Hadith 2314.
[51] Z bin Ibrahim bin Muhammad Ibn Nujaim al-Maṣrī, *al-Ashbāh wa al-Naẓā'ir 'alā Madh'hab Abi Hanifata al-Nu'mān* (Dar al-Kutub al-'Ilmiyyah, Beirut, 1991) 247.
[52] A bin Ali al-Rāzī Al-Jaṣṣāṣ, *Aḥkām al-Qur'an* (Dar Ihyā' al-Turāth al-Arabī, Beirut, 1405H), 5:334.
[53] Muslim, Hadith No. 1641.
[54] A Musa Yusuf bin Abdullah bin ABdulBarr al-Namrī al-Qurṭubī, *al-Istidhkār al-Jāmi' li Madhāhib Fuqahā' al-Amṣār* (Dar Qutaibah, Damascus, 1993), 14:349.
[55] Al-Jaṣṣāṣ, *Aḥkām al-Qur'an*, 5:334.
[56] Abu Zakariyyā Muḥyuddīn Yahya bin Sharaf al-Nawawī, *Rauḍat al-ṭālibīn wa 'Umdat al-Muftīn* (Al-Maktab al-Islāmī, Beirut, 1991), 5:390; 'Alā'uddīn Abu al-ḥasan Ali bin Sulaiman al-Mardāwī, *Al-Inṣāf fī Ma'rifat al-Rājih min al-Khilāf 'alā Madh'hab al-Imām Ahmad bin Ḥanbal* (Maṭba'at al-Sunnah al-Muhammadiyyah, Cairo, 1956) 11:152.

3.3.2 *Unilateral Contracts under the CC*

Both the civil and common law traditions are cautious about conferring a binding character on promises and unilateral acts. In English law this is easily explained because of the absence of consideration. In the civil law, promises are not generally viewed as binding on the promisor unless several layers of formalities are satisfied, chiefly notarial approval.

Article 192 CC regulates acts of unilateral disposition in a manner that reflects the general position in both the civil and common law traditions. It states that

1. A legal act by sole will shall not create any obligation or amend or terminate any existing obligation, other than where provided by law.
2. If the law provides that an obligation is created, amended or terminated by such legal act made by sole will, such act shall extend to the provisions of the law that govern the contract in general, other than those in conflict with acting by sole will.

As a general rule, therefore, a promise does not bind the promisor to the promisee. Of course, where the promisor does give effect to the promise, such as by actually making a gift or a donation, then these may not be retrieved as they are no longer part of the sphere of the promise.[57]

Certain promises are, nonetheless, binding on the promisor.[58] Article 193 CC concerns those situations where the promisor makes a promise of a reward to the public in exchange for performing a certain act. Article 193 CC speaks of this relationship as entailing 'consideration', which although overlaps with its common law counterpart under the same name, should not be conflated with it. Article 193 CC explains that the promise of a reward in exchange for something is binding on the promisor, in which case the promise is no longer a unilateral act but is contingent on another's performance under the terms demanded by the promisor. Following well-established civil law tradition, article 193 CC goes on to say that such promises are enforceable 'even where [the promisee] performed the promised act prior to receiving [the] promise, or without thought of the promise of reward, or without knowledge thereof'. Article 197 CC provides a significant insight into the legal nature of promises made to the public. It stipulates that the promisor is not entitled as a right to

---

[57] See Art 203 of Law No 22 of 2006 [Family Law], as well as Arts 507 and 508 CC. For a commentary on these see Court of Cassation Judgment 46/2013.

[58] Exceptionally, the Court of Cassation in Judgment 31/2009, in a case concerning *res judicata*, held that the extension of an existing lease by means of a promise made by the lessor 'becomes a full-fledged lease between the successors of the original lessor and the lessee'.

the performance associated to the prize, unless the conditions of the promise provide otherwise.

The promisor, of course, may withdraw his or her promise made to the public in exchange for a performance. However, such withdrawal/retraction shall be effective only from the date it is so declared. If a person performed the required act prior to the promisor's declaration of withdrawal, such person has a lawful claim to the reward.[59] Where a person commenced but not completed performance (in respect of the prize) upon the promisor's declaration of withdrawal, such person may demand payment from the promisor with respect to 'any expenses incurred … within the limits of the prize'.[60] Such expenses are due only where the promisee can prove that 'he could have completed the job in a timely manner'.[61]

Promises to the general public are not of an indefinite duration. Where the promisor determines a timeframe for completion of the performance associated with the prize/promise, he may not withdraw the promise during such period.[62] The promise shall, however, lapse after the expiry of this period. Where no such timeframe has been set out in advance, the prize/promise may be withdrawn 'by notice to the public in the same manner as the promise was offered, or in a similar manner through other media'.[63] In any event, the promisor shall decide whether the prize is payable or not within six months from the expiry date of the period set out in the notice, unless such notice contains another date.[64] In equal measure, the 'suit to claim a prize or other rights arising from the promise shall prescribe after a period of six months from the date of the decision referred to in Article 196 … or from the date of declaring the withdrawal of the promise, as the case may be'.[65]

3.3.3 *Promises Giving Rise to Reasonable Reliance*

The CC does not expressly regulate the exceptional situation where a promise creates a reasonable reliance on the promisee, who then acts (while incurring expenses and time) on the basis of the promise. This is wholly different to promises that do not give rise to reasonable reliance, other than promises in

---

[59] Art 195(1) CC.
[60] Art 195(2) CC.
[61] Ibid.
[62] Art 194(1) CC.
[63] Art 194(2) CC.
[64] Art 196 CC.
[65] Art 198 CC.

the form of awards to the public, discussed in the previous section. Given that reasonable reliance on a promise generally entails the enforceability of the promise,[66] and in conjunction with the express language of article 193 CC, it is reasonable to assume that such reasonable reliance suffices under Qatari law to render the promise enforceable.

3.4 CAUSE

'Cause' does not correspond to the requirement of 'consideration' under the common law. Its purpose in the civil law tradition has served to enhance the legality of contracts, even at the expense of party autonomy. Even so, 'cause' or '*causa*' (*causa obligationis*) was abandoned in the latest round of amendments to the French Civil Code.[67] As things stand, articles 155 to 157 CC not only retain the importance of cause but render it effectively the fourth element in the establishment of a valid contract, after offer, acceptance and an intention to be bound.

Article 155(1) CC stipulates that a contract shall be revoked where the obligation of a contracting party is 'without good cause or unlawful'. There is a clear demarcation between 'good cause' and unlawful purpose, although some overlap between the two is evident. Although paragraphs 1 and 2 of article 155 CC refer specifically to 'good cause' and not to 'cause', article 157 refers to 'cause'. If a meaningful distinction is to be made between good cause and unlawful [cause] in article 155 CC, this must necessarily mean that the former refers to unethical, immoral or grossly imbalanced causes,[68] such as that remuneration (wages) is only due for work undertaken,[69] whereas the latter only to illegal and unlawful causes.[70] Of course, both instances are already covered in the CC, so there is little to no need to include them again as a necessary condition of the contract. In any event, paragraph 2 of article 155 CC goes on to say that

> In the determination of good cause, the motive for concluding the contract shall be taken into account if the other contracting party was aware or must have been aware thereof.

---

[66] See Art 1.8 UNIDROIT PICC.

[67] Art 1128 French CC (2016 revision) no longer requires *causa* for the valid formation of a contract under French law.

[68] For the Islamic origins of good cause, see (n 42); see Court of Cassation Judgment 131/2014.

[69] Court of Cassation Judgment 50/2012.

[70] The Court of Cassation, in Judgment 123/2011, held that the payment of the sale price by the buyer did not necessarily lead to the formation of a contract where the sold object was not owned by the seller.

This somewhat lends credence to the distinction between good and unlawful cause. If a party takes advantage of gross disparity with its counterpart, then such a contract clearly does not start off with a good cause; yet, it is not unlawful as such, unless it is an adhesion contract. Article 155 CC puts forth what is known in the civil law tradition as objective and subjective *causa*. Objective *causa* generally prevents the formation of a contract where one or more of the parties' obligations cannot, objectively speaking, be realised. Subjective *causa*, on the other hand, refers to the parties' personal circumstances and how these make performance onerous, unfair or grossly disproportionate.

Article 156 CC introduces an evidentiary rule, whereby an obligation is generally deemed to be lawful and with good cause, unless evidence to the contrary is provided. Presumably, the burden is on the party claiming the absence of good cause and the standard must be one of reasonableness.[71]

Article 157 CC, although seemingly innovative, adds nothing to the discussion in article 155 CC. It reads as follows:

1. The cause of the contract shall be its true cause until evidence to the contrary is provided.
2. Where the cause is fictitious, any party alleging that the obligation has another lawful cause shall provide evidence to support this allegation.

A fictitious or untrue cause would prevent formation of the contract under article 155 CC, because there is an absence of 'good cause' or worse because the fictitious or untrue cause gives rise to some type of illegality.

---

[71] See Art 98, Law No 13 of 1990 (Civil Procedure Law).

4

Capacity and Authority to Contract

4.1 INTRODUCTION

As a liberal legal system, Qatari law provides for significantly broad contractual freedom. Even so, several limitations are placed not so much on the substantive exercise of such freedom, but on its procedural dimension. Hence, natural persons considered under the law as lacking partial or full competence will have their contractual will substituted (and sometimes even replaced) by a guardian. In equal manner, foreign or other entities desirous of trading in Qatar must do so through a registered Qatari commercial agent. As a result, this chapter will discuss the regulation of personal capacity (*ahliya*) and agency under the civil law of Qatar and will not deal with the issue of competence pertinent to foreign investors,[1] or specific competence of state (or administrative) entities, even if said competence concerns contractual freedom.[2] The chapter deals with the most important types of agency and hence several are missing from this discussion.[3] It will become clear from the

---

[1]   It is beyond the scope of this chapter to examine the regulation of competence of foreign investors in the Qatari legal order. Foreign investment law and its regulation of investment and investors is *lex specialis* in relation to commercial agency contractual arrangements. Overall, Law No. 1/2019 Regulating the investment of non-Qatari Capital allows for a limited number of instances where a foreign investor possesses autonomous competence and under its own name. Even the decision of the MoCI No. 142/2006, which provides that foreign firms may open representational offices without a local partner, only allows sourcing activities that do not involve financial transactions. See J Truby, 'Free Zones, Foreign Ownership and Tax Incentives for Foreign Direct Investment in Qatar' (2016) Global Trade & Customs Journal 11.

[2]   See, for example, Art 2(2) of Law No 2/2017 Promulgating the Civil and Commercial Arbitration Law [Arbitration Law], which requires the approval of the Prime Minister for an agreement to submit to arbitration disputes arising from administrative contracts.

[3]   For example, subsidiary warranty lawsuits are excluded here. This arises where the warranty applicant entrusts its guarantor to enter into an existing dispute between itself and a third party in order to be represented in court and potentially offer compensation in respect of the

discussion relating to personal capacity that several (but not all) principles underpinning classical Islamic law have been incorporated in the Qatari CC, despite the fact that they are to a large degree antiquated and out of touch with Qatar's international obligations.

4.2 LEGAL PERSONALITY

4.2.1 *Legal Personality and Competence to Contract*

Legal personality, competence or capacity are all synonyms for the deceptively simple notion of having rights and duties under a legal system and a capacity to enforce or have them enforced against the entity in question. The CC confers such capacity upon both physical (or natural) persons, as well as legal persons – the latter under certain circumstances. Just like other legal systems, the Qatari CC further permits delegation of capacity upon a third entity through a contract of agency. It should be noted from the outset that the rights and duties that comprise one's personality may vary in quantity and quality from those enjoyed by other entities. By way of illustration, minors cannot, as a rule, enter into real estate transactions in their own name and corporations cannot enter into marriage contracts.

Article 39 CC stipulates that personality commences upon birth – assuming the person is alive – and ceases upon death. These in turn are the outer limits of contractual freedom. Even so, the *foetus in utero* is capable of rights, provided it is born alive.[4] There is nothing in Qatari law, however, suggesting that the *foetus* can contract in its name or through a third entity.

Legal personality, as described above, and competence, although generally synonymous and overlapping in nature, may at times give rise to subtle differences. An entity, such as a physical person, may generally enjoy broad legal personality (i.e. rights and duties) and yet be temporarily prevented from exercising said rights. Such *incapacity* may come about as a result of consent (e.g. A agrees with B not to engage in business deals with C and D), or by the operation of the law. In the latter case the law might prevent certain people from their ordinary freedom of contract because of perceived defects in their consent, or because of a defective personal status.[5] Article 109 CC goes on to say that persons declared by law to be totally or partially incapacitated shall

---

damage that the warranty claimant suffers from the ruling in the original lawsuit. See Court of Appeal Judgment 255 and 277/2017.

[4]   Art 40 CC.

[5]   By way of illustration, under Art 20 CL, persons who have filed for bankruptcy or convicted of fraud-related offences are not considered competent to enter into trading transactions.

not possess legal capacity to conclude a contract. Incapacity will be explored in more detail in a subsequent section of this chapter. Absence or loss of legal capacity, subject to the exceptions mentioned in subsequent sections,[6] invalidates offer and acceptance.[7]

From the point of view of Qatari private international law, article 11(1) CC provides that the legal capacity of persons is governed by the law of the country to which they belong by reason of their nationality.

Paragraph 2 of article 11 CC, however, goes on to note that in respect of financial transactions concluded and being effective in Qatar, if one of the parties is an incapacitated foreigner, where 'such incapacity is due to a cause neither apparent to nor easily detected by the other party, such cause shall have no effect on the legal capacity of such foreigner'.

4.2.2 *Age of Majority and Discretion*

Minors are capable of contracting in their own name. The CC distinguishes between the age of *majority* (bulūgh) and the age of *discretion* (rushd) or *maturity*. The age of majority is 18 years, irrespective of sex.[8] Article 49(1) CC stipulates that a person that has attained the age of majority and in possession of its mental faculties possesses full legal personality to contract in its own name and perform legal acts.[9] Such capacity is suspended under the same provision where the courts have imposed guardianship or custody of the minor and its property, or where the minor is otherwise incapacitated.[10] Article 189 of the Qatari Family Law No. 22 of 2006 stipulates that: 'A person who has attained the age of majority by attaining eighteen years of age shall have full legal capacity, unless he is placed under guardianship'.[11] However, considering the nature of the family laws, Welchman reminds us that the setting of an age of full capacity is related to the notion of marriage.

---

[6] See, for example, Art 98(2) CC, which provides that the promisor's loss of legal capacity shall not preclude the conclusion of the promised contract if it has already been dispatched to and accepted by the promise.

[7] Art 71 CC.

[8] Art 49(2) CC.

[9] Art 17 CL equally provides that freedom to trade is available for those reaching the age of majority. The age of majority is of seminal importance in Islamic law as it represents the dawn of full capacity. But there exist significant differences concerning the age of puberty. See Nawawī, Yaḥyā ibn Sharaf, Muhammad Najīb Mutīʿī, and Abū Ishāq Shīrāzī, *Kitāb Al-Majmūʿ: Sharh al-Muhadhdhab Lil-Shīrāzī*. (Dār Ihyāʾ al-Turāth al-ʿArabī, 2001) 36off.

[10] See also Art 18 CL, which caters for the guardianship of a minor's assets in a business activity.

[11] It should not be forgotten, however, that the age of majority in this family law context chiefly relates to capacity for marriage, where capacity is dependent on a guardian for females. L Welchman 'First Time Family Law Codifications in Three Gulf States' [2010] Int'l Surv. Fam. L. 163, 166.

The age of discretion is generally perceived as the milestone in a minor's life whereby some degree of maturity has been achieved. As a result, the minor is no longer considered worthy of full protection (i.e. guardianship or other mechanism) and can enter into certain contracts in its own name. Although the age of maturity is a matter of assessment on a case-by-case basis, article 50(2) CC makes it clear that no person below seven years is to be considered as having reached the age of discretion. In respect of particular contracts, the CC combines the minor's age with its discretion/discernment.[12] Hence, article 112 CC stipulates that a discerning sixteen-year old in lawful possession of his or her property may validly undertake any acts related to the management of such property. Article 115(2) CC states that a discerning fifteen-year old possesses partial competence (as the court may place restrictions for the minor's interest) to dispose of wages earned. Moreover, article 116 CC allows discerning sixteen-year olds to conclude wills.

Maturity or discretion is not only a question of age. Article 50(1) CC clarifies that lack of discretion may also arise by reason of 'imbecility (*al-ma'tūh*) or insanity', in which case the person is considered incompetent to exercise its civil rights, including the absolute freedom to contract. Mental incapacity will be considered more fully in a subsequent section of this chapter.

Article 51 CC further limits capacity to contract by stating that persons attaining discretion but not majority, as well as persons that have achieved majority but who are 'prodigal or negligent' lack capacity.[13] No doubt, the latter limitation (i.e. prodigality [*safah*] and negligence) can be abused and does not sit well with western notions of contractual freedom. It is important for the higher courts and the legislator to either specifically limit the application of this provision, or otherwise eliminate it.

4.3 CAPACITY OF MINORS

'Minors' are not defined as such, albeit it is clear that the term encompasses persons that have not attained the age of majority. Article 110 CC specifies

---

[12] This distinction has its origin in Islamic law. The Malikīs and Hanafīs set out two types of development in the life of a minor, namely, non-discerning (*ghayr mumayyiz*) and discerning (*mumayyiz*). The Hanbalīs argued that even in respect of a discerning minor, its transactions were valid if authorised by its guardian (*wali*). See Wahbah al-Zuhaylī, *Financial Transactions in Islamic Jurisprudence* (Translated by Mahmoud Al. El-Gamal, Dar al-Fikr, 2003) vol 3, at 358.

[13] On the capacity of the discerning minor, see I Bantekas, J Ercanbrack et al, *Islamic Contract Law* (OUP 2023) chp 4.

that dispositions of property by a minor lacking discretion shall be deemed void. This is clearly the general rule and hence persons contracting with minors must ensure that discretion is fully evident and attested, or that its absence is well compensated by guardianship or other mechanism. Where a minor possesses discretion, disposition of property is valid where its effects as a whole are without doubt to the advantage of the minor.[14] If the effects of such disposition are not overwhelmingly beneficial to the minor, it will be declared void, unless immediately ratified by the minor's guardian, the courts, or the minor itself after attaining the age of majority.[15] In the previous sections it was pointed out that a discerning sixteen-year old may dispose of property lawfully in its possession. Equally, discerning minors entrusted with the administration of property may validly enter into any contract in respect of said administration, save for lease agreements whose duration is longer than a year.[16] Obligations assumed by minors not authorised to transfer, arising from their signatures on bills of exchange as drawers, endorsers or in any other capacity, shall be null and void. This is true even where the holder of the bill of exchange acted in good faith and without realising that its counterparty was a minor.[17]

Apart from capacity to administer and dispose property, which is generally unrestricted, the capacity of discerning minors to conclude an individual employment contract may be limited by a request to the court of the guardian, trustee, or other interested person if this is in the benefit of the minor.[18] In such cases, the courts may terminate the contract.

From the point of view of Qatari private international law, article 22 CC provides that where a person is not Qatari, all matters relating to natural and legal guardianship, trusteeship/receivership and custodianship, and systems established to protect minors, incapacitated persons and absent persons, shall be governed by the law of nationality of the person in question.

4.4 PARTIAL COMPETENCE

The CC distinguishes between mental incapacity and incomplete or partial competence. The terminology is not always consistent. Mental incapacity is defined to in article 52 CC as possessing no, or defective, capacity. Incomplete

[14] Art 111(1) CC.
[15] Art 111(2) CC.
[16] Art 113 CC. See also Art 114 CC concerning property entrusted or delivered to the minor for the purpose of maintenance.
[17] Art 459 CL.
[18] Art 115(1) CC.

or partial competence concerns the contractual freedom of persons that otherwise possess an effective mental capacity, but who are nonetheless deemed as 'suffering from inattentiveness or prodigality'.[19] Incomplete competence also arises in those situations where discerning minors possess limited contractual freedom, as is the case with individual employment contracts. Prodigality and inattentiveness are not defined in the CC and do not constitute recognised disabilities or other forms of impairments that inhibit or otherwise disadvantage contractual freedom.[20] Prodigality has its origins in classic Islamic law where there was considerable agreement between scholars concerning persons squandering the property of their family, therefore justifying interdiction.[21] The competence of persons considered prodigal and inattentive is equated *mutatis mutandis* to that of discerning minors. This is expressly stipulated in articles 120 to 125 CC.

It is not clear how they operate in practice,[22] but in any event, they should under no circumstances be employed arbitrarily by the courts to diminish or limit contractual freedom. Limitation of contractual freedom on these two grounds constitutes a significant violation of personal liberty and fundamental human rights[23] and is inconsistent with Qatar's international obligations. Article 119 CC stipulates that persons with partial (incomplete) competence entering into contracts while claiming to be fully competent may rely on their partial incompetence to escape the legal effects of their offer or acceptance. Exceptionally, however, minors fraudulently concealing their partial incompetence in a way that leads to a reasonable belief of full competence are liable for any damages caused under their contract.

The place of article 126 CC just after the provisions relating to discerning minors suggests that it is applicable thereto and not to the provisions on

---

[19] See Arts 117 and 118(1) CC. It should be emphasized that Art 118(1) CC makes no distinction between insanity/imbecility (i.e. mental incapacity) and inattentiveness/prodigality. Such a distinction is, however, necessary as the two sets of circumstances are wholly different and cannot possibly produce the same effects. This reasoning seems to also be confirmed by Art 120(1) CC, which stipulates that contracts concluded by prodigal or inattentive persons shall be governed by Art 111 CC, which refers to minors possessing discretion.

[20] See Art 1 Law No 40 of 2004 on the Guardianship over Minors' Funds, which defines several types of incapacity, albeit in very demeaning terms that lack scientific merit.

[21] Abū al-Walīd Ibn Rushd, *Bidāyat al-Mujtahid wa Nihāyat al-Muqtasid* (Garnet Publishing, Translated by Imran Ahsan Khan Nyazee, vol 1, 1994) 334, in Bantekas and Ercanbrack (n 13).

[22] But see, Art 35, Law No 40/2004 (on the Guardianship over Minors' Funds), which concerns the validity of financial dispositions made by interdicted persons.

[23] Of course, the law must and does place sensible limitations especially where the parties' power imbalance is significant. See F Kessler, 'Contracts of Adhesion: Some Thoughts about Freedom of Contract' (1943) 43 Colum L Rev 629.

mental disability which follow. Article 126 CC allows natural guardians (e.g. parents), legal guardians (e.g. *kafīls*)[24] and curators (*qawama*) to contract on behalf of discerning minors within the limits of the law.

4.5 MENTAL INCAPACITY

Article 118(1) CC suggests that persons suffering from insanity (*junūn*) and imbecility,[25] (as well as prodigality (*safah*) and inattentiveness, examined in the previous section) lack contractual freedom altogether. In fact, the courts are under an obligation to *interdict* (*hajr*) such persons and the pertinent judgments must be recorded in special registers.[26] Although insanity is not defined,[27] article 119 CC spells out its effects. A person suffering from insanity and dementia and interdicted on this basis by the courts lacks the competence to enter into contracts. Any contract entered after the interdiction is null and void. Where the contract was entered prior to the judicial interdiction, it shall only be null and void if the other party was aware of the condition or if it was a matter of common knowledge.

The outright and absolute constriction of contractual freedom to persons with mental disabilities constitutes a fundamental violation of article 12 of the UN Convention on the Rights of Persons with Disabilities (CRPD), which has been ratified and supported by Qatar.[28] Article 12 CRPD states in relevant part that

2. States Parties shall recognize that persons with disabilities enjoy legal capacity on an equal basis with others in all aspects of life.

---

[24] A *kafala* relationship establishes a bond of legal guardianship between the *makful* and the *kafil* (legal guardian). See U M Assim, J Sloth-Nielsen, 'Islamic Kafala as an Alternative Care Option for Children Deprived of a Family Environment' (2014) 14 AHRLJ 322.

[25] Again, this rather outdated (and offensive) characterisation is a remnant of classic Islamic law. It refers to a person who by reason of intellectual defects its decision-making ability is crucially undermined. 'Abd al-Karīm Zīdān, *Wajīz fī Uṣūl al-Fiqh* (Mu'assasat Qurṭuba, n.d.) 104, in Bantekas and Ercanbrack (n 13).

[26] The Court of Appeal in Case 94/2008 made it clear that unless a person has been interdicted by the courts under Art 118 CC, judgments restricting contractual or other freedom produce no legal consequence. Such *hajr* is reflected in various sources, including Art 957 Majallah, which stipulates that 'minors, lunatics and imbeciles are ipso facto interdicted'. See Bantekas and Ercanbrack (n 13) for a more comprehensive discussion.

[27] As already stated, mental incapacity is referred to in Art 52 CC as possessing no, or defective, capacity.

[28] In fact, unlike many states, Qatar was one of the few that did not enter into any reservations. See I Bantekas, 'Reservations to the Disabilities Convention: Peer Engagement and the Value of a Clear Object and Purpose' (2020) 33 NY Intl L Rev 65.

3. States Parties shall take appropriate measures to provide access by persons with disabilities to the support they may require in exercising their legal capacity.

5. Subject to the provisions of this article, States Parties shall take all appropriate and effective measures to ensure the equal right of persons with disabilities to own or inherit property, to control their own financial affairs and to have equal access to bank loans, mortgages and other forms of financial credit, and shall ensure that persons with disabilities are not arbitrarily deprived of their property.

Article 12 CRPD clearly suggests that persons with disabilities, and irrespective of the disability, are presumed to possess legal competence and personality no less than non-disabled persons, which necessarily encompasses contractual freedom. That disabled persons may require assistance under certain circumstances does not entail that such assistance should substitute their decision-making authority; rather, it should be merely assistive.[29] Article 127 CC seemingly supports decision-making assistance (as opposed to substitute decision-making) to persons with physical, sensory, or mental disabilities, where they are unable to 'understand the contents or surrounding circumstances of a contract'. In such cases the courts have authority to appoint a judicial assistant to 'assist such person as may be necessary in its best interests'. Article 128 CC stipulates that where a disabled person under court-ordered judicial assistance undertakes a transaction not authorised by the assistant, this shall be declared invalid. Such an outcome is clearly incompatible with the rationale of assistive decision-making, thus rendering the assistance in article 127 CC in the form of substitute decision-making.[30] In extreme cases of 'severe debilitating illness' the courts are authorised to substitute the will of the disabled person through that of the judicial assistant, if failure to act threatens the interests of the disabled person.[31] This is a welcome step towards more assistive decision-making and should be encouraged by the courts in line with Qatar's obligations under the CRPD.

---

[29] See L Series, 'Article 12: Equal Recognition before the Law' in I Bantekas, MA Stein, D Anastasiou (eds), *Convention on the Rights of Persons with Disabilities: A Commentary* (OUP 2018) 350, 364–65. See also CRPD Committee, Concluding Observations on the Initial Report of Qatar, UN Doc CRPD/C/QAT/CO/1/Add.2 (6 December 2017) paras 23–34, where the Committee recommended that Qatar carry out a review of its legislation with a view to repealing regimes of substituted decision-making and replacing them with supported decision-making regimes, which uphold the autonomy, will and preferences of persons with disabilities.

[30] Such an outcome against disabled persons' personal liberty and freedom of contract could be avoided by reference to Art 144 CC, which provides for invalidation or adaptation of contracts producing 'excessive injustice' to a party with limited capacity.

[31] Art 129 CC.

4.6 CAPACITY OF JURIDICAL/LEGAL PERSONS TO ENTER INTO CONTRACTS

Article 54 (chapeau) CC sets forth the principle that juridical persons enjoy juridical (otherwise known as legal) personality.[32] This means that, inter alia, they can contract in their own name and incur liability solely in their own person. Paragraph 2 of article 54 CC specifies that the will of the juridical person shall be expressed by its representative, which shall be a natural person.[33] The provisions on agency in the CC apply as residual rules to the authority of the juridical person's representative. More specialised laws may, and usually do, set more specific agency requirements.[34] Articles 295 and 296 of the Commercial Companies Law, for example, stipulate that the authority of the managers or the board of directors ends with the dissolution of the company.[35] In equal measure, a limited partnership company is managed by the general partners in tandem, one of them, or a non-partner manager. It is not permissible for silent partners to take over the management, even on the basis of a power of attorney.[36]

The authority to act as a representative of a juridical person may be express or implied. Express authority is typically conferred by an entity's articles of association (by-laws) or other corporate resolutions. In some instances default authority may be conferred by the law, as is the case with article 242 of the Commercial

---

[32] It goes without saying that certain entities, which are not *prima facie* natural persons, are not viewed as legal persons. This is the case with sole proprietorships, in respect of which the Court of Cassation has been at pains to emphasize that they lack the qualities of legal persons. See Judgment 19/2016. See Court of Cassation Judgment 283/2019, where the Court defined the essential characteristics of a legal person as follows: (1) there must be a group of natural persons or assets allocated to a specific objective and (2) express recognition by the law of the status of such a group as a juridical person with a separate legal personality; see equally in this respect, namely, the capacity of the legal person to litigate, Court of Appeal Judgment 347/2015.

[33] The Court of Cassation has held that a legal person (in this case a foreign bank) enjoys capacity to claim entitlements owed to individual board members, since the respondent (a Qatari bank) had requested the claimant to appoint said board members and as a result the claimant could pursue actions on their behalf. Court of Cassation Judgment (May 2016, unknown number). Reported by H Hussiem, 'Qatar Court of Cassation Finds Individual Company Members can Represent Company' (June-July 2016), available at: www.tamimi.com/law-update-articles/qatar-court-of-cassation-finds-individual-company-members-can-represent-company/

[34] Readers should refer to Law No 11/2015, on Promulgating the Commercial Companies Law (Company Law). Relying on Art 102 of Law No 5 of 2002 on Promulgating the Commercial Companies Law, the Court of Cassation held that a joint-stock company is represented before others and before the judiciary by its chairman of the board and he or she has the right to delegate some of its powers to other members of the board. Court of Cassation Judgment 107/2013.

[35] See, to this effect, Court of Cassation Judgment 208/2014.

[36] Court of Appeal Judgment 12/2018.

Companies Law No 11 of 2015, whereby, unless otherwise stated in the by-laws, managers of limited liability companies possess full managerial authority and their acts, including contracts signed by them on behalf of the company, bind the company.[37] Implied authority may arise either because a particular action is necessary to carry out one's express authority, or because it has otherwise been granted outside the framework of a company's by-laws, for example by tacit approval or orally. A representative or employee of a legal person, while transacting in a personal capacity, does not bind the legal person.[38]

Legal persons, chiefly corporate entities, may also engage with agents that are external to the legal person. The Court of Cassation has held that where a power of attorney is issued by the representative of the legal person, the agent (e.g. a lawyer) submitting an appeal in the courts must deposit with its proxy document proof of the capacity of the legal representative of the legal person who authorised it to file the appeal until the court ascertains that capacity.[39]

The Court of Cassation, relying on Article 3 of the Commercial Registration Law, emphasised that a company branch does not, by registration in the Commercial Registry, acquire a legal personality that is independent from that of the parent company.[40] All rights and duties acquired by a branch equally encumber the parent company and form part of its own rights and duties and all liability is borne by the parent; so, it alone has the capacity to sue and be sued.[41]

From the lens of Qatari private international law, article 12(1) CC stipulates that the legal personality of foreign legal persons shall be subject to the law of the state 'where they have established their respective headquarters'. However, in accordance with paragraph 2 of article 12 CC, where a foreign legal person conducts its main activity in Qatar, even if its headquarters are abroad, it shall be subject to Qatari law.

4.7 AGENCY

Agency is a common feature of the law of contract, which serves to facilitate business and transactions by substituting the principal with another entity to act on its behalf. While agency is recognised in all legal systems as

---

[37] It is well settled by the Court of Cassation that the effect of Arts 225 and 240 of Law 5 of 2002 [Commercial Companies Law] is that the manager of the LLC has full authority to manage the company unless the Memorandum of Association of the company provided for its authority, and that its acts are binding upon the company. See Court of Cassation Judgment 164/2010.

[38] Court of Appeal Judgment 53/2019.

[39] Court of Cassation Judgment 51/2013; equally, Court of Cassation Judgment 63/2014.

[40] Court of Cassation Judgment 283/2019.

[41] Court of Appeal Judgment 289/2017; equally Court of Appeal Judgment 238/2019.

a contractual relationship between principal and agent, as indeed in Qatar,[42] there is some divergence as to the boundaries of authority conferred on the agent by contract or the operation of law. The legal consequence arising from the agreement of agency is that the principal is bound by contracts entered by the agent acting within the scope of authority conferred upon him or her.[43]

4.7.1 *Agency as a Contract and Power of Attorney*

The establishment of an agency relationship is not a unilateral act and hence must be predicated on the same criteria underlying contracts, namely, offer, acceptance and an intention to be bound.[44] Moreover, the agent must possess sufficient capacity to act on behalf of the principal.[45] The agreement establishing an agency relationship requires some degree of formality under Qatari law.[46] It must be made in writing, signed by the principal, the agent and a witness, as well as be duly authenticated by the authentication department of the Ministry of Justice.[47] The authority conferred by the principal on the agent is known as a power of attorney (POE),[48] which itself may be of a general nature, or otherwise concern well-specified actions. The formality of the POE does not serve to invalidate the *bona fide* actions of the agent undertaken without an authenticated POE. Rather, it is meant to ensure that third parties transacting with the agent are aware of its authority, as well as that the agent does not arbitrarily exceed the authority conferred by the principal. As a result, where the principal commits a mistake that leads a *bona fide* third party to believe that the agency upon which the agent contracted with this third party is still

---

[42] See Art 81 CC; equally Art 61 QFC Contract Regulations.

[43] Art 84 CC. See, to this effect, Court of Cassation Judgment 242/2015.

[44] Art 716 CC. Hence, the beginning and termination of an agency on the basis of an agreement is crucial, because absent a valid agreement the agent may compete against the principal and act in its own name. See Court of Cassation Judgment 84/2009.

[45] Art 717 CC.

[46] Art 718 CC. See also Court of Cassation Judgment 18/2010, where it was held that a lawyer may not be challenged on the ground that its power of attorney has not been authenticated before the procedure was carried out, unless otherwise stipulated by law.

[47] See Court of Cassation Judgment 64/2011, spelling out some formalities; equally, Court of Cassation Judgment 236/2011.

[48] In some contractual relationships, such as the right of the representative of a new creditor to collect payment, the POE would be in the form of a letter of subrogation, in accordance with Art 362 CC. The Court of Cassation in its Judgment 28/2010 held that representation of the state in litigation is a kind of a legal power of attorney to act on its behalf, and such power shall be made by referring to its source which is the law. In principle, the Minister is the representative of the State regarding the affairs related to its ministry, except where the law delegates a person other than the Minister.

valid, the agent's actions are binding on the principal.[49] This is in line *mutatis mutandis* with article 209 CC, whereby an employer is liable for the acts of its employees during the ordinary course of their employment.[50]

Article 82(2) CC makes it clear that if the principal announces its agent's authority to third parties and such announcement departs (exceeds) from the authority granted under the agency agreement, the authority under the principal's announcement supersedes the authority in the formal agency agreement.[51] The formality of the instrument/deed containing the POE is confirmed by article 90 CC, which compels the agent to surrender the deed immediately upon its expiration.

4.7.2 *The Authority of the Agent*

As a general rule, the agent is limited by the powers conferred upon him or her by the POE.[52] The authority of the agent, where this is unclear, will be assessed on the 'texts and the circumstances in which the power of attorney was issued and the circumstances of the mandate'.[53] According to article 719 CC, the mere designation of agency in an agreement without any further specification of the powers conferred on the agent shall not grant the latter any capacity other than in respect of 'administrative acts'.[54] Anything other than mere administrative acts requires a *special agency*, particularly for gifts, sale, reconciliation, mortgage, acknowledgement, arbitration, oaths and pleadings before the courts.[55] The agent does not possess authority to exceed the powers stipulated in the agency agreement, save if the principal so announces, or subsequently so concedes, in accordance with the discussion in the previous section.[56] The agent may, however, exercise implied powers in accordance

---

[49] Court of Cassation Judgment 209/2015.
[50] Court of Cassation Judgment 36/2015.
[51] It has been rightly held that the capacity of the representative ceases before the date of the beginning of the contractual representation. It is not permissible for the representative to contract in the name of the principal or to claim authority against third parties on behalf of the principal, except from the day following the fulfilment of the power of attorney. See Court of Appeal Judgment 25/2018.
[52] Art 82(1) CC.
[53] Court of Cassation Judgment 22/2013.
[54] Art 719 CC encompasses within the concept of 'administrative acts': 'leases, provided they do not exceed three years; maintenance and safekeeping works; collection of rights; and repayment of debts'.
[55] Art 721(1) CC.
[56] Art 722(2) CC. In any event the agent may exceed its powers where it is impossible to notify the principal and the circumstances are such that the principal would have consented to the exercise of the excess powers.

with the nature of the task for which the agency is conferred and in accordance with applicable practice.[57] As a result, where a contract is entered into by an agent without the necessary authority, it is the agent and not the principal that is liable for all acts relating to defects of consent.[58] Article 83(2) CC does make the point that where the agent acted in accordance with the principal's authority and precise instructions,[59] the principal may not plead the ignorance of the agent in respect of facts and circumstances which the principal knew or should have known.

4.7.3 *Disclosure of the Agency*

In most cases the agent will be authorised to disclose its relationship with the principal and correspondingly the third party may well require the disclosure of agency. Even so, one should not be oblivious to the fact that a principal may have a serious business interest in not disclosing to potential competitors its commercial intentions. Equally, politically exposed persons may be unwilling to make their assets or acquisitions known to the general public. Undisclosed agency makes sense in all these situations. Such undisclosed agency is generally permitted under Qatari law, but it is not free from consequences. Article 85 CC stipulates that where an agency is undisclosed the contract shall be deemed to have been concluded between the agent in its personal capacity and not on behalf of the principal. This presumption is inapplicable where the third party knew or should have known of the agent's authority, or it makes no difference to the third party whether the contract is concluded between the agent or the principal. This is generally known as *ostensible* or *apparent* authority.[60] Good faith is an integral aspect of the relationship between agents and third parties. This is clear in article 86 CC where agency is deemed to remain valid even where it had terminated, assuming both the agent and the third party were unaware that the agent's authority had terminated, or they could not have known even if they had exercised suitable due diligence.[61]

---

[57] Art 720 CC.
[58] Art 83(1) CC.
[59] It is of course likely that the agent's instructions are limited. In such circumstances, the agent, if he or she is to take urgent action, must always act in the best interests of the principal and defer to the latter where possible, especially in respect of matters falling outside the agency's express authority. See Art 276 CL.
[60] Despite the clear wording of Art 85 CC, certain practitioners claim that ostensible authority is not recognized under the CC, but only under the QFC Contract Regulations. See F Lucente et al, 'Corporate Authority in Qatar: To Bind or not to Bind?' (2014), available at www.tamimi .com/law-update-articles/corporate-authority-in-qatar-to-bind-or-not-to-bind/
[61] *Mutatis mutandis* stipulated also in Art 288 CL.

It is evident from this discussion that where an entity has not been granted agency authority by a principal, or if an agency exists but the agent exceeds its authority, then the effects of the contract entered between the 'agent' and the third party do not bind the principal.[62] It is, therefore, in the interest of the principal to avoid contracting on its own behalf if such an outcome was not intended. Article 88 CC recognises that agents may under certain (presumably narrow) circumstances be asked by the principal to conclude a contract with their own person (i.e. agent to agent). If these are approved by the principal or are standard practice under the terms of a business custom, they bind the principal. Article 139 CL sets out a mandatory rule against the possibility of a self-contract – absent consent of the principal – by the agent as follows:

> Whoever acts on behalf of third party under any agreement or provision may not buy for himself, directly or under a pseudonym, even at auction, an item that he has been entrusted with selling under such representation, except by permission of the judge, and without prejudice to what has been provided for in the law to the contrary.

The same is true in respect of brokers or other experts purchasing property in respect of which the principal authorised them to sell or provide an estimate.[63] Even so, self-contracts under articles 139 and 140 CL are valid if consented to by the principal.

4.7.4 *Standard of Care*

Agency involves a recognizable task undertaken by the agent on behalf of the principal. The appropriate exercise of this agency function is crucial to the interests of the principal. As a result, a certain duty of care must be imputed in the contract or the law. Article 723(1) CC distinguishes between agency with consideration and without. Unless otherwise specified, article 729(1) CC stipulates an agency shall be without consideration, save if the contrary was implicitly understood by the agent. In the event that the agency is deemed to be without consideration, the agent shall use 'the same standard of care as for its own acts, but not beyond that of a reasonable person'. Where the agent is acting with consideration its duty of care is that of 'a reasonable person at all times'.[64] This is an important distinction that is not

---

[62] Art 87(1) CC. An additional consequence for the 'agent' under such circumstances is that not only is he or she bound by the contract with the third party, but the absence of authority may give rise to an autonomous claim for damages, in accordance with para 2 of Art 87 CC.

[63] Art 140 CL.

[64] Art 723(2) CC.

always expressly made by civil codes. As part of the duty of care, the agent is responsible, unless the agreement or the nature of the transaction otherwise demand, for providing appropriate information about the exercise of the agency to the principal.[65] The Court of Cassation has emphasised that lawyers must refrain from accepting a power of attorney, providing assistance or expressing an opinion to the opponent of their client throughout the period of consideration of the original dispute. This is considered a professional misconduct that exposes lawyers to disciplinary accountability[66] without, however, causing nullity or affecting the validity of the work undertaken or terminating the agency.[67]

The agent, unless otherwise agreed, is not permitted to use the assets of the principal for its own account. If so, the agent is liable to damages against the principal.[68] Such unlawful misuse of the assets of the principal may also amount to a tort.

4.7.5 *Obligations of the Principal to the Agent*

Clearly, in the event of an agency with consideration the principal must pay the agent's fee, or a share in the profits, as explained below in the sections dealing with the various forms of commercial agency. Moreover, given that the exercise of an agency typically involves a series of expenses incurred by the agent, the principal is under an obligation to reimburse the agent for such expenses, 'irrespective of how successful the agent [was] in such performance'.[69] In equal measure the principal must, at the request of the agent, provide him or her with all the necessary amounts for the performance of the agency.[70] Hence, the agent is justified in not performing the agency where pre-payment of expenses was not made by the principal, in which case the principal may also be in breach of the agency contract.

Article 731 CC makes the point that the principal shall be liable for any damage suffered by the agent in the normal performance of the agency, save for any damage incurred as a result of the agent's mistakes. It is, of course, taken for granted that the agent performs its duties in accordance with the appropriate standard of care, as explained in the previous sub-section. Where more than one principal appoints a single agent to perform a common act, all

---

[65] Art 724 CC.
[66] Art 49 of Law No 23 of 2006 Enacting the Code of Law Practice.
[67] Court of Cassation Judgment 26/2014.
[68] Art 725 CC.
[69] Art 730(1) CC.
[70] Art 730(2) CC.

such principals shall be jointly liable against the agent for the performance of the agency, unless agreed otherwise.[71]

4.7.6 *Delegation by an Agent to a Sub-agent*

Article 89 CC, following well-established international practice, permits further delegation by the agent to another person, as long as pertinent authority was granted in the POE.[72] Where such authority was not granted, the agent shall be liable for the acts of the sub-agent as if such act is the act of the agent itself. In such event, the agent and is delegate shall be jointly liable.[73] Where the agent is authorised to delegate performance of the agency but no delegate is designated, the agent shall be liable only for its mistake in nominating or giving instructions to the delegate.[74]

4.7.7 *Multiple Agents*

Where multiple (joint) agents have been contracted by the principal in respect of the same act, but under a distinct contract, each of them may individually perform the required acts unless the principal authorises the agents to act jointly.[75] Where, however, multiple agents are assigned under a single contract without any authority to act individually, they shall act jointly, unless the exchange of opinion is not required for a specific act.[76]

In accordance with article 727(1) CC, multiple agents shall be jointly liable where the agency is indivisible or where the damage suffered by the principal arises from a common mistake of the agents. Paragraph 2 of article 727 CC limits joint liability where the impugned act of the agent in question exceeds the limits of or abuses the agency.

4.7.8 *Termination of the Agency*

Readers should consult the discussion in Chapter 11. The agency shall terminate upon the completion of the acts described in the agency agreement or upon the expiry of its term. The agency shall also terminate on the death of the agent or the principal unless it is granted in favour of the agent or a

---

[71] Art 732 CC.
[72] Equally Art 274 CL.
[73] Art 728(1) CC.
[74] Art 728(2) CC.
[75] Art 726(1) CC.
[76] Art 726(2) CC.

third party, or unless it is intended to be completed upon the death of the principal.[77] Article 736(1) CC allows the principal to terminate or limit the agency at any time, even if there is an agreement to the contrary. However, where the agency is issued in favour of the agent or a third party, the principal may not terminate or limit such agency without the consent of such agent or third party.[78] Of course, where the agency is terminated without good cause and in a manner that causes harm to the agent, the latter is entitled to indemnification.[79]

Just like the power of the principal to terminate the agency, so too the agent may at any time withdraw, even if there is an agreement to the contrary, by giving notice to the principal. In this case, the agent shall indemnify the principal where the withdrawal is not without good cause and which moreover causes harm to the principal.[80] Unless the agent has compelling reasons, it may not withdraw from the agency if a third party has an interest therein, provided that such third party shall be notified of such withdrawal in order to offer adequate time to decide what is in its best interest.[81] Where the principal dismisses the agent without good cause or does not renew the agency absent a fault by the principal, the agent is entitled to compensation.[82]

Irrespective of the manner of termination of the agency, the agent shall complete the acts commenced to such stage where no damage may be suffered by the principal.[83]

4.8 COMMERCIAL AGENCY

Commercial agency is regulated by three distinct pieces of legislation, namely, the general provisions of the CC; Law No 8 on the Organization of Business of Commercial Agents 2002 (Agency Law); and articles 272–317 of the Commercial Law. The interpretation of these statutes has been aided by a small amount of case law by the Court of Cassation and in addition the legal profession has made efforts to clarify agency-type arrangements. There is some overlap between the provisions of these three instruments and several rules are thus repeated.

---

[77] Art 734 CC.
[78] Art 735(2) CC.
[79] Art 735(3) CC.
[80] Art 736(1) CC.
[81] Art 736(2) CC.
[82] Arts 300 and 301 CL, as well as Art 735 CC. See, to this effect, Court of Cassation Judgment 335/2016; equally, Court of Cassation Judgment 163/2016.
[83] Art 737(1) CC.

Commercial agency is an important feature of the Qatari economy. This is because the import, distribution and sale of foreign goods and services can only be effectuated through a Qatari entity[84] in the form of a commercial agent. As a result, all foreign companies intending to do business in Qatar must appoint a Qatari commercial agent. Article 2 of the Agency Law stipulates that the key elements of commercial agency are as follows: a) exclusivity; b) scope of the agency on behalf of the principal; and c) consideration.[85] Exclusivity is fundamental despite narrow exceptions set out in the Commercial Law.[86] The benefits and privileges of commercial agency,[87] predominantly for the agent, arise only if the agency is registered on the Commercial Agents Register[88] held by the Ministry of Commerce and Industry (MoCI).[89] Failure to do so will render the agency void *ab initio*, as well as give rise to criminal sanctions on the part of the fraudulent agent.[90] The tighter regulation of commercial agency was meant to put an end to the practice of non-Qataris trading under a license or registration held by a Qatari entity.[91]

There are several differences between a commercial agency and general agency under the CC. Firstly, commercial agency confers authority on the agent only in respect of business actions.[92] While such POE may be absolute, it does not affect the personal relations of the principal. Secondly, a commercial agency should involve some consideration (unless otherwise agreed),

---

[84] Art 11, Agency Law, as amended by Law No 2/2016 (Commercial Agents Law).

[85] Iterated in Court of Cassation Judgment 84/2009. In Judgment 24/2009, the Qatari Court of Cassation held that in the commercial agency in question the local agent had failed to successfully establish the scope of the agency on behalf of the foreign company and hence the agency was void. See equally Court of Cassation Judgment 22/2013 to the same effect, albeit this judgment has been criticized on the ground that it did not address the issue of scope, being satisfied that a valid commercial agency agreement had been established by reference to the other two conditions.

[86] Some professional commentators argue that exclusivity depends on the type of agency arrangement and that certain categories, such as sales representatives, are exempted. It is also claimed that legal structuring may serve to bypass exclusivity requirements under the CL and the Agency Law. See Squire Patton Boggs, 'What Rules and Regulations Govern Matters of Commercial Agency in Qatar?' (2012), available at www.squirepattonboggs.com/en/insights/publications/2012/05/qatar-law-qa-commercial-agency-matters-in-qatar

[87] For example, upon registration, exclusivity over products and services commences, as well as a 5 per cent commission over the value of goods imported, in accordance with Art 5(1) Agency Law.

[88] See Law No 25/2005 (Commercial Registry Law), as amended by Law No 20/2014.

[89] Arts 10–16, Agency Law.

[90] Art 22 Agency Law.

[91] This was achieved by Law No 25/2004, known also as Proxy Law. See, to this effect, Court of Cassation Judgment 60/2016.

[92] Art 272 CL.

typically through the payment of a fee or a commission[93] that may, or may not, be stipulated in the agency agreement.[94] As a result, commercial agents owe a duty of care to the principal and the latter is liable for the agent's fees and expenses.[95] Thirdly, because the commercial agent is typically engaged under a fee and owes a duty of care to the principal, he or she is obliged to adhere to the principal's instructions and is liable for any damage arising from failure to adhere to ordinary standards of care.[96] This duty of care is quintessential in the relationship between commercial agents and principals.[97] Commercial agents owe extensive duties of care and best interests obligations to their principals,[98] irrespective of the fact that article 275 CL specifies that commercial agents possess 'freedom of action' in carrying out their mandates. As a result, blind adherence to the principal's instructions despite overwhelming evidence that damage to the principal's interests will follow is inexcusable. In such circumstances the agent must defer to the principal for further review.[99]

Commercial agents are vested with powers similar to those conferred on ordinary agents under the CC. Such powers must under all circumstances arise expressly or implicitly from the agency agreement. Article 278 CL provides for three types of circumstances under which the agent can contract in its own name (second party) with a third party, in which case, however, the agent is not entitled to a fee for representing the principal.

The duration of commercial agency is inextricably linked to the rights and duties of the parties. The Agency Law recognises two types of commercial agencies in terms of their duration: a) *limited duration*, whose fixed term nature is clearly expressed in the contract; and b) *unlimited duration*, requiring the parties' common consent for termination.[100] As regards the former, commercial agency comes to an end where the agreement expires or the work

---

[93] The obligation to pay agency fees gives rise to several privileges for the agent by which to secure such fee, particularly through sale of goods in the agent's possession. See, for example, Arts 282–285 CL.

[94] Art 273 CL. See Court of Cassation Judgment 65/2011, which held that in case of lack of agreement, common remuneration or tradition, the court shall have the power to identify the remuneration according to the subject, extent, and results of the agency.

[95] Ibid.

[96] Art 275 CL.

[97] Ordinary standards of care may involve actions that are customary or intrinsic in the exercise of the agency in question, such as insurance under Art 277 CL. See also Art 280 CL, concerning the agent's duty of care in respect of property damaged by transportation. Equally, Art 281 CL requires accurate book keeping.

[98] 'Best interests', subject to reasonable precaution is specifically spelt out in Art 276 CL.

[99] Art 275 CL.

[100] Art 9(a) Agency Law.

is completed.[101] Even so, the privileged position of the agent is emphasised by the fact that successful agents are entitled to compensation when a fixed term agency agreement is terminated by the principal.[102] Moreover, the same is true where the agent becomes bankrupt or incapacitated.[103]

4.8.1 Contract Agency

Articles 290–303 CL set out a particular species of commercial agency, namely contract agency. Article 290 CL defines this as 'a contract under which the agent continuously seeks and negotiates the conclusion of transactions in a specific field of activity for the benefit of the client against consideration'. Typically, the contract agent's task will be to conclude and implement transactions on behalf of the principal. Just like general forms of commercial agency, the contract agency agreement must be recorded in writing and spell out in detail the parties' mutual obligations, the agent's authority and fee,[104] as well as its duration.[105] An important dimension of contract agency is that the agent is to manage the commercial activity independently, through its own business or trade, while bearing all pertinent expenses.[106] Given that the contract agent effectively represents the principal's services, brands and products in the area managed by the agent, the latter may receive requests for the execution of contracts that are concluded by him as well as complaints about non-implementation of these contracts.[107] It is clear therefore that the contract agent does not assume the financial rights of the principal, absent the latter's express consent.[108]

Article 292 CL makes it clear that the contract agent assumes a significant financial commitment and is in turn dependent on the principal's services, brands, or products, as well as the principal's continued cooperation. As a result, the Qatari legislator is adamant that the contract agent should not be exposed to arbitrary competition by the principal. This is expressly stipulated in article 293 CL. Accordingly and in the same vein, article 294 CL states that where the implementation of the contract requires a significant amount of expense on the part of the agent, the duration of the agency cannot be less than five years.

---

[101] Art 8(a) Agency Law.
[102] Art 8(c) Agency Law.
[103] Art 287 CL.
[104] Given the nature of this type of agency, the fee may well be a percentage from the sales, in accordance with Art 296 CL. See also Art 297 CL in respect of other expenses that may be claimed by the agent.
[105] Art 291 CL.
[106] Art 292 CL.
[107] Art 295 CL.
[108] Art 295 CL.

Because agency contracts are presumed by the law to be in the joint interest of both parties, article 300 CL stipulates in emphatic terms that the principal may not terminate the contract where the agent was not at fault but shall compensate the agent for damages resulting therefrom. Any agreement contrary to this shall be invalid. Equally, the agent shall also be obliged to compensate the principal for damages arising from the agent's resignation 'at an inappropriate time and without an acceptable excuse'. While the parties may agree a fixed term, if this is not renewed by the principal the latter shall pay a fair amount of compensation to the agent that was diligent and whose work led to a successful promotion of the business interests of the principal.[109] Compensation is also due where the agent is replaced as a result of collusion between the principal and the new agent.[110]

4.8.2 *Commission Agency*

According to article 305 CL, 'a commission agency is a contract under which an agent legally conducts business under its own name on behalf of the client for a consideration'.[111] Unlike other agency arrangements, articles 306–309 CL consider the principal's instructions as providing general guidelines to the agent; the latter may well deviate from these according to its business judgment and if the price received as a result is higher he or she may retain the difference. If this turns out to be lower, then the difference to the principal should in principle be compensated. In any event, the general principles of commercial agency apply *mutatis mutandis* to commission agency. A particularity of the commission agency model is that unless otherwise agreed the agent must not disclose the identity of the principal and in equal manner the agent must not disclose the identity of the third party to the principal.[112] Moreover, the commission agent contracts in its own name and is bound in its own name, with the third party, and subsequently, the principal is not bound to the third party and neither can have recourse against the other.[113]

The agent is entitled to reimbursement of expenses related to its mandate, save if they arose from the agent's mistake.[114] The same rule applies where the agent incurred harm or damage arising from the mandate.[115]

---

[109] Art 301 CL.
[110] Art 303 CL.
[111] Court of Cassation Judgment 65/2011. The Court emphasised that it may be proven by all methods of evidence, even a presumption.
[112] Art 311 CL.
[113] Art 315 CL.
[114] Art 312 CL.
[115] Art 313 CL.

4.8.3 *Distributorship*

Article 304 CL is the only provision in the CL specifically discussing distributorship arrangements. Since it is situated in the part of the CL dealing with commercial agency, it too is regulated by the agency provisions of the CL and the CC.[116] Some commentators note that where a distributor does not fall within the definition of a commercial agent under the Commercial Law and/or the agency is not registered (as discussed above), article 304 CL still allows the distributorship agreement[117] where

> a trader undertakes to market and distribute products of an industrial or commercial establishment in a particular territory shall be considered to be a commercial agency provided that he is the sole distributor of such products.

The Court of Cassation has held that in order for the distribution contract to be considered a commercial agency contract, it must meet two conditions combined: a) the first is that the contract is accompanied by a condition whereby the producer or the wholesaler assigns to a local distributor the right to limit the sale of its products only to others in a specific area, and b) that the distributor does so within the scope of the agency and on behalf of its client, in return for a consideration, whether profit, commission, or wages. If both conditions are fulfilled in the contract, the contract is considered a commercial agency and falls within the scope of the Commercial Agents Regulation Law No 8 of 2002.[118] A contract for distributing the products of an industrial or commercial establishment in a specific area is considered a commercial agency if the distribution is exclusive to the product.[119]

4.8.4 *Trade Representative*

Unlike the preceding forms of agency, a trade representative is engaged in a contract of employment with the trader to carry on trading activities on behalf of and in the name of the trader.[120] As an employee, the trade representative cannot contract in its own name[121] and the trader or traders so employing

[116] In fact, Art 304 specifies that distributorship is governed by Arts 294, 300–303 CL.
[117] Al Tamimi, 'Doing Business in Qatar' (2019), at 22, available at www.tamimi.com/wp-content/uploads/2019/04/Doing-Business-in-Qatar.pdf
[118] Court of Cassation Judgment 171/2013.
[119] Court of Cassation Judgment 335/2016.
[120] Art 318 CL.
[121] In fact, the trade representative's employee status prevents him or her from conducting own business or that of another person, without the express permission of the trader(s), in accordance with Art 323 CL.

the representative are liable for all contracts entered into by him or her.[122] It is therefore imperative that the trade representative disclose at the time of contracting the full identity of the trader.[123] Where the authority of the representative is not expressly stipulated in the agreement, this 'shall be deemed to include all transactions relating to the type of trade that he has been authorized to conduct'.[124]

4.8.5 *Brokerage*

The contract of brokerage involves authorisation, for a fee,[125] to a broker by a client to find and negotiate with a second party a specific contract under conditions laid down by the client.[126] The existence of a brokerage agreement is a question of fact that may be deduced on the basis of available documentation, witnesses and the circumstances.[127] Unless otherwise agreed, the broker may not be a party to the contract it is authorised to negotiate and conclude. If it does become a party he or she is not entitled to a fee.[128] In accordance with article 340 CL, 'where a number of brokers are authorized in a single contract, they shall be jointly responsible for the work assigned to them, unless each is licensed to work individually, or specific duties are assigned to a particular broker'.

---

[122] Art 319 CL.
[123] Art 321 CL.
[124] Art 320(1) CL.
[125] For a determination of the fee, see Arts 328–33 CL.
[126] Art 327 CL. See Court of Cassation Judgment 102/2010; see also Court of Cassation Judgment 175/2016.
[127] Court of Cassation Judgment 126/2009.
[128] Art 334 CL.

5

Formality

5.1 INTRODUCTION

In Chapter 2, we discussed contract formation in general, whereas here we shall dive deeper into formality and delivery in particular. Before doing so, we need to lay the foundations by which to evaluate the legal impact of formality and delivery on civil and commercial contracts. It will be recalled that under the civil law tradition, contracts are predicated on three general pillars, namely (i) consent (الرضاء), consisting of offer, acceptance and intention to be legally bound; (ii) subject matter (المحل) and (iii) cause (السبب). In addition, there may, although not necessarily, exist two further requirements (special pillars), namely (iv) formality[1] (الشكلية) and (v) delivery (التسليم).[2]

---

[1] According to the Court of Cassation Judgment 20/2007, formality is a fundamental pillar for the formation of any *sale contract* concerning the sale of *retail stores*. Thus, the law requires such sale contract be notarised in an official document and issued by the concerned public body, that is, the Documentation Department of the Ministry of Justice. The contracting parties are prohibited from agreeing to circumvent this pillar and any contrary agreement is deemed null and void (absolute nullity). Moreover, the contracting parties cannot elect to authorise (affirm) the sale contract. However, once the contracting parties complete the statutory requirement of 'formality', then the sale contract becomes binding because all its pillars will have materialised.

[2] According to the Court of Cassation Judgment 274/2015, delivery is a fundamental pillar for the formation of any *sale contract* concerning the sale of *real estate* (immovable properties). Registering any property conveyance with the Real-Estate Registration Department of the Ministry of Justice, is a regulatory requirement for the completion of the conveyance but *it is not* a pillar serving the formation of the sale contract. This means that any real estate sale contract whereby the seller *does not* deliver the property to the buyer is invalid (absolute nullity) and the mere formality of completing the registration process *does not* authorise (affirm) this void contract. Thus, the seller is obligated by law to deliver the sold real estate to the buyer and in turn the buyer is obligated to make payment to the seller. Following this the sale contract becomes valid and produces full legal effects; see also G Mahgoub Ali, *The General Theory of Obligation: Part One – Sources of Obligation in Qatari Law* (Doha Modern Printing Press, 2016) 302.

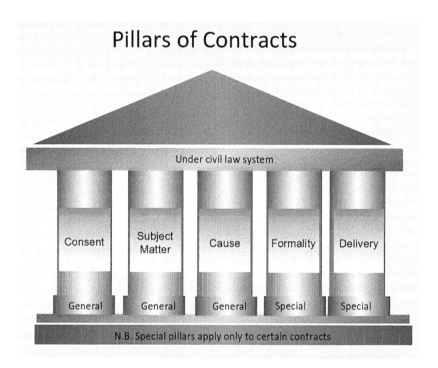

FIGURE 5.1 Pillars of contracts

The principle of formality in the civil law tradition is actually *an exception* to the general rule of 'informality', where the latter simply dictates that contracts may be concluded in any form. It makes sense that the law does not intend to further encumber civil and commercial transactions by requiring contracting parties to draft and execute all contracts, whether complex or simple, for example buying a cup of coffee. Although the general rule of 'informality' has not been codified in the French CC, from which both the Egyptian CC and Qatari CC were derived, the exception of formality is explicitly mentioned; whenever, it is required throughout the CC. Figure 5.1 will be provided as the discussion progresses in this chapter.

5.2 REASONS FOR FORMALITIES

In general, there are three rationales underlying the need for formality, namely (i) the warning function; (ii) information function and (iii) evidentiary function. For specific contracts only mandated by law, the requirement of such formality most likely encompasses a combination of more than a single rationale.

Starting with the warning function, it serves the purpose of 'alarming' potential contracting parties to the risks associated with entering a transaction deemed either legally or financially dangerous. Its objective is to incentivise the parties to pause and think about the consequences of such transaction prior to granting their consent. For example, consumer credit agreements in many jurisdictions are rightly viewed as financially dangerous because they typically subject the debtor to high interest rates, which in turn expose it to likely hardship over long periods. Another example concerns consumer guarantee agreements, whereby one party promises to repay the debts of its counterparty if the latter fails to perform its obligation to the creditor (a third party). This type of financial security is also deemed dangerous because the guarantor could be a 'victim' of potential exploitation of trust by the debtor, for example a mother providing financial security to guarantee the payment of her child's debt. Because family relationships involve emotional considerations, these play a major role in the decision-making process, which may lead to undesired consequences such as bankruptcy. Thus, the law intends to warn such individuals by mandating the formality process, in order to provide an opportunity to reconsider their position prior to finalising the 'dangerous' transaction.[3]

Moving to the second rationale, namely the information function, formality here serves the purpose of providing contracting parties with sufficient information. We can see this function visible in immovable property conveyance transactions, where it is mandatory for a civil law notary to draft the notarial deed and warn the contracting parties of the legal consequences. Lastly, the third rationale, the evidentiary function, as its name indicates serves the purpose of securing evidence of the contract in question. When a contract is put into writing, certainty about the mere existence and content of such contract are no longer disputed. However, the certainty of a written contract does not prevent the contracting parties from interpreting its terms and conditions differently in practice.[4] The types of formalities required under Qatari law will be discussed further in this chapter.

5.3 CONTRACTS TO BE MADE BY NOTARIAL DEED

5.3.1 *Gifts and Donations*

Gifts in the civil law tradition are encompassed under the umbrella of donation contracts, which include, among others, instruments such as wills, trusts,

---

[3]   Mahgoub (n 2) 102.
[4]   Ibid, 102–103.

loans, deposits without consideration and agency without consideration.[5] Formality by notarial deed is considered a condition for a valid gift contract in many civil law jurisdictions such as Egypt, Kuwait and the United Arab Emirates (UAE). Article 488 of the Egyptian CC states that 'A gift shall be put into a *notarial deed*, otherwise it is null and void with the exception of being disguised into another [type of] contract'. Article 525 of the Kuwaiti CC and article 615 of the UAE CC have followed suit.[6] However, the Qatari CC has deviated from this established tradition and did not mandate formality as a prerequisite for a valid gift contract. According to article 493(1) CC: 'A gift shall be valid by consent and acceptance and shall be completed by collection'. There is no explicit mention of formality in this provision. Furthermore, article 493(3) CC states that: 'The enforceability of a gift agreement shall depend on *any procedure to transfer title* in accordance with any laws. Either party may complete the required procedures'; thus, the Qatari legislator has mandated *an exception to the general rule* and demanded that contracting parties must comply with any registration and/or formality requirements concerning the conveyance of property, especially real estate. The Qatari Court of Cassation in its judgment 224/2016 held that: 'The legislator did not mandate that a gift shall be put into a notarial deed, but made it subject to the general rules of evidence, which are applicable to all contracts'.[7]

---

[5] The term consideration in this context *is not* tantamount to the common law doctrine of 'consideration' because the latter does not exist as a pillar for valid contracts under the civil law systems as discussed earlier. Consideration here means 'profit' and/or 'charging a fee', that is, the donor intends to expend wealth by giving up something of value (whether material or moral) to the donee without expecting something else in return for its generous act. However, this general rule *is not absolute* and is usually limited by applicable laws. For example, the rules governing gifts limit the prohibition of consideration. We will discuss this issue in a subsequent section.

[6] A Al-Sanhuri, *The Mediator in Explaining the Civil Code* (Egypt House for Publishing and Distribution, 2020) vol 5, at 37.

[7] Gifts under Qatari law are regulated by Arts 191 to 205 of the Family Law ('**FL**', Law no. 22 of 2006) and Arts 498 to 504 of the CC (Law no. 22 of 2004). As a rule of thumb, rules mandated by a special law supersede their counterparts. The courts apply the rules mandated by a general law only when (i) a special law is silent about a certain issue already regulated by the general law; or (ii) the case in dispute falls outside the ambit of the special law, hence the general rule shall apply (Court of Cassation Judgement 224/2016). The ambit of FL over disputes arising from gifts is directly linked to the definition of family under Qatari law. Surprisingly, the FL does not define 'family', and thus one must rely on Arts 45 to 48 CC. Art 45 CC states that '(i) The family of a person shall consist of the person's spouse and relatives; and (ii) persons having a common ancestor are deemed to be relatives'. So, it is clear that Qatari legislator defined the term 'family' to include both the person's (i) immediate family members (i.e. spouse and children); and extended family members (i.e. parents, siblings, uncles, and aunties). This is a reflection of collectivism as a main characteristic of the Qatari society compared to western societies, Thus, under Qatari law any dispute arising between contracting parties not recognised as family members falls under the terms of the CC.

In a nutshell, a gift under Qatari law pursuant to article 191(1) FL is defined as a donation (a transfer of ownership for something of value) made by a donor *during his or her lifetime* to a *donee without consideration*. Thus, such a gift shall be offered to the donee while the donor is still alive and not in its deathbed;[8] otherwise, the gift will be deemed as constituting a will and consequently the rules of wills will apply,[9] pursuant to article 202 FL and article 497 CC. Furthermore, article 191(2) FL made it crystal clear that 'conditional' gifts, that is a gift with attached consideration will be deemed as a sale and consequently the rules of sales will apply. This strict prohibition of 'gifts with attached consideration' under the FL differs from the permissible approach adopted under article 492(2) CC, under which the latter permits a donor to offer a gift to a donee subject to fulfilling a specific obligation or condition in return. In this scenario, the value of such 'limited consideration' *shall not* exceed the actual value of the donation, otherwise the donee's liability will be capped to the actual value of the donation. Moreover, articles 500(2), 501, 503 CC and 504(1) CC regulate other matters associated with conditional gifts.

The gift is formed when a valid offer made by a donor meets a 'matching' acceptance that is expressed by the donee. The gift itself must be owned by the donor and exist at the time of making the offer. Compatibility with *Sharia* law is the main rationale behind this condition, since gifts cannot be constituted by something that the donor expects or foresees to own sometime in the future, such as money gained through derivative contracts (futures and forwards) and hedging activities.[10] As a general rule, the donee must express its intention to accept the gift offer, either explicitly or implicitly. However, the donee's silence *must not* be deemed as acceptance because the law here recognises that donees may have some reservations about the acceptance of a gift offer and, thus, must not be obliged to accept it in the first place. The only exception to this general rule is mandated in articles 195 FL and 493(2) CC, whereby the donee's acceptance *is not* mandatory when the donor is the parent or legal guardian/custodian of the donee. Lastly, the donor may unilaterally retract[11] the gift contract, if he or

---

[8] According to the Court of Cassation in Judgments 152/2012 and 187/2012, a gift contract that was concluded during the lifetime of the donor, but its essence was to divide the donor's estate among its wife and children in a specific manner must takes place after the donor's death. It concluded that this gift contract was actually a 'will' in disguise.

[9] Art 202 FL and Art 497 CC.

[10] Art 199 FL and Art 494 CC.

[11] According to the Court of Cassation Judgment 110/2008, retraction of a gift contract for an item that was not handed to the donee (no possession over the gift item) has a retroactive effect, that is, the gift contract is null and void from the date of its inception. The Court added that any gift contract concluded during the enforcement of the currently obsolete law (Law No. 16/1971 concerning the Law of Civil and Commercial Articles), that is, prior to the enactment of Qatar's CC, shall be governed by Islamic law.

she meets one of the legal conditions mandated by the law pursuant to articles 203 to 205 FL and articles 505 to 512 CC as applicable. Gift contracts are legally enforced upon taking possession of the gift item by the donee as stipulated in articles 192(2) FL ('A gift shall become enforceable only upon possession or delivery and receipt') and 194 FL. This is equally true in respect of article 493(1) CC, whereby, 'A gift shall be completed by collection' as applicable.[12] In addition, taking possession of the gift may substitute the donee's acceptance, if the latter was not expressed previously, because the donee's action in this scenario is more affirmative according to article 194(1) FL.

5.3.2 *Agency Contracts (Power of Attorney)*

Pursuant to Article 716 CC, an 'Agency shall be defined as a contract under which the agent undertakes to do any legal act for the account of the principal'. The Qatari legislator has defined the contracting parties (principal and agent) and the contractual obligations as an undertaking to do a 'legal act'. It is a crystal clear that agency contracts constitute a 'delegation' from a principal to an agent to do something on its behalf. It is worth noting here that the legal act itself could be either (i) civil or (ii) commercial. The differentiation between the two types of legal acts is important in order to distinguish the following: (i) which courts possess jurisdiction over a claim arising from an agency contract, that is civil courts or commercial courts and (ii) which statute is applicable to the claim, that is the Civil Code, or the Commercial Law.

Formality in agency contracts depends on the legal requirements for the legal act itself in accordance with article 718 CC, which states that 'The agency contract shall have such form as required to be available in the subject-matter of the legal act'. Thus, we may conclude here that 'formality' is *an exception* to the general rule, which is not *a prerequisite* from the outset for most agency contracts. An important example of 'an exception' relates to gift contracts. As discussed earlier, gifts do not require formality under Qatari law in order to be legally binding. However, an agency contract in circumstances where the legal act consists of a donation from the principal's assets (in whole or in part)

---

[12] According to the judgment of the Court of Cassation 110/2008, the rules of gift pursuant to the Hanbali school mandate that title (ownership) of a gift item passes from a doner to a donee only upon the latter taking possession of it. Thus, a gift transaction entails two stages; namely (i) a 'pre-possession' stage where the gift contract is not legally binding, hence no transfer of title (ownership) and the donor may retract it unilaterally; and (ii) 'post-possession' stage where the gift contract is legally binding, and transfer of title (ownership) materialises. The only exception to the 'post-possession' stage is the permissible retraction of a gift contract where the donor is the parent of the donee.

to a third party does require formality pursuant to article 721 CC, that is a private power of attorney made on a notarial deed. The rationale behind this exception is to protect principals from the misuse or abuse of a 'non-authenti-cated' agency contracts by their agents, where the latter donate the estate to a third party without consent. Another legal act that requires formality is related to a company's articles of association. According to article 515(1) CC, 'The contract of the company shall be in writing, otherwise it shall be invalid. Any amendments to the contract not reflected on such form as applicable in the contract shall be also be invalid'. Thus, an agency contract (power of attorney) concerning a company's association articles *must be made in writing* but not necessarily in a notarial deed.

In general, there are two types of agency contracts (power of attorney) namely (i) general power of attorney and (ii) private power of attorney. The general power of attorney grants the agent authority to administer the prin-cipal's affairs without the power to transfer title/ownership of the principal's assets, unless these are necessary as a matter of administration as may be required of the agent. According to article 719 CC,

> Agency in general, without specific designation of the subject-matter of the agency, shall not grant the agent any capacity other than in administrative acts. The term 'administrative act' shall include lease, provided that it does not exceed three years; maintenance and safekeeping works; collection of rights; and repayment of debts. This expression shall also include any dispo-sition as required for management.

The law here provided a list of legal acts that are deemed administrative in nature, which include (i) rent of real estate or chattel that does not exceed three years in period; (ii) maintenance works; (iii) collection of rights, for example collection of credits lent to third parties; and (iv) repayment of debts owed to third parties. Furthermore, the law is very strict about adherence to the wording of agency contracts, where the rights are delegated from the principal to the agent. Article 720 CC states that

> The agency contract shall not grant the agent any capacity other than to do such acts as stated therein and any ancillary things in accordance with the nature of such acts and the applicable practice.

Thus, agents shall not be granted authority that goes above and beyond the scope of the legal act that the principal was intended to grant in the first place, that is managing the principal's estate rather than transferring the ownership of such estates.[13]

---

[13] See Court of Cassation Judgment 174/2018.

The second type of agency contacts is the private power of attorney. In this context, article 721 CC states that

> (i) Any act other than administrative acts shall require a special agency, particularly for gifts, sale, reconciliation, mortgage, acknowledgment, arbitration, oaths and pleading before the courts of law; (ii) A special agency shall be valid in a particular type of legal acts, even if the subject-matter of such act is not specifically determined, unless it is an act of gift.

The Qatari legislator has emphasised the risk associated with delegating legal acts pertaining to donations, sales or mortgage of the principal's estate to its agent (substantive), where transfer of title would most likely occur. Thus, the law intends to *warn the principal* by requiring it to issue a private power of attorney through a notarial deed. Another type of legal act granted equal importance is associated with legal actions before the courts (procedural), such as making of oaths, giving testimony, acknowledging a material fact, pleading before the court, or even reconciling a legal dispute out of court. All these legal actions create a significant impact on the principal's rights, all of which are protected by law. If the principal is not warned beforehand about the consequences of delegating such legal acts, it may consequently be severely disadvantaged.

Lawyers in the State of Qatar cannot represent their clients before the courts or other governmental authorities without an 'authenticated' agency contract (power of attorney), that is in this scenario, the law requires the 'private' agency contract to be made in a 'notarial deed' as a general rule. Pursuant to article 54 of the Code of Law Practice,[14]

> (i) The lawyer shall represent his client by virtue of a power-of-attorney authenticated pursuant to the law, and he shall deposit the power-of-attorney in the case file if belonging thereto, but if the power-of-attorney is of a general nature, it shall be sufficient for the court to review and record its number, date and authenticating authority in the hearing's transcript and enclose a photocopy thereof in the case file'. (ii) If the client appears in a court accompanied by the lawyer, the court shall record such appearance in the hearing's transcript, and such appearance shall be deemed as an authenticated power-of-attorney, and the fees prescribed for authenticating the power-of-attorney shall then be charged.

The law here prescribes *two exceptions* to the general rule whereby lawyers may legally represent their clients before the courts and/or public authorities. First, if a lawyer possesses an authenticated 'general' power of attorney, it may

---

[14] Law No 23/2006.

request the court to be granted with the right to legally represent the client. The lawyer must file the authenticated 'general' power of attorney to the court, whereupon the court will review such request in the hearing's transcript and grant such power. A copy of the authenticated general power of attorney will be enclosed in the case file. Secondly, another exception applies when neither 'private' nor 'general' power of attorney exists beforehand between lawyer and client. In this scenario, the law will deem their *appearance together* before the courts as a legal act of granting the lawyer a specific power of attorney. Consequently, the lawyer will be granted the right to legally represent its client and the court will charge the authentication fees to the client.

5.3.3 *Immovables (Real-Estate Conveyance and Mortgage)*

Contracts concerning conveyance and mortgage of immovable properties are subject to strict formality due to the associated high risk and value of these transactions in addition to their impact on the economy at large. The law intends to fulfil the public policy of stabilising transactions between all stakeholders. In order to achieve these objectives, the Qatari legislator has mandated several conditions, as set out in articles 919 and 246 CC.

5.3.3.1 Real-Estate Conveyance

Article 919 CC states that,

> As in the case of other rights in kind,[15] title to a movable asset and real property shall be transferred by any legal act, provided that the disposing party is the owner of the disposed right, subject to the provisions of article 246 and 247 herein.

This provision is complemented more specifically by article 246 CC, which goes on to stipulate that

> The obligation to transfer title or any other right in kind shall automatically transfer such right, provided that the subject-matter of the obligation is a self-identified thing held by the obligor and subject to the rules in connection with registration.[16]

---

[15] According to Art 837 CC, ownership *in rem* encompasses the following exclusive rights: (i) use; (ii) utilisation or exploitation; and the (iii) disposal (sell or lease).

[16] For real estate registration, see Court of Cassation Judgments: 227/2015 and 180/2015. Art 247 CC states that: '(i) Where the obligation relates to the transfer of a right in kind to a thing identifiable only by its kind, such right shall not be transferred until such thing is apportioned. (ii) Where the obligor fails to perform his [or her] obligation, the obligee may, with the permission of the court, or without its permission in the case of emergency, obtain a thing of the same kind at the expense of the obligor. The obligee may also demand the value of the thing, without prejudice in either event to his [or her] right to indemnity'.

Here, the first condition concerns the 'absolute' and 'untarnished' ownership of a property by the disposing party or the seller. In common law jurisdictions, this is known as 'Fee Simple Absolute' under the law of property. This condition is essential for the transfer of title and risk to the receiving party or the buyer. However, anything less than absolute ownership, such as the right to possess or the right to use said property may be transferred by a third party who holds such right *in rem*. For example, a tenant with a right to possess and use a property may sublease it to a sub-tenant unless the tenancy contract prohibits this. Also, the general rule of conveyance does not entail that a property which is encumbered with a particular right *in rem*, such as easement or mortgage cannot be transferred. The law permits such transactions under specific rules.

The second condition is essential to the validity of property conveyance, namely 'the legal act' to initiate such transaction. In the civil law tradition, legal obligations arise from (i) legal acts or (ii) legal facts law (legislation). Legal acts are defined as manifestations of will intended to produce legal effects. They may be based on agreement [bilateral or multilateral] or unilateral disposition. Legal acts are subject, as to their validity and effects, to the rules governing contracts. Legal facts are defined as 'behaviours or events to which legislation attaches legal consequences'. Legal facts are governed, according to the circumstances, by the sub-title relating to extra-contractual liability or the sub-title relating to other sources of obligations.[17] The above definition of both legal acts and legal facts are obtained directly from articles 1100, 1100(1), and 1100(2) of the French CC as amended by Ordonnance No 2016-131 of 10 February 2016. Neither the Qatari CC nor the Egyptian CC contains any explicit definition of legal acts and legal facts. However, both Egyptian and Qatari jurisprudence acknowledge these definitions despite the lack of statutory text.

Abdulrazzaq Al-Sanhuri, the 'god father' of civil codes in the Middle East, has explained that a legal act is a voluntary performance made by a person (natural or legal) intended to create legal consequences. Unlike legal acts, legal facts arise from either an (i) event (natural or man-made) creating legal consequences or (ii) performance made by a person (natural or legal) *without intention* to create legal consequences, such as civil wrongdoings (delicts) and enrichment without cause.[18] When the Qatari legislator was in the process of drafting article 919 CC, it deliberately deviated from the original text of article 932 of the Egyptian CC. The key difference here is apparent by substituting

---

[17] J Cartwright, B Fauvarque-Cosson and S Whittaker, 'French Civil Code of 2016' (English translation) www.trans-lex.org/601101 accessed 26 October 2022.
[18] Al-Sanhuri, (n 6) vol 1, Part 1, at 112–114 and 141–142. See also M Al-Ouji, *The Legal Basis of the Civil Code* (Al-Halabi Law Publications, 2010) 221 and 261.

the word 'contract' with the word 'legal act'. The rationale behind this change from the Qatari perspective is that the term 'legal acts' cover both contracts and unilateral dispositions. Thus, its use in the statutory text is more accurate than limiting this condition to property conveyance arising from contracts only.

The third condition is formality that manifests in the process of registration. Besides the mandatory requirement of registration as stipulated in article 246 CC, which is general in its application, Qatari legislators have enacted a special law to deal specifically with the Real-Estate Registration System ('RERS').[19] Here, we highlight the relevant provision that mandates formality, namely article 4, which states that

> All [legal] acts that would create, remove, or change a property right or another property right-in-kind, as well as final judgements confirming the same, shall be registered. The lack of registration shall mean that the aforementioned rights shall not be moved, transferred, or changed whether between the stakeholders or third-parties. Non-registered contracts shall have no effect other than the personal obligations between the contracting parties.

Thus, the law makes it crystal clear that title (ownership) and other rights *in rem* cannot be transferred between contracting parties until the formality of registration is complete.[20] Once the formality condition is met, the legal effect of such transaction is deemed from the effective date of the legal act (whether it is a contract or a unilateral disposition) and not from the registration date. The rationale behind this is that the legal act is the main source of obligation for such transaction (conveyance or mortgage), and the registration project is a mere formality to 'activate' its legal effects upon all stakeholders.[21]

5.3.3.2 Real-Estate Mortgage

In the civil law tradition, there are two types of mortgages namely (i) official mortgage; and (ii) possessory mortgage.[22] In the context of this chapter, we will be focusing on the former because as the name indicates, this contractual obligation requires formality to manifest its legally binding effects. According to articles 1058 CC and 1059 CC, an official mortgage is defined as follows:

> An official mortgage shall be defined as *a contract* in which the creditor requires *a right over real property for the settlement of a debt* owed to him [or her] by the debtor. This right entitles the creditor *to take precedence* over ordinary creditors and over creditors who are lower rank to him [or her] in

---

[19] Qatar Law No. 14 of 1964, as amended.
[20] See Court of Cassation Judgments 142/2018 and 420/2017.
[21] Al-Sanhuri (n 6), vol 9, Part 1, a 299–307.
[22] For further discussion on possessory mortgages, see Al-Sanhuri, ibid, 511.

the settlement of his [or her] right out of the proceeds of the sale of such property, no matter who purchases it [emphasis added]

In-line with article 1058 CC, article 1059 CC reads as follows:

(i) An *Official mortgage* shall not be established unless made under *an official paper*[23] reviewed and signed according to the law. (ii) The mortgagor shall bear the costs of the mortgage contract unless there is an agreement to the contrary.

The statutory texts describe the rules which govern an official mortgage under Qatari law. First, an official mortgage is a contract between a mortgagor and mortgagee; henceforth, the general rules of contract law apply to their relationship during the term of the agreement. Second, it is important to note that an official mortgage as a legal instrument can be created for real-estate properties exclusively, that is chattels (movable properties) are not included.

Third, an official mortgage is used as a 'collateral' to secure payment of a debt between the contracting parties. The mortgagor (the debtor) grants the mortgagee (the creditor) a right in kind over a real estate that is owned by the former in order to secure a loan borrowed from the latter. The loan becomes a 'secured credit', and the mortgagee (the creditor) acquires a 'security interest' over the mortgaged property (right in kind). Fourth, an official mortgage must be issued on a notarial deed and properly filed with the real-estate registration system in accordance with the Qatari CC and RERS. This prerequisite of formality serves multiple purposes, namely to (i) protect the interests of all stakeholders for this transaction; (ii) warn the mortgagor of the potential risk of losing the mortgaged property due to default payments, even though the said property remains under his or her ownership and possession during the term of the contract; (iii) grant the mortgagee enough information to make an informed choice about the transaction prior to its conclusion; (iv) grant the mortgagee a notarial deed, which it may use to settle the default payments without the need to seek a court order; (v) allow the mortgagee to register its right in kind with the relevant authorities in order to protect their rank in the secured credit and (vi) allow potential new creditors to retrieve any previous mortgages made on the said property from the public registration in order to figure out their rank among secured creditors and consequently estimate the potential risk of such transaction. It is worth highlighting that only the first mortgagee who registers or files its right in kind with the real property registration system will be granted the right to 'perfection' among the other secured creditors. Perfection means that in the case at hand, the mortgagor becomes

---

[23] See Court of Cassation Judgment 167/2016.

unable to settle the secured credit, and then the creditor will have a 'supreme' security interest in the settlement of its credit over any other secured creditors who are in lower rank, or against ordinary creditors.

Failure to comply with the formality requirement will nullify the official mortgage transaction; however, the loan agreement between the contracting parties remains valid because the latter does not require formality. The creditor may sue the debtor (as an ordinary creditor) for damages under the general rules of contracts which govern loan contracts but cannot claim a right in kind on the property as collateral.[24]

5.4 CONTRACTS TO BE MADE IN WRITING

5.4.1 *Company Articles of Association*

Articles of association constitute a supreme contract acting as the company's 'constitution' or 'charter' and its rules supersede any other internal contract or agreement made by the company. A company's articles of association include, but not limited to, the name of the company as a legal person, its nationality (place of domicile), its commercial activities, the company's capital, the type of company as per the Qatar Companies Law ('**QCL**') (Law No. 11 of 2015), or any other relevant law passed by the government, the name of the owners or shareholders, their share of the capital, their role in the company, their authorisations to sign and approve, and the appointed managing directors (senior management). Furthermore, the articles of association are governed by multiple pieces of legislation under Qatari law, namely (i) the CC, (ii) QCL and Commercial Registry Law ('**CRL**') (Law No. 25 of 2005 as amended by Law No. 20 of 2014). Articles of association are known to have a relatively 'long-term' lifespan and protect the rights of both owner(s) (among themselves) and third parties (others) who may engage with the company in a potential business transaction, knowing that the said company is well established in accordance with the law.[25]

Article 513 CC has defined the company's article association as follows:

> a company is a contract between two or more persons to contribute money or work to a financial project and to divide the profit or loss that may arise therefrom.

Thus, the law makes it a crystal clear as a general rule that a company must be established through a contract between the parties (bilateral or multilateral) for the purpose of collaborating in a business endeavour in which the parties will

---

[24] Al-Sanhuri (n 6), vol 10, 199–203.
[25] Y Al-Shazhly, *Qatar Corporate Law* (LexisNexis, 2017, in Arabic) 83.

share both resulting profits and losses. However, article 2 CL has established *an exception to the general* rule in accordance with article 513 CC by stating that

> (i) A commercial company is an agreement under which two or more natural or legal persons commit to contribute to a profit-generating project, by way of providing capital or work and sharing the profit generated or loss sustained from the project. (ii) The company may comprise only one person in accordance with the provisions of Chapter 8 of this law.

Reading Article 228 CL states that

> '(i) A limited liability company is a company that consists of one or more persons and the number of partners shall not exceed fifty (50) persons. (ii) A partner will only be liable up to their share in the capital. The shares of the partners shall not be negotiable securities'.

Henceforth, a limited liability company ('**LLC**') can be established by one person only. It is worth noting here that an LLC under Qatari law differs from the common law business organisation that is known as 'sole proprietorship'. The key difference can be summarised as follows: (i) a sole proprietorship[26] *does not* create a legal person that is separate from its owner (natural person); thus, risk and liability in case of the owner's bankruptcy pass to its estate; whereas, (ii) the LLC *creates* a legal person[27] that is separate from its owner (natural person); thus, the risk and liability in case of the company's insolvency are limited to its capital as per the company's article of association, that is risk and liability *do not* go all the way to the owner's estate (due to the protection of the legal principle of 'corporate veil', which may only be pierced by a court order.[28]

Formality is an important prerequisite for the validity of a company's articles of association.[29] In accordance with article 515 CC

> (i) The contract of the company shall be in writing, otherwise it shall be invalid.[30] Any amendments to the contract not reflected on such form as applicable in the contract shall also be invalid. (ii) However,

---

[26] See Court of Cassation judgments on sole proprietorship, 42/2016; and 19/2016.

[27] See Court of Cassation Judgments 347/2015; 138/2016; 91/2008; and 49/2010.

[28] According to Court of Cassation Judgment 306/2019, the liability of a limited liability company shareholder is limited to its share of the company's capital. The law aims to protect third parties who intend to engage in a potential business venture with the company by adding the abbreviation (L.L.C.) to the company's name, so others from the outset become aware of the company's legal form and its limitations.

[29] See Court of Cassation Judgment 352/2016.

[30] The Court of Cassation in Judgment 5/2007, held that 'when the legislator mandated a particular formality for a specific contract [i.e. company's article of association] to be valid, such formality becomes mandatory and without it the said contract is null and void. This nullity

such invalidity may not be held thereto by the shareholders against third-parties and such invalidity shall not be effective as between the shareholders themselves, other than from the time a shareholder demands that invalidity be ruled.

Article 6 CL added more rules governing the formalities of the company's articles of association as follows

> (i) Except for joint venture companies, a company's contract as well as any amendment thereto shall be in Arabic and authenticated; otherwise, the company's contract or the amendment shall be invalid. (ii) The procedure for the authentication of the company's contract shall be set by a decision of the competent authority in liaison with the Minister. (iii) The company's contract or any amendment thereto may be accompanied by a translation in any other foreign language, and in the event of discrepancy, the Arabic version shall prevail.

It is worth highlighting here that the formality of 'writing' is a condition for the validity of the company's articles of association (substantive) and not proof of its existence (procedural). The lack of this particular formality serves to render the contract null and void (absolute nullity). Moreover, the Qatari legislator mandated that any amendment to an existing company's articles of association must be made under the same formality requirements (i.e. writing). The official language of a company's articles of association must be Arabic. However, article 6(2) of CL has granted *an exception to the general* rule as mandated in article 515 CC, whereby foreign language translations may accompany the Arabic original version. In the event of discrepancy between the original version and its translations, the original version in Arabic supersedes other translations.

Article 8 CL places great emphasis on the company's veil and legal personality, by stating that,

> Except for joint venture companies, a company shall not have a legal personality until it is declared in accordance with the provisions of this law. The company's manager or members of its board, as the case may be, shall be jointly liable for the damages caused to third parties due to their failure to declare the company.

The above article must be read in conjunction with article 7 CRL, which states that

> extends to those contract's amendments that did not fulfil the formality'. Formalities mandated by the law *aim to protect public interest*, and any failure thereof serves to nullify the contract from its effective date (retroactively)'.

No natural or legal person may engage in trade or establish a business unless it is entered in the Commercial Registry.

The formality concerning the registration[31] of a company as a legal person with the relevant authority (i.e. the Department of Commercial Affairs at the Ministry of Economy and Commerce) aims to create a public database for all Qatari legal persons authorised to conduct business transactions domestically and abroad. Thus, all third parties who intend to engage with Qatari companies in potential business ventures, may have access to such a commercial registry from the outset. Concerns about 'real' or 'sham' companies is rife before the courts; pertinent public policy through such formality thus aims to (i) minimise this risk of dispute; (ii) stabilise all business transactions and (iii) protect the Qatari economy at large.[32]

5.5 CONTRACTS TO BE EVIDENCED IN WRITING

5.5.1 *Guarantees (Suretyship)*

In the civil law tradition, a guarantee is considered a contract (commonly bilateral but also multilateral), where the guarantor promises to settle the outstanding debt of the borrower (debtor) in the event the debtor defaults in its credit agreement with the creditor. It is worth highlighting that the *contracting parties* in this legal instrument are the guarantor and the creditor. Consequently, the debtor who is the main beneficiary is not a contracting party, but a mere third party to the agreement. Article 808 CC defines a guarantee contract as follows:

> A guarantee shall be defined as a contract under which a person undertakes to the creditor to accept responsibility for the performance of an obligation by the debtor where the debtor fails to perform such obligation.

The guarantee as a contract *does not* require *formality* to become legally binding. Consent between the guarantor and the creditor is sufficient. However, the law mandates that *a guarantee contract must be evidenced in writing* in accordance with article 809 CC, which states that 'a guarantee shall be evidenced[33] in writing, even if the original obligation may be established by

---

[31] For the role of the commercial registry, see Court of Cassation Judgments 127/2015 and 167/2015.

[32] Al-Shazhly (n 25), 88–90.

[33] In the original Arabic text of Art 809 CC the Arabic word (ثبت) was mistranslated to 'made' instead of the correct word 'evidenced'. The English translation with this error is available on the official Al-Meezan portal (Qatar's Ministry of Justice). Also, the Arabic word (بينة) in the

proof. For example, if a guarantor's offer to settle a debt was met with the creditor's acceptance during the contract session, then the guarantee contract is legally formed without the need to put it in writing. However, if a dispute arises from an oral guarantee contract, then the claimant may file to the court any official correspondence that was made in writing between the contracting parties, in which it makes an explicit reference to the valid guarantee agreement, that is the correspondence proves the existence of such a guarantee contract in the first place. The type of correspondences that may be included encompasses notice letters, registered mails, e-mails (subject to the rules of evidence in accordance with civil procedure rules) and others.

One visible characteristic of the guarantee contract is that it encumbers one party only, that is the guarantor to settle the debt to the creditor. Hence, the creditor has no obligation to fulfil. However, this *does not mean* that a guarantee as a contract may be formed by a unilateral disposition because the consent of both the guarantor and the creditor is mandatory for its valid. It is worth highlighting that despite the general rule governing guarantees, which mandates that the obligation to fulfil the main undertaking is unilateral (by the guarantor), the law does not prohibit a bilateral undertaking, especially if the contracting parties elect to do so. This is especially so where the creditor promises to grant the debtor a specific amount of money in exchange for the guarantor's promise to settle the outstanding amount in case of default by the debtor.[34] Another characteristic of the guarantee contract is that the debtor's knowledge of it is not required. In fact, the contract may be formed even against the debtor's consent. According to article 811 CC: 'The debtor may be guaranteed without his [or her] knowledge or without his [or her] consent'. Moreover, a guarantee contract may take the form of a commercial instrument such as a promissory note.[35] Last but not least, as discussed earlier, the formation of a guarantee does not require formality, but must be evidenced in writing. The public policy behind this rule is that the guarantor's consent must be evidenced in writing in order to warn of the high risk associated with such legal instrument.[36]

second part of the legislative text was translated as 'evidence', which does not flow well with the first part of the article, thus it has been substituted with the word 'proof'.

[34] Al-Sanhuri (n 6), vol 10, at 20.
[35] Ibid, at 60.
[36] Ibid, at 62.

6

Interpretation and Gap Filling by the Courts

6.1 INTRODUCTION

This chapter examines an important, yet relatively obscure dimension in the life cycle of a contract. Whenever the parties, upon formation, disagree about the meaning of a particular term, they will turn to the courts for clarification. Consequently, the courts must determine but effectively interpret/construe the term in question in light of the contract as a whole. The CC sets out several interpretative tools that guide the courts in this process. These consist of literal interpretation, ascertainment of the parties' common intention or their shared subjective understanding, as well as maxims such as the *contra preferentem* rule. Contractual interpretation under the CC is predicated on rules and principles typically associated with the civil law tradition, but there do exist several differences that are peculiar to the CC.[1] A particular form of interpretation is also constituted by the exceptional gap-filling authority of the civil courts, despite the sanctity of party autonomy. The CC allows the courts in exceptional circumstances to intervene in the life cycle of the contract in order to either flesh out an assumed, but not expressed, intention of the parties, or in order to remedy an inappropriate imbalance or an overriding injustice.

6.2 CLARITY OF WORDING

The CC provides only two articles on contractual interpretation, namely 169 and 170. Despite their brevity, they are consistent with the body of practice on

---

[1] It is taken for granted that the courts must have jurisdiction to accept a request to interpret a contract. Where the same issue has become *res judicata* or is otherwise the subject matter of an arbitral award, the enforcement of which is sought in Qatar, the courts do not possess authority to interpret the underlying contract. Hence, the Court of Cassation's Judgment 33/2008, in *International Trading and Industrial Investment v DynCorp Aerospace Technology* must be seen as aberration that carries no precedential value.

interpretation that is common in both civil and common law jurisdictions. Article 169(1) CC implicitly distinguishes between contracts requiring interpretation from those that do not. A contract whose wording is clear, in that it leaves no doubts about what the parties intended to achieve or how to apportion rights and obligations, shall not be subject to construction by the courts. What is meant by construction in this context, is that the courts must not apply any principle or rule of construction to a contract whose wording is clear and unambiguous. The construction of clear and unambiguous terms dilutes the clarity of such terms and risks altering the parties' intention.[2]

As a result, when the courts are asked to determine the parties' obligation in a contract whose terms are clear and unambiguous, they must apply said terms literally. This should not be confused or conflated with the literal interpretation of contractual terms, which constitutes a method of interpretation.

6.3 LACK OF CLARITY

Not infrequently the parties fail, whether intentionally or inadvertently, to clarify the qualitative or quantitative elements of one or more contractual obligations. When this occurs and one of the parties so demands, the courts will resort to an interpretation of the relevant terms. If the parties perform their obligations, despite an objective lack of clarity, it is presumed that they internalised their understanding of said terms. The following sub-sections discuss several principles of interpretation put forth by the CC in the event that one of the parties requests a judicial construction of unclear terms. Where, however, the terms of a contract are clear, the courts are not permitted to 'interpret' it. They should rely on the relevant clear meaning.[3]

6.3.1 *Literal Construction*

Article 169(1) CC implies that where the terms of a contract are unclear, the intent of the parties may be construed by the courts. In this case, the courts may resort to a literal interpretation of the words used by the parties and ascribe to these words their ordinary meaning. The possibility of a literal construction is mentioned in paragraph 2 of article 169 CC, but not as an autonomous and self-contained method of interpretation. Rather, its application is conditional to other mandatory principles, namely good faith, the parties' common intention and public policy. These will be explored in the next sub-sections.

---

[2]   The Court of Cassation in its Judgment 114/2009 emphasized the sanctity of party autonomy in consonance with the parties' agreement.
[3]   Court of Cassation Judgment 8/2016.

As a result, a literal interpretation is only possible where there is no *prima facie* inconsistency with the three principles and assuming that the disputed terms are deemed by the courts unclear.[4] The CC does not provide any indication as to how a literal construction is to be conducted. The authors are not aware of any limitations to the general principles underpinning the literal construction of contracts, and hence, these are part of the CC. More specifically, a) unless otherwise indicated, words and phrases must be construed in accordance with their ordinary meaning; b) a party claiming the existence of a meaning other than the ordinary meaning of a word or phrase must provide evidence of such common meaning; and c) a literal interpretation must not lead to absurd or unjust outcomes.

It is not uncommon for the Court of Cassation to employ a literal construction in order to arrive at the parties' common intention. In one case, the meaning of the word 'hazard' was debated. The Court went on to say that it was well settled that although the hazard linguistically means risk, and the majority of jurists identified it as associated with hidden consequences – and as additionally forbidden by the Shari'a – this was nonetheless the meaning intended in a contract whose main object was the taking of risks.[5]

6.3.2 *The Parties' Common Intention*

Article 172 CC is not particularly useful for the purposes of interpreting what the parties intended, but only for assessing whether the parties perform their obligations in good faith once the contract has come into operation. The interpretation of contracts by its very nature concerns the parties' subjective intention when drafting their contract, and this process predates their respective performance. As a result, it is important for the courts to assess the parties' true intention prior to the formation of the contract, at a time when they were putting words on paper, although this process does not fall within the sphere of contractual interpretation. Article 169(2) CC demands that construction must be predicated on the 'common intention' of the parties:

> … without restriction to the literal meaning of the words, taking into account the nature of the transaction as well as the honesty and confidence that should prevail between the parties in accordance with commercial custom.

In line with transnational practice, the parties' common intention is imputed by the courts and is generally demonstrated by reference to objective standards

---

[4] Court of Cassation Judgment 392/2015.
[5] Court of Cassation Judgment 87/2010.

under the particular circumstances of the parties. There is no indication that
the situation is any different in the Qatari CC.[6] The parties' common intention
may just as well be demonstrated by what the contract aims to achieve, in which
case the individualistic pursuits of one of the parties, contrary to the expressed
common pursuit, will not prevail over the common intention. Where the parties' common subjective intention is not susceptible to accurate verification
(and it usually will not be), then such common intention will be inferred on
the basis of the average person under the circumstances of the parties.[7] Article
169(2) CC makes the task a lot easier for the courts by adding another possible
inference as to the parties' common intention, namely prevailing commercial
custom.[8] The importance of this admonition here is that the courts are justified
in inferring the parties' common intention from private instruments reflective
of commercial custom relied upon, directly or indirectly by the parties, such
as the UNIDROIT Principles of International Commercial Contracts or the
FIDIC rules. In the absence of such admonition, reliance on commercial custom as an interpretative device would be arbitrary and subject to appeal and
cassation. As already stated in the previous section, the courts' pursuit of the
parties' common intention must not deviate from the apparent meaning of
the terms of the contract and associated documents, without, however, being
restricted to what is indicated by a specific phrase or words.[9]

Qatari courts all the way to the Court of Cassation employ standard language
to emphasise the 'complete' authority of the trial court to interpret both the
contract and related documents in order to ascertain the common intention
of the parties.[10] As will become evident in a following sub-section relating to
the permissibility of all probative evidence, the courts are under an obligation
'not to deviate from the apparent meaning of the terms of the contract or other
written documents and should consider what a particular expression or phrase
therein truly indicates. The courts must be guided by the nature of the transaction and the degree of trust expected, in accordance with the current custom in

---

[6] In its Judgment 86/2008, the Court of Cassation was asked to determine whether the parties
    to a contract providing for arbitration held the same intention following two addenda to their
    initial contract, one of which clearly opted for litigation. The Court of Cassation held that the
    lower court was entitled to infer the parties' intention in a manner that it is more fulfilling to
    their purpose, on the basis of tolerable grounds and without transcending the apparent mean-
    ing of words.
[7] Art 4.1(2) UNIDROIT PICC.
[8] This is common to all legal systems, e.g. s 346 of the German Commercial Code states that
    'due consideration shall be given to prevailing commercial custom and usages concerning
    the meaning and effect of acts and omissions among merchants' and Art 1511(2) of the French
    CCP, which states that tribunals 'shall take into account trade usages'.
[9] Court of Cassation Judgment 5/2012.
[10] Court of Cassation Judgments 44/2010; 87/2010; 113/2012; 53/2012; 40/2013; 394/2015.

transactions'.[11] Where the courts in ascertaining the parties' common intention determine that the apparent meaning of contractual terms is different to the parties' common intention, they are bound to fully justify how the non-apparent meaning best reflects the parties' common intention.[12] Hence, the overall context of the parties' contractual relationship is central to the construction of the parties' common intention.[13] Under no circumstances should the courts exceed the explicit statement or words in the parties' contract.[14] The Court of Cassation has emphasised that the courts should not put too much emphasis on the meaning of a specific sentence, but on the overall meaning of all its sentences and conditions, guided by the nature of the transaction and the honesty and trust that should guide the parties in the fulfilment of their transaction.[15]

6.3.3 *Shared Subjective Understanding*

The parties' common intention is different from their understanding of a word or term. While there might be no doubt about their common intention as a whole, the parties may well differ about their understanding of a particular word or term. Although the CC does not specifically address this issue, it does clearly stipulate that the literal interpretation of words or terms does not supersede the parties' common understanding. Where a party intended a crucial word or term to possess a particular meaning and, at the time of conclusion of the contract, the other party could not have been unaware of the first party's intention, the first party's intention/understanding of that word or term prevails.[16] Where the second party's intention was different to that of the first party and the second party could not have been aware of the first party's intention, the contract lacks a common intention, and hence, it has not been properly formed.

6.3.4 *Interpretation of Imbalanced Contracts:* *The* Contra Preferentum *Maxim*

Contractual fairness requires appropriate construction/interpretation by the courts in order to counter the deficiencies associated with the incorporation problem and the use of standard terms. Qatari law has adopted most

---

[11] Court of Cassation Judgment 219/2011.
[12] Court of Cassation Judgments 23/2012; 323/2014; 18/2015.
[13] See Court of Cassation Judgment 126/2013, where it was held that the courts must be led by what is stated in the contract as a whole and the circumstances of its issuance; see also Court of Cassation Judgments 120/2014; 80/2015 and; 437/2018.
[14] Court of Cassation Judgments 82/2011 and 84/2011.
[15] Court of Cassation Judgment 219/2012.
[16] See Art 4.1 UNIDROIT PICC.

construction principles developed in the common and civil law traditions. Article 107 CC goes on to establish the so-called *contra preferentum* rule, according to which an ambiguous term in an adhesion contract shall always be construed in favour of the adhering party. It is, therefore, in the interest of the stronger party to clarify the content of its standard terms, in accordance with the analysis in the previous section. This allows for fairer contracting.

Article 170(1) CC takes the mantle even further by providing that if doubt arises as to the wording or meaning of words or phrases in the contract, these shall be construed in favour of the obligor. Where, however, the contract contains a clause discharging a party from liability, such provision shall be construed narrowly.[17] Paragraph 2 of article 170 CC must be read alongside article 160 CC and applicable consumer legislation.

Article 80(1) CC makes the point that where the parties have agreed that their affairs shall be governed by standard terms and conditions these shall apply only when sufficient notice has been served on the adhering party. Paragraph 2 of article 80 CC goes on to say that where such provisions of which no notice has been taken are essential, the contract shall be invalid. If the provisions are auxiliary, the judge shall resolve any dispute arising therefrom in accordance with the nature of the transaction, current usage, and rules of justice.

6.4 EVIDENCE FOR CONTRACTUAL INTERPRETATION

There is no discussion on this issue in the CC or the CCP. The key question here is what kind of evidence the courts may rely on in deciphering the parties' common intention. Is this a documents-only process or are witnesses also permitted to testify? Moreover, should all documents be permitted or only those that are official and those private documents that satisfy formality requirements? Finally, should evidence arising from the parties' negotiations phase be considered admissible, given that such a phase is outside the scope of good faith?[18]

Article 216 CCP distinguishes between official exhibits and conventional documents, both of which must satisfy several formalities. Articles 217 and 218 CCP specify that official exhibits may be used as evidence without any limitations, and this is also possible with respect to photocopies of official exhibits. With respect to conventional documents, article 220 CCP makes it clear that if found to have been signed by a party and their authenticity is not in doubt they possess unlimited evidentiary value. The only exception

---

[17] Art 170(2) CC.
[18] Art 172(1) CC.

concerns ledgers kept by businessmen. These may not be used as evidence against non-businessmen.[19] As regards witness-based evidence, articles 260 to 262 CCP generally permit such evidence in commercial disputes, as well as non-commercial disputes of a high value.

Exceptionally, litigants may request that the other party take a so-called decisive oath, in accordance with article 314 CCP. The court may compel a party to take this oath, even if it is intended to prove a fact to the contrary of a written contract, even in respect of a formal document, except for formal documents whose authenticity may not be challenged.[20]

As a result, and in line with civil law principles, the Qatari CCP does not ascribe to the so-called parol evidence rule, whereby evidence that is extrinsic to the contract, such as draft contracts, statements and emails exchanged during the negotiation of the contract, travaux or witness statements are inadmissible.[21] The CCP implicitly allows all such evidence in order to allow the judge to ascertain the parties' common intention and excludes nothing that has probative value, subject to the requirements demanded of each evidence as discussed.[22] This is clear in the language and practice of the Court of Cassation, through which it has supported the authority of trial courts to examine and interpret all relevant evidence pertaining to contracts, so long 'as judgments are reasoned and based on reasonable grounds'.[23] The existence of an employment relationship (which by extension evinces an employment contract) has been viewed as a question of fact by the Court of Cassation,[24] and the same is true with the renewal of a lease.[25] As a result, all evidence with a probative value is admissible.[26] This may include the appointment of an expert, which is at the discretion of the courts.[27] The Court has made it clear that probative value is tantamount to the 'truth'.[28] In several instances, the Court of Cassation has ordered that the parties provide

---

[19] Art 223 CCP. See also Arts 226 and 227 CCP for two particular exceptions.

[20] Court of Cassation Judgments 3/2010 and 97/2011.

[21] See Art 4.3 UNIDROIT PICC, which refers to a list of five extrinsic factors as relevant circumstances in interpretating a contract. This is consistent with the Qatari CC, save for the fact that extrinsic factors are expressly permitted in the PICC but not the CC.

[22] It is established that photocopies of originals, whether written documents or photographs have no probative effect except to the extent they lead to the signed originals, if any. See Court of Cassation Judgment 9/2010.

[23] Court of Cassation Judgments 161/2010; 45/2011; 74/2011; 22/2012 and 113/2012.

[24] Court of Cassation Judgment 89/2011.

[25] Court of Cassation Judgments 33/2012 and 158/2012.

[26] Court of Cassation Judgment 89/2011.

[27] Court of Cassation Judgments 93/2012 and 191/2012.

[28] Court of Cassation Judgments 90/2011; 154/2012; Court of Cassation Judgment 22/2013; 369/2014; 139/2014 and 258/2016.

oral evidence in court where the material presented, including their contract, did not provide sufficient clarity.[29] This rationale is aided by specialist
legislation. Article 38 of Labor Law No. 14 of 2004 indicates that if the contract was not in writing, the employee may prove the work relationship by all
means of proof.[30] No doubt, such instances are exceptional, and the general
rule remains whereby it is not permissible to disprove a written document
except by another written document.[31]

6.5 GAP FILLING

The relationship between gap filling and contractual interpretation is obvious.
In interpreting a contract, the courts are not allowed to infer facts which neither the parties nor the law intend or imply.[32] By extension, the courts do not
possess power to alter the parties' requests.[33] However, just because the parties
failed to cater for each and every issue that could arise in their relationship
does not and should not mean that the contract becomes inoperable. The bor-
derline between inference/construction and substituting the parties' intention
(gap filling) is not always clear. The Court of Cassation has aptly demarcated
the two by stipulating that the courts may not create contracts for the parties
but possesses full power for interpreting and construing agreements in order
to infer the common intention of the parties, as this appears from the facts and
circumstances. 'The interpretation of the contract [and supporting documen-
tation] may not go beyond the obvious meanings implied by their wordings'.[34]
The Court of Cassation has expressly employed the term 'adaptation', albeit
subject to the considerations mentioned throughout this chapter.[35]

The common law does not view ad hoc gap filling as a means of contractual
interpretation, but as supplementing terms missing from the contract, which
the parties clearly assumed. Common law courts refer to these as *terms implied
in fact*. Just like other civil codes, the Qatari CC does not contain general
provisions on gap filling. However, the foundational principle whereby party
autonomy is supreme makes it clear that gap filling is exceptional, subject also
to the interpretative tools set out in the previous sections of this chapter.

---

[29] See Court of Cassation Judgment 10/2011. This was viewed by the Court as a valid exception
to the principle of material evidence only as articulated in Arts 261 and 262 CCP; see equally
Court of Cassation Judgment 47/2011.

[30] See Court of Cassation Judgment 98/2014.

[31] Court of Cassation Judgment 115/2012.

[32] Court of Cassation Judgments 335/2016 and 92/2016.

[33] Court of Cassation Judgment 55/2012.

[34] Court of Cassation Judgment 63/2008.

[35] See eg Court of Cassation Judgments 16/2013 and 115/2015.

6.5.1 Terms Implied by Fact

The CC does specifically refer to terms implied, yet not expressed, in the parties' contract. Even so, implied factual terms are beyond doubt encompassed within the gap filling authority of the Qatari courts. Unlike the common law tradition, terms implied by fact are a matter of interpretation in the civil law tradition and by extension the Qatari civil law. Article 169(2) CC, which we have already examined, allows the courts to fill gaps in the parties' mutual obligations by reference to the 'nature of the transaction', the 'honesty and confidence that should prevail', as well as 'commercial custom'. Hence, where the contract refers to standard terms or private rules, such as those under FIDIC, the courts will construe the entire body of such terms and rules as being part of the contract, unless the parties specifically excluded some rules, or if the nature of the transaction otherwise demands. In exceptional cases, the law requires that certain stipulations be evidenced only in writing. This is the case with an agreement to arbitrate under article 7(3) of the 2017 Arbitration Law or guarantees under article 809 CC.

That terms implied in fact are a matter of interpretation should assist in distinguishing this function of article 169(2) CC from article 150 CC, which does not set out a rule of construction. Article 150 CC stipulates that where the object of a contractual obligation is a material thing it shall be identified with precision in terms of its type/kind, quality, and quantity. Where it is identified by its type, 'it shall be sufficient to include in the contract such provision as may be required to identify the quantity of such thing. Where there is no agreement on the degree of quality and such quality cannot be ascertained by use or by any other circumstances, the obligee must supply an article of average quality.'

6.5.2 Terms Implied by Law

Mandatory provisions that apply to all contracts – otherwise known as *terms implied in law* in common law jurisdictions – are binding on parties to all contracts and cannot be waived by mutual consent. Many of these concern public policy and good faith, and in general, their purpose is to prevent injustice; others serve the public interest.[36] The courts may amend the parties' obligations in such circumstances in order to remedy any imbalance or counter injustice. Article 106 CC, for example, stipulates that if a contract

---

[36] For example, Law No. 30 of 2002 on Environment Protection (Environment Law) obliges the project owner to take all necessary precautions and measures to prevent air or water pollution. This includes the submission of environmental impact assessments (EIAs).

is made by adhesion and contains arbitrary conditions, the judge may at the request of the adhering party amend such conditions so as to expunge them fully, even if the adhering party proves to have known thereof as prescribed by justice. Similarly, article 140 CC makes the point that 'where a person exploits another person out of need, obvious frivolity, visible vulnerability, or sudden heat of passion, or his moral influence over the other person causes that other person to conclude a contract in his own or a third party's favour, and such contract contains an excessive imbalance between the obligations he must perform and the material or moral benefits he shall obtain from the contract, the judge may, at the request of the affected party, reduce his obligations, or increase the obligations of the other party, or void the contract'. In equal vein, article 141 CC stipulates that the courts may annul or reduce the amount of contracts of gift where the donor is exploited, taking into consideration due process and fairness.

In a subsequent sub-section dealing with public policy, it will become evident that the existence of a public policy rule overrides the parties' common intention and such rule is always part of their contract. Examples include the violation of the rule conferring 51% ownership to Qatari nationals in commerce conducted in Qatar,[37] as well as peremptory laws regulating labour relations.[38]

In another chapter, we go on to examine the authority of the courts to intervene in the parties' contractual obligations where said obligations have become onerous for one of the parties.[39] Article 171(2) CC suggests that the courts have authority to 'reduce the excessive obligation to a reasonable level'. Similarly, in order to avoid rescission of a contract the courts may 'determine a period of grace within which the obligor shall perform his obligation'. Finally, where the parties have agreed that a contract may be rescinded without a court order, such agreement 'may not limit the authority of the judge to terminate the contract, unless the wording of the contract expressly indicates that this is the parties' mutual intention'. In 2013 the Court of Cassation issued an important judgment, which has some relevance to this sub-section. There, the Court emphasised that 'it is not permissible for a judge to rescind or amend a valid contract on the ground that the revocation or modification is required by the rules of justice. Justice completes the will of the contracting parties, but does not abrogate it'.[40]

---

[37] Court of Cassation Judgment 11/2015.
[38] Court of Appeal Judgment 268/2018.
[39] See Chapter 12.
[40] Court of Cassation Judgments 122/2013 and 109/2015.

6.5.2.1 Good Faith

We shall encounter good faith in Chapter 7 as a mandatory statutory mechanism that applies to all contracts. In this chapter, we shall examine good faith as a principle of interpretation. We have explained that article 172(1) CC points out that good faith concerns the performance of contractual obligations.[41] What this excludes from the scope of article 172(1) CC is the application of good faith in the phases of *negotiation* and *formation* of the contract. Article 172(2) CC expands the good faith requirement by stating that obligations arising from a contract encompass, in addition to what the parties have agreed, whatever 'is required by law, customary practice and justice' in accordance with the nature of the obligations in the contract. This no doubt covers industry practices, such as commercial custom,[42] as well as fair dealing in accordance with the law and accepted public policy. Article 169(2) CC renders good faith an interpretative method above literal construction ('honesty and confidence that should prevail between the parties') and side by side with the parties' common intention.

It is not possible to apply good faith as an interpretative tool to the pre-contractual phase, albeit the courts construe the parties' performance on the basis of good faith. In Chapter 7, we explain those limited circumstances where the parties are free to waive good faith.

6.5.2.2 Public Policy, Custom and the *Sharia*

Contractual terms in violation of public policy render the contract void.[43] At the same time, although it seems obvious, Qatari courts must construe a contract in conformity with the public policy or public order of Qatar. The mandatory nature of public policy is, therefore, implied by the law in the parties' contract.[44] As a result, the parties are not allowed to waive public policy requirements. The Court of Cassation has defined public order as follows: 'a set of basic principles that foster the political system, social consensus, economic rules, and moral values on which society is based, and through which the public interest is achieved'.[45] Qatari courts often

---

[41] This, of course, is hardly unusual and most legal systems apply the same principle. See Art 242 BGB.

[42] The Court of Cassation has consistently held that interest rates shall be upheld in accordance with prevailing business custom. See Judgments 66/2014; 40/2013 and Judgment 208/2014.

[43] Arts 151 and 154(1) CC.

[44] The Court of Cassation in its Judgement 62/2006 emphasized that the agreement must not conflict with public order or ethics; equally Court of Cassation Judgment 63/2008.

[45] Court of Cassation Judgment 141/2015.

refer to conduct or principles that reflect public policy, from which the parties may not deviate. These include labour rights, particularly the restricted right to termination by the employer;[46] commercial activities in violation of the requirement that a Qatari partner hold at least 51% of shares;[47] exercising a profession without proper license and registration;[48] rental value and eviction from leased properties[49] and not bypassing the proper jurisdiction of Qatari courts.[50]

On the other hand, the courts are bound to construe a contract in accordance with the *Sharia* where the particular subject matter is not regulated by statute.[51] The parties may not exclude the *Sharia* where their contract is governed by Qatari law, and the latter lacks a statutory provision regulating a particular issue under the contract.[52] This is not an easy venture nor is it free from contention. Article 1(2) CC provides a hierarchy, with statute at the apex, followed by the *Sharia* ('if any'), customary practices and finally 'rules of justice'.[53] While it seems that the two provisions serve distinct purposes, namely that article 1(2) CC merely attempts to posit the *Sharia* as a secondary source of law, whereas article 169(2) CC refers to commercial custom as an interpretative tool, article 1(2) CC is effectively transformed into an interpretative tool where a statutory provision is deemed to be lacking.[54]

The *Sharia*, no doubt, becomes a primary source of law in interpreting a dispute where Islamic law is the governing law of the parties' contract, or where the subject matter of the dispute concerns a contractual type predicated

---

[46] Court of Cassation Judgments 44/2010 and 73/2010.
[47] Court of Cassation Judgments 74/2010 and 102/2010; see also Court of Cassation Judgment 73/2016 on a similar employment issue.
[48] Court of Cassation Judgment 226/2011.
[49] Court of Cassation Judgments 19/2011 and 32/2015.
[50] Court of Cassation Judgment 62/2011.
[51] Art 1(2) CC; see Court of Cassation Judgment 323/2014.
[52] In practice, it seems that several issues in the CC are regulated by the *Sharia* and CC in tandem, especially where it is deemed that the *Sharia* is more elaborate. The Court of Cassation in Judgment 21/2008 accepted the applicability of the *Sharia* concerning the acquisition of property by prescription, despite the existence of a relevant provision in the CC (Art 404). While ultimately the Court did not agree with the lower court's interpretation of Islamic law, neither the Court nor the parties expressed any concern about the use of *Sharia* despite the existence of express provisions in the CC. Hence, it is evident that the courts will apply the *Sharia* not only where the CC is silent on a particular issue, but also where the *Sharia* is more elaborate.
[53] See Court of Cassation Judgment 122/2013 on the limitations of justice as a rule that is trumped by the mutual intention of the parties; see equally Court of Cassation Judgment 26/2015.
[54] The best approach in the event where the *Sharia* becomes applicable is to apply only its contractual dimension. See I Bantekas, J Ercanbrack, U Oseni, I Ullah, *Islamic Contract Law* (OUP 2023).

on Islamic law.[55] The consistent practice in the GCC is that in interpreting such contracts, the courts are not to accept the parties' stipulations that the contract is in conformity with the *Sharia*; rather, the courts have authority to undertake an objective analysis of said conformity.[56]

Article 169(2) CC allows the courts to infer the parties' common intention by reference to commercial custom.[57] The Court of Appeal has relied on custom on several occasions and hardly sees it as peripheral. In one case, it relied on the report of an expert to declare the existence of a customary rule whereby airlines have the right to prevent a passenger from travelling permanently or temporarily in certain cases. This was considered as having a customary value despite the fact that the practice in question was subject to variation and instability.[58] The Court of Cassation has not relied on the *Sharia* in any significant degree, at least in the construction of contractual relationships. Conversely, it has relied extensively on custom, even if the same subject matter is somehow regulated by the *Sharia*. The reason for this preference lies clearly in the fact that recourse to the *Sharia* in some cases would serve to invalidate the contract (e.g. delay interest), but not if business custom is applied.

---

[55] The Court of Cassation, although it rarely refers to the *Sharia* in contractual disputes, sometimes does refer to it as the origin of a rule. See Judgment 94/2013.

[56] See Dubai Cassation Court Judgment 898–927/2019, which concluded that for a *murabaha* contract to be *Sharia*-compliant, it has to satisfy the criteria of the Maliki school and that a certificate of compliance from an Islamic bank or financial institution is insufficient.

[57] The Court of Cassation does not shy away from identifying business custom through standard phraseology. Eg in Court of Cassation Judgment 148/2010, it held that the bank's exposure to the lender is significant and hence compensation for late payments (delay interest) is justified by reference to banking custom, whereby it is 'common knowledge' that proof is not required; equally Court of Cassation Judgment 220/2011; to the same effect see also Court of Cassation Judgment 40/2013. The Court of Cassation in Judgment 107/2013, stated that where a special commercial/trade law is silent 'commercial custom shall be applied, with the special custom or local custom being given precedence over the general custom'. If there is no commercial custom, the provisions of the civil law shall apply. This was also reiterated in Court of Cassation Judgment 66/2014; see equally Court of Cassation Judgments 371/2014 and 208/2014.

[58] Court of Appeal Judgment 526/2018.

7

Good Faith and Unfair Terms

7.1 INTRODUCTION

In other chapters, we examined how party autonomy shapes the parties' contractual relations. Indeed, party autonomy is the cornerstone of the law of contracts, and in general terms, the law intervenes in this process only sparingly with mandatory rules. In this chapter, we examine those circumstances where the civil law (both the CC and special laws) not only intervenes but invalidates the parties' express consent on the ground that their agreement lacked good faith or imposed unfair terms on the weaker party. This is an unusual mechanism that is justified to avoid injustice and exploitation[1] against one of the parties (unfair terms), typically arising in relation to adhesion or consumer contracts. The imposition of good faith is equally justified by reference to public policy even if not expressly spelt out. This 'parental' regulation of contracts is not without contention, and as the reader will come to realise, the contours of the application of good faith differ among jurisdictions, although our emphasis here is on the Qatari experience.

7.2 GOOD FAITH

Just like other legal systems, the Qatari CC does not attempt to define good faith. Its meaning is assumed to be self-evident. There are numerous provisions in the CC that refer to good faith, although the majority concern the law of property and not contracts. There are certain issues of contention but what is absolutely clear is that good faith is a foundational principle of Qatari private law; yet, it does not seem to be absolute and may be waived under certain

---

[1]   These grounds were also encountered in the context of defective consent, particularly Arts
     140–147 CC. See Chapter 8 for a more comprehensive discussion.

circumstances, as explained below. In a case concerning the construction of a building outside (or contiguous to) the limits of the owner's property (land), thus, taking up part of the neighbour's land, the Court of Cassation was asked to determine whether the building should remain – subject to fair compensation – under the condition that the owner was in good faith concerning the boundaries of its own land. The Court of Cassation agreed with the Court of First Instance in that the meaning of good faith in article 916 CC requires the building owner, while building, to possess an absolute and justified belief that it is doing so in its own land and not trespassing in the land of its neighbour. This, in turn, entails that it has exerted all habitual effort to verify the borders of its own land and not made a mistake out of rashness, indifference or negligence.[2]

Unlike article 1104(1) of the French Civil Code, which stipulates that contracts must be negotiated, formed and performed in good faith, article 172(1) of the Qatari CC points out that good faith concerns the performance of contractual obligations.[3] The inspiration behind this provision is the Egyptian Civil Code of 1948.[4] What this excludes from the scope of article 172(1) CC is the application of good faith in the phases of *negotiation* and *formation* of the contract. It might well be that Islamic law recognises a role for good faith in the pre-contractual formation phases, chiefly the parties' negotiations.[5] However, it should be pointed out that Islamic law and business custom are supplementary sources to the primacy of the CC.[6] They are only applicable where the CC is silent on a particular issue. In the opinion of the authors, article 172(1) CC is not silent on this issue; rather, it purposely excludes the application of good faith from all pre-contractual phases, thus, rendering this a matter for party autonomy. The pertinent provisions in the Qatari CC dealing with the formation of contract are deemed sufficient to deal with bad faith, in the sense that if the offeror were to grossly misrepresent the quality or quantity of

---

[2] Court of Cassation Judgment 10/2008.
[3] This, of course, is hardly unusual and most legal systems apply the same principle. See Art 242 BGB.
[4] Art 148(1) Egyptian CC; see also Art 129 Bahraini CC; Art 197 Kuwaiti CC; Art 246 UAE CC.
[5] See N Majeed, 'Good Faith and Due Process: Lessons from the Shari'ah', (2004) 20 Arbitration International 97. In fact, evidence suggests that Islamic law requires good faith during negotiations too. This is generally derived from a number of *hadith*, namely: 'a person does not believe until he prefers for his brother what he prefers for himself', which is construed as requiring fair dealing and diligent examination of terms and conditions of a sale. It is equally forbidden to conceal or misrepresent the qualities of a good. See Muslim bin Hajjah, 'Ṣaḥīḥ Muslim, Book of Faith' No. 459; equally, Al-Bukhari 3/67, concerning the narration of a negotiation for the purchase of a camel.
[6] Art 1(2) CC.

the good or service that is the subject matter of the contract, there would be a dissensus between the offer and acceptance. As a result of such dissensus, no contract would come about. Misrepresentation during negotiations may in turn give rise to a tort where harm was caused to the offeror or offeree.[7]

Article 172(2) CC expands the good faith requirement by stating that obligations arising from a contract encompass, in addition to what the parties have agreed, whatever 'is required by law, customary practice and justice' in accordance with the nature of the obligations in the contract. This no doubt covers industry practices, such as commercial custom,[8] as well as fair dealing in accordance with the law and accepted public policy. The importance of public policy in this regard will be examined in a subsequent section dealing with party autonomy to exclude or waive good faith in contractual relationships. The two following subsections will deal with subjective and objective good faith.

7.2.1 *Subjective Good Faith*

Subjective good faith generally refers to a person's state of mind by which to ascertain whether or not that person knew or had reason to know of a certain fact. A person possessing actual or other knowledge about a fact and yet acts or behaves as though it did not have such knowledge is said to be acting in bad faith. Article 800 CC is a good illustration of the law requiring good faith by the stronger party to a transaction. There, it is stipulated that the ordinary three-year prescription period for insurance claims does not arise where the insurer fails to provide information in its possession concerning risk.[9] The law generally posits certain consequences to bad faith of a subjective nature. Article 165(1) CC notes, for example that the invalidity of title-transferring contracts shall not be effective against a special successor receiving a right in kind from either contracting party, provided that such successor received such right as indemnity in good faith. A special successor is considered as acting in good faith if at the time of the transfer, it 'was not aware of the reason for revoking the contract of its predecessor and could not have known of such reason if the successor exercised prudent and reasonable judgment'.[10] Equally, article 226 CC stipulates that where a person receiving a pre-payment acts

---

[7] See Arts 199–219 CC.
[8] The Court of Cassation has consistently held that interest rates shall be upheld in accordance with prevailing business custom. See Judgments 66/2014; 40/2013 and 208/2014.
[9] See Court of Cassation Judgments 141/2015; 36/2015 and 182/2016.
[10] Art 165(2) CC. See equally Art 186 CC.

in good faith, such person shall not be required to repay any further amount other than that which was prepaid. If, however, such person is found to have been prepaid in bad faith, it shall be obliged to repay any benefits, in addition to the prepaid amount. The Court of Cassation has further ruled that an employer slurring or defaming an employee with a view to avoid paying end of service gratuity is acting in bad faith.[11] As a rule, therefore, subjective good faith operates to validate an action or transaction.[12]

Conversely, subjective bad faith invalidates (after the act) the act or transaction. This is in line with the Court of Cassation's emphasis whereby an aggrieved contractual party can only seek damages for harm that it could have avoided or in respect of which it could have taken reasonable steps.[13]

Another important function of subjective good faith is to deter abuse of right and, hence, act as a form of estoppel against said abuse of rights.[14] This principle is entrenched in several provisions of the Qatari CC,[15] including article 132, and has equally been enunciated by the Egyptian Court of Cassation,[16] and the Qatari Cassation Court.[17] This states that a party whose consent was the result of a mistake may not insist on such mistake in a manner contrary to the principle of good faith. Equally, article 333 CL emphasises that a broker may not request a fee or recover expenses if its actions damage the interests of the contractor instructing him to the advantage of another party for whom it was not acting as negotiator or where he is promised a benefit by the latter contractor, contrary to the dictates of good faith.[18]

Exceptionally, good faith alone is not always enough. In certain circumstances, the law requires a party to a transaction, particularly experts and

---

[11] Court of Cassation Judgment 50/2012.

[12] See also Art 960 CC; Art 82 CL provides that payment of a commercial debt shall be valid 'if it has been made to a person who possesses a receipt of debt or carries a form of discharge from the creditor and the debtor has acted in good faith. A debtor shall be deemed to have acted in good faith if unaware that the certificate of debt or the discharge form is illegal'.

[13] Court of Cassation Judgment 13/2010.

[14] The invocation of financial distress to terminate a contract or reduce the burden of an existing contractual obligation is poignant in this context. See Court of Cassation Judgment 61/2011, where it reversed the ruling of a lower court which had terminated a lease contract on account of the applicant's financial distress which followed from the global financial crisis. The Court required proof that the crisis had a serious impact on the applicant's finances so as to justify termination or adaptation of the lease agreement.

[15] But chiefly Arts 62 and 63 CC.

[16] Egyptian Court of Cassation Judgment 3473/2006.

[17] Court of Cassation Judgment 176/2014.

[18] At least one commentator suggests that Qatari courts frequently imply good faith obligations in contracts. See M Khayal, *The General Theory of Obligation under Qatari Law*, vol 1 (Qatar University Press, 2015, in Arabic) 248–249.

professionals, to act diligently and in accordance with the precautions required
by their industry. In such circumstances, the absence of due diligence cannot
be remedied by the presence of good faith. Article 476(3) CC, for example,
stipulates that where the buyer's title to property is invalidated by the courts
without the buyer's knowledge that the property was in fact owned by a third
party, the seller is liable for damages even if he or she acted in good faith as
to the ownership of said property.[19] Equally, article 459 CL notes that obligations assumed by minors not authorised to transfer funds or property, and
which obligations arise from their signatures on bills of exchange as drawers,
endorsers or in any other capacity, shall be null and void. Such nullity applies
in respect of any holder of a bill of exchange, even where the latter has acted
in good faith.

7.2.2 *Objective Good Faith*

Objective good faith is embodied in article 172(1) CC. Following well-
established – although by no means fully uniform – civil law tradition in this
respect, article 172(1) CC obliges all parties to a contract to fulfil their obligations thereto in accordance with good faith.[20] This effectively requires that all
parties are bound to ensure, to the best of their knowledge and abilities, that
the terms of the contract are fulfilled at all times and that they strive towards
such fulfilment. Good faith in this sense is best viewed as a form of cooperation and not as an individualistic and self-serving pursuit.[21] By way of illustration, if a party is in possession of information that could assist its counterpart to
comply with its obligations under the contract but intentionally omits to con-
vey such information, not only is it unable to rely on the other party's failure,
but it itself is also in breach of its contractual obligations, namely, the statutory
obligation to fulfil contractual obligations in accordance with good faith. In
equal measure, where a party to a contract has contributed (even if not the
sole cause) to damages through poor or non-fulfilment of its own obligations,
it is not entitled to the full extent of damage that it would otherwise be entitled
to.[22] No doubt, if assistance to the other party is required at the expense of

---

[19] See equally Art 945(1) CC.
[20] It is important here to distinguish between acting in good and nonetheless failing to fulfil
      contractual obligations. See Court of Appeal Judgment 378/2019.
[21] The Egyptian Court of Cassation in Judgments 4726/2004 and 4733/2004 has emphasised the
      obligation of all parties to a contract to avoid any third-party communications and all actions
      that may harm or adversely impact the fulfilment of the contract.
[22] Court of Cassation Judgment 8/2012. This judgment was no doubt inspired by the Egyptian
      Court of Cassation Judgment 152/1980.

the assisting party, such costs are recoverable. If the cost is detrimental to the assisting party and outweighs the overall benefit from the contract, it would be unreasonable to suggest that its omission to assist is in violation of good faith. Overall, especially in long-term contracts, the parties may not claim damages (or the right to terminate) as a result of breach by the other party, if they were able to avert the breach with or without cost.

The significance of objective good faith in the Qatari civil code should not be under-estimated, particularly since it does not extend to the negotiating (or pre-contractual) phase. No doubt, the courts are at liberty to impute good faith broadly in their construction of contracts and following the Egyptian approach this should extend to administrative contracts.[23]

7.3 WAIVING GOOD FAITH

Article 945(3) CC, which refers to possession of property emphasises that 'good faith shall always be presumed unless evidence to the contrary is provided and unless the law provides otherwise'. Although this provision is unrelated to contracts, it gives rise to an important principle, namely that good faith may be waived by the parties, at least expressly, save if the law provides otherwise.[24] Such an outcome has expressly been iterated by the Court of Cassation in judgment 10/2008, whose facts have already been set out in an earlier section of this chapter. The Court emphasised that good faith is a rebuttable presumption if there are no reasons preventing such presumption in the first place. Although the Court was specifically referring to article 916 CC, which concerns immovable property, it did not seem to be positing a limited principle and there is no good reason why the rebuttable nature of the presumption should not apply elsewhere in the CC. Some commentators suggest that limitations in the exclusion of certain types of liability, such as article 267 CC, are consistent with good faith, in the sense that a right cannot be exercised unlawfully.[25]

This issue is further complicated by the fact that it is common practice in Qatar for parties to transnational contracts, including administrative contracts, to insert choice of law clauses designating a foreign law, typically English law,

---

[23] Egyptian Supreme Administrative Court Judgment 303/2006; equally iterated by the State Council, General Assembly for Advice and Legislation, Opinion No. 793/2017.
[24] Adhesion contracts provide a good example. In accordance with Arts 105–107 CC the parties may not, even by mutual agreement, waive the liability of the stronger party or any arbitrary provisions in the contract.
[25] M H Al-Kaabi, 'Is it Possible to Introduce Efficient Breach Theory to a Civil Law Country? The Case of Qatar' (2020) 34 Arab LQ 13.

as the governing law.[26] Although this is consistent with international practice,[27] it does give rise to an important question; namely, whether the absence
of *implied* (but not express) good faith in English contract law[28] is compatible with the Qatari civil code. The two would only be compatible where the
Qatari Civil Code is found to permit the parties to waive or exclude good faith
requirements in their contractual undertakings. Given our analysis, thus far,
the authors are of the opinion that this is indeed possible, save where such
exclusion creates a gross imbalance between the parties and, thus, risks causing a serious harm to one of the parties. General principles of justice would
no doubt equally be applicable.[29]

Naturally the same question would be answered differently by English and
Qatari courts. It, therefore, requires further analysis from the lens of Qatari
conflicts of laws rules. The starting point is article 29(2) CC, which stipulates
that the 'law governing the contract in its substantive provisions, the law of
the domicile of the contracting parties, or their common national law, may
apply'.[30] Two caveats apply with respect to this rule. The first is situated in
article 10 CC. It states that 'where a dispute arises in the application of different laws ... the dispute shall be resolved by reference to Qatari law'. This
provision is clearly inapplicable where the parties have chosen English law
as the governing law of their agreement. The second restriction stems from
article 38 CC, according to which a foreign law, even if chosen by the parties,
shall not be applied if it is in conflict with Qatari public order and morals.[31]
The aforementioned discussion hopefully serves as a basis to argue that the

---

[26] See I Bantekas, 'The Globalization of English Contract Law: Three Salient Illustrations'
(2021) 137 LQR 130.
[27] Even where the governing law of a contract is not English law, the QICDRC still relies on
English contract law to flesh out general principles. In *Obayashi Qatar LLC v Qatar First
Bank LLC* [2020] QIC (F.) 5, para 90, Qatari law was the contract's governing law. Yet, the
court relied predominantly on the English law of demand guarantees, as well as the fraud
exception therein, as a condition freeing the debtor from its obligation.
[28] It is impossible to do justice to this subject but see generally *Walford v Miles* (1992) 2 AC
128 and *Chapman v Honig* (1963) 2 QB 502, per Pearson LJ. Even so, good faith has been
introduced on the basis of other mechanisms and principles, such as: contracts of utmost
good faith, as in *International Management Group UK Ltd v Simmonds* (2003) EWHC 177
(Comm); fiduciary relationships; unfair terms in consumer contracts requiring open and fair
dealing, as chiefly expounded in *Director General of Fair Trading v First National Bank* (2001)
UKHL 52 and; where English courts have accepted that good faith is part of English law
through EU law and principles: *Yam Seng Pte v International Trade Corp Ltd* [2013] 1 All E.R.
(Comm.) 1321, paras 119–154, but especially para 24.
[29] See Art 1(2) CC, which refers to justice, business custom and Islamic law as supplementary
sources to the primacy of the CC.
[30] See Art 27(1) CC concerning contracts containing no choice of law clause.
[31] See Court of Cassation Judgment 226/2012.

CC is supportive of excluding good faith under certain circumstances, and no Qatari court has ever rejected the application of English law on the ground that its stance on implied good faith is contrary to Qatari public policy and public morals.

7.4 UNFAIR TERMS IN CONTRACTS

Qatari law, generally speaking, aims to strike a reasonable balance between the parties' reasonable expectations, respect for public policy and justice,[32] while at the same time ensure that the weaker parties' obligations are not grossly imbalanced. In this respect, it is no different to the same set of aims set out by the common law and civil law traditions. This section is chiefly focused on adhesion and consumer contracts, albeit the same principles apply to all contracts, *mutatis mutandis*. Qatari judicial practice clearly suggests that certain commercial contractual practices are unfair, as is the case with receiving compensation for the same loss more than once (so-called double recovery).[33] Although it is beyond the scope of this book to focus on employment contracts, it suffices to say that labour relationships are subject to several public policy limitations. This includes among others: labour rights, particularly the restricted right to termination by the employer[34] and the prevalence of the employment contract over and above the employer's bylaws.[35]

The discussion in the beginning of this chapter, dealing with good faith, is very much relevant to the application and construction of unfair terms in contracts, particularly consumer contracts. Good faith plays a central role in the construction of such contracts,[36] because the law requires the more powerful party to avoid exclusion or limitation (of liability) clauses that cause significant harm to the weaker party, especially where the latter possesses little, or no, bargaining power. Agreements entered under such circumstances are known as adhesion contracts and the terms effectively imposed by the stronger

---

[32] Art 1(2) CC provides a hierarchy of sources, with statute at the apex, followed by the Sharia ('if any'), customary practices and finally 'rules of justice'. See Court of Cassation Judgment 122/2013 on the limitations of justice as a rule that is trumped by the mutual intention of the parties; see equally Court of Cassation Judgment 26/2015.

[33] See N Mahasneh, 'Delay Damages: The Application of Qatari National Law to Article 8(8) of the 2017 Red Book' (2020) 34 Arab LQ 10.

[34] Court of Cassation Judgments 44/2010 and 73/2010.

[35] Court of Cassation Judgment 32/2011.

[36] For the position in Islamic law, see M Fayyad, 'Measures of the Principle of Good Faith in European Consumer Protection and Islamic Law: A Comparative Analysis' (2014) 28 Arab LQ 205.

party are standard terms[37] (and conditions). It is not always easy, however, to draw the line between economic disparity that gives rise to an adhesion contract and disparity that does not. The discussion is crucial, of course, because if a particular type of contract is not considered adhesive, then an otherwise arbitrary or unfair term would be valid. Insurance contracts offer an excellent illustration. There is clearly a significant financial disparity between the insurer and the insured, but this is not always the case, and in any event, it is not always compulsory to take out insurance. The Court of Appeal has iterated that in case of doubt, insurance contracts must be viewed as adhesion agreements under the terms of article 107 CC.[38] On the contrary, Qatari courts have viewed other contractual relationships involving some form of standard terms as not satisfying the requirements for adhesion contracts. This is true particularly in respect of real estate agreements,[39] interest in loan agreements[40] and sales terms restricting the buyer's right to damages.[41] This is also the case with respect to the obligations of guarantors to another person's loan or the imposition of interest for delayed payments.[42] The Court of Cassation has recognised these obligations as stemming from business custom.[43]

One of the ways through which the CC counters unfair clauses is by requiring sign-posting of the adhering party's statutory rights in the adhesion contract. By way of illustration, article 778 CC requires the insurer to insert a

---

[37] Standard terms are not defined in the CC. Art 1110 of the French CC defines 'standard form contracts' as contracts whose general conditions are determined in advance by one of the parties without negotiation. See N Mahasneh, 'Standard Terms Contracts: The Approaches of the Qatari Civil Law and the UNIDROIT Principles 2016: A Comparative Study' (2018) 32 Arab LQ 462.

[38] Court of Appeal Judgment 1272/2015. See also Arts 775 and 775 CC, which address void terms and conditions in insurance contracts, as well as a variation of the *contra preferentum* rule.

[39] Court of First Instance (CFI) Judgment 114/2016, cited in Mahasneh (n 37) 473. In one case involving a real estate transaction, the Court of Cassation (Judgment 74/2011) noted that consumers may not reject unfair and unjust conditions in adhesion contracts. This seems an aberration and does not count as good law.

[40] CFI Judgment 114/2016, ibid, 474.

[41] Court of Cassation Judgment 74/2011.

[42] s 110 of Decree Law No 33 of 2006 on the Qatar Central Bank.

[43] The Court of Cassation does not shy away from identifying business custom through standard phraseology. For example, in Court of Cassation Judgment 148/2010, it held that the bank's exposure to the lender is significant and hence compensation for late payments (delay interest) is justified by reference to banking custom, which is moreover 'common knowledge' that does not require proof; equally Court of Cassation Judgment 220/2011; to the same effect see also Court of Cassation Judgments 40/2013 and 107/2013, where it was stated that where a special commercial/trade law is silent 'commercial custom shall be applied, with the special custom or local custom being given precedence over the general custom. If there is no commercial custom, the provisions of the civil law shall apply'. This was also reiterated in Court of Cassation Judgments 66/2014; 371/2014 and 208/2014.

provision in insurance contracts exceeding five years that termination takes effect every five years by a six-month notice to the other party.

Article 105 CC underscores the inherent imbalance of power in adhesion contracts, acknowledging in the process that the absence of negotiations as a result of the stronger party's (effective imposition of) standard terms does not entail that the other party has not expressed its acceptance of the offer.[44] This is known as the *incorporation problem*. Following well-established civil law tradition,[45] article 106 CC goes on to emphasise that adhesion contracts may not contain arbitrary terms and where they do the adhering party may request the courts to expunge them fully. This is true even where the adhering party was aware that the term was arbitrary.[46] In most cases, the adhering party will be aware of the arbitrary nature of the underlying standard term but will have little practical choice in the matter. Clearly, therefore, arbitrary contractual terms in adhesion contracts are prohibited as a matter of public policy and the adhering party's knowledge is not considered an abuse of right.[47] It is not surprising as a result that article 106 CC prohibits any agreement to the contrary; that is, the parties are not at liberty to agree that such terms shall remain in force. There is no definition as to what constitutes 'arbitrary' terms, but at the very least, this encompasses clauses that produce a gross imbalance to the interests of the adhering party, as well as those that exclude or limit the liability of the stronger party.

7.4.1 *Exemption Clauses*

That the law allows stronger parties to effectively impose standard terms does not mean that said terms can contain arbitrary conditions, including those that exempt the stronger party from full or partial liability, all of which are detrimental to the interests of the weaker party. Qatari law curtails the use and validity of exemption clauses in several ways. As explained elsewhere, article 170(2) CC posits the general rule, according to which if the contract contains

---

[44] See Court of Appeal Judgment 241/2010; Court of Cassation Judgment 74/2011.

[45] The revised French CC, which was a source of inspiration for the Qatari CC, provides in Art 1170 that terms which serve to deprive the debtor's essential obligation of its substance are invalid. Art 1171 of the French CC produces the same result in respect of terms that create a significant imbalance to the parties' rights and obligations.

[46] Commentators argue that this is in contrast to the historical predecessor of Art 106 CC, namely Art 148 Egyptian CC, which does not address the adhering party's knowledge of the arbitrary term. See Mahasneh (n 37) 478.

[47] See Court of Cassation Judgment 17/2012, where it was held that a guarantee for a future obligation under Art 1812 CC is invalid, unless the two parties specify in advance in the guarantee contract the amount of the debt guaranteed by the guarantor.

a clause discharging a party from liability, such provision shall be construed narrowly. Article 24 of the 2008 Consumer Law is expressed in more absolute terms. It states that

> Any condition referred to in a contract, document, or other similar instrument in respect of contracting with the consumer shall be null and void where such condition relieves the supplier of any of his obligations stipulated in this Law.

Suppliers (businesses or stronger parties to adhesion contracts) cannot impose blanket exemptions from liability clauses in their contracts with consumers. Their duties as suppliers towards consumers are prescribed by law[48], and hence, because they are statute based, they may not be exempted by contract. Article 3 of the Consumer Law further provides that the consumer shall be entitled to fair compensation for any property or financial damages sustained as a result of the purchase or use of commodities and services. Any contrary agreement between consumer and supplier shall be deemed null and void.

A poignant illustration is also offered in articles 801 and 802 CC which stipulate that insurance contracts may not impose conditions that are not in the best interests of the insured or beneficiaries, including extending or decreasing the applicable period of prescription.[49]

7.4.2 *Incorporation*

We have slightly touched on the incorporation problem in the previous section, but it is worth further analysis because of its importance to contractual fairness and the debates it has given rise to in other jurisdictions. The key question is to what extent standard terms should be notified and made clear to the adhering party. To illustrate its importance, it is instructive that under German law, if a term contained in standard terms is so unusual that the other party would not have expected to encounter it, it is deemed inapplicable.[50] In similar vein, Lord Denning, as far back as 1956 demanded that the more unreasonable a standard clause is the greater the notice which must be given

---

[48] See, for example, Art 12 Consumer Law, which concerns a duty to include in consumer contracts details about returns, repairs and maintenance; see also Art 789 CC, which provides that any agreement in insurance contracts by which to discharge the insurer from his obligation to notify the insured or to shorten the time of suspension or termination notices is null and void.

[49] See Court of Cassation Judgment 140/2014, which held that a clause in the insurance contract that did not guarantee loss or damage of the insured object as a result of repairs undertaken was invalid.

[50] Art 305(c)(1) BGB.

of it.[51] This is known as the *red hand rule*, because Lord Denning jokingly suggested that such a clause would need to be printed with a red hand pointing to it. We have already examined how article 106 CC tackles the incorporation problem by prohibiting arbitrary terms. This is hardly enough, however. Article 80(1) CC stipulates that where the contracting parties agree to standard terms and conditions, such terms shall apply 'unless any party proves that they had no notice of such provisions, or had no opportunity to discover them at the time of the agreement'. Paragraph 2 of article 80 CC continues by saying that where standard terms of which no notice has been taken are essential, the contract shall be invalid. 'If the provisions are auxiliary, the courts shall resolve any dispute arising therefrom in accordance with the nature of the transaction, current usage and the rules of justice'. As a result, conspicuous or unexpected general conditions are not binding on the weaker party, unless drawn to its attention in a manner that renders them fully noticeable. The subsequent section on fairness provides more insights on the notice requirements generally demanded, or which should be demanded.

7.4.3 *Interpretative Rules for Assessing Unfair Terms*

The policing of contractual fairness requires appropriate construction/interpretation by the courts in order to counter the deficiencies associated with the incorporation problem and the use of standard terms. Qatari law has adopted most construction principles developed in the common and civil law traditions. Article 107 CC goes on to establish the so-called *contra preferentum* rule, according to which an ambiguous term in an adhesion contract shall always be construed in favour of the adhering party. It is, therefore, in the interest of the stronger party to clarify the content of its standard terms, in accordance with the analysis in the previous section. This allows for fairer contracting. In one case, the applicant had acquired a credit card from a bank and withdrew large amounts. The bank treated its agreement with the applicant as a loan agreement, rather than a credit card agreement, and imposed significantly larger amounts of interest on withdrawals. The Court of Cassation found this to be contrary to pertinent business custom and restored the parties' contractual relationship to that of a credit card agreement.[52]

Article 170(1) CC takes the mantle even further by providing that if doubt arises as to the wording or meaning of words or phrases in the contract, these shall be construed in favour of the obligor. Where, however, the contract

---

[51] *Spurling Ltd v Bradshaw* (1956) 1 WLR 461.
[52] Court of Cassation Judgment 107/2013.

contains a clause discharging a party from liability, such provision shall be construed narrowly.[53] Paragraph 2 of article 170 must be read alongside article 160 CC and consumer legislation.

7.5 FAIRNESS

The question of fairness is central to the enforcement of unfair clauses in consumer contracts. While the 2008 Consumer Law and CC provide general guidance that arbitrary terms will be invalid, as well as that unfair exemption clauses will suffer the same fate, the courts would have to assess each claim anew. It is for this reason that most jurisdictions in Europe, as well as the EU, have set out lists of unfair terms. Although several variations exist, these are typically distinguished between terms falling within *grey lists* and *black lists*. Terms in grey lists may be binding if they do not encompass disproportionate obligations. Terms in black lists can under no circumstances be considered binding.[54] Under Qatari law, there are no grey or black lists for consumers and the courts to rely upon, and hence, much will depend on the particular content of terms in adhesion contracts, as well as the attitude of the courts in construing arbitrariness and good faith in such contracts. A good illustration may be derived by the rights of guarantors against the debt of a third party. The Court of Appeal has made it clear that the guarantor has the right to warn the creditor to take measures against the debtor (when the debt is due) within six months from the date of the warning, and failure to do so clears the guarantor and the surety contract expires unless the debtor provides a sufficient guarantee.[55]

---

[53] Art 170(2) CC.
[54] See Arts 308 and 309 BGB; Arts R 212-1 and R 212-2 of the French CC; Annex [to Art 3] of EC Directive 93/13 on Unfair Terms in Consumer Contracts.
[55] Court of Appeal Judgment 54/2018.

8

Defects of Consent

8.1 THE GENERAL RULE

In the previous chapter, we examined the notion of capacity and legal personality under the Qatari civil and commercial law. In general, article 108 CC conflates capacity and consent by stating that consent (to contract) is only valid in respect of entities that possess capacity under the law. Overall, the law distinguishes between persons with full legal capacity and those with partial or no legal capacity. Persons with limited capacity may contract through a guardian and in limited circumstances not involving a significant financial commitment they are free to contract without guardianship.[1] Entities with full capacity may freely contract in their person.

The types of defects envisaged in articles 130–147 CC encompass circumstances that inhibit free and informed consent by the offeror or offeree. The CC follows the civil law tradition of grouping these grounds in one section. The existence of a threat, coercion, mistake or exploitation prevents the offeror or offeree from forming a valid intention to be bound by the offer or acceptance.[2] The offeror or offeree would have bargained differently or not at all had these circumstances not been present when the offer or acceptance was made. The CC sets out a fifth type of defect, in the form of injustice against the interests of the state or a state entity. The law renders contracts concluded under such defects of consent voidable,[3] as opposed to void or null. This is a very importance consequence, whose effects will be explored at the end of this chapter.

---

[1]   See Chapter 4 and Arts 118–126 CC.
[2]   Hence, this chapter will not discuss the forgery of contracts or associated documents where they do not give rise to defects in forming intent. The Court of Cassation has long held that the invocation of forgery must be done according to the procedures and time limits afforded by law. See Court of Cassation Judgment 81/2010.
[3]   Arts 158–162 CC.

It should be stated that the types of defects analyzed in this chapter arise subsequent to the formation of the contract. Hence, if proven, any of these grounds serves to extinguish an existing contract. Defects of consent prior to the conclusion of a contract typically challenge the existence of mutual consent (so called *dissensus*), or even the identity of the parties themselves (i.e. who is the buyer and seller). A defective common consent under those circumstances prevents the formation of a contract in the first place.

8.2 MISTAKES

It would be unfair for a party to plead a mistake in the formation of its consent (even if true) in order to escape its obligations under the contract. It would be equally unfair, however, if a mistake that was not obvious from the outset causes significant harm to the party acting in ignorance of that mistake. Given that the concept of 'mistake' is key to this discussion, it is worthwhile explaining how this is conceptualised in the architecture of article 130 CC. It refers not to arithmetical or spelling mistakes,[4] but fundamental mistakes of substance that are crucial for the formation of consent of either the offeror or the offeree. In one case, the buyer of two plots of land contracted with an intermediary to buy the land in its name and then transfer the two plots to the buyer once full payment had been made. The intermediary proceeded to buy the two plots but when he registered these in the land registry it transpired that he had in fact bought plots that were different to those inspected and approved by the buyer. Such a mistake was viewed by the Court of Cassation as being fundamental in nature, thus, justifying the annulment of the contracts between intermediary and buyer.[5]

Article 130(1) CC places greater emphasis on the impact of the mistake upon the ignorant party by stipulating that if said party would have not provided consent had it known about the mistake, it may subsequently demand voidance of the contract. The mistaken party's mistake may only be pleaded against its counterpart if the latter in ignorance committed the same mistake (so-called common mistake), or where it was aware of its occurrence, or if it could have easily detected such mistake.[6] By implication, where the mistaken party entered into a contract requiring due diligence from both parties, it may not plead a mistake predicated on its own due diligence failures, as this would

---

4 Art 133 CC. See also Court of Cassation Judgment 113/2012 to this effect. The courts may correct such simple errors in accordance with Art 138 CCP.
5 Court of Cassation judgment 87/2011. See also Court of Cassation judgment 242/2016 to the same effect, although this case is mostly centered on fraud under Art 134 CC.
6 Art 130(1) CC.

constitute among others an abuse of right. Conversely, where the mistake arose out of the failure of the other party to provide or disclose information under its possession or knowledge,[7] or where it was under a statutory obligation to provide information,[8] the mistake may be pleaded against said party. This is further confirmed by paragraph 2 of article 130 CC, which provides that gifts (promises) based on a mistake are voidable without the need to establish whether or not the beneficiary participated in or was aware of the mistake.

The duty to disclose relevant information is particularly important in the consumer context. Article 7 of the 2008 Consumer Law[9] provides that suppliers displaying goods for trading must clearly indicate on the packaging the type, nature, ingredients and other information relating to the good. Moreover, where the good involves a certain risk, the consumer shall be clearly warned against such risk. There equally exists an obligation to disclose to the consumer all the fees and expenses associated with payment of goods in instalments,[10] as well as all relevant facts about the characteristics and price of goods or services.[11]

Just like the civil law tradition with its emphasis on good faith, mistaken consent that is contrary to good faith does not serve to invalidate the contract.[12] Good faith is central to the CC[13] and the parties to a contract may not plead a 'mistake' if they were either aware of the mistake (although undisclosed by the other party) or they would have provided consent anyway. The other

---

[7] Withholding of information in one's possession is different from intentional misrepresentation of circumstances under the contract by one of the parties. Misrepresentation, which effectively amounts to fraud, is regulated under Arts 134ff CC. Despite the appearance of 'misrepresentation' in Art 134 CC, this should not be confused with its common law namesake. Under the leading case of *Smith v Hughes* (1871) LR 6 QB 597, it was famously held that there exists no general duty to disclose information and in principle mere silence is not a ground for avoiding a contract. The English Misrepresentation Act 1967 identifies three types of misrepresentation, namely: fraudulent, negligent and innocent.

[8] Law No 13/2012 on Issuing the Law on Qatar Central Bank, provides in Art 142 that financial institutions shall not offer, provide, promote or advertise any financial service that is misleading or incorrect. Any advertisement shall be clear, unambiguous and in plain language that is neither misleading nor deceptive, and shall include the essential data, merits, characteristics and prices of the financial service advertised as well as the terms and conditions relating to accessing such services and educating consumers about the risks of the financial product or service offered.

[9] Law No 8/2008 on Consumer Protection. See also Decree No. 68 of 2012 on the issuance of the Regulations on the implementation of the Consumer Protection Law No. 8 of 2008 (Consumer Protection Regulation).

[10] Art 15 Consumer Law.

[11] Id, Art 11.

[12] Art 132 CC.

[13] Besides Art 132 CC, this is chiefly prescribed as a foundational principle of Qatari contract law in 172(1) CC, whereby all contracts must be performed in accordance with good faith.

(non-mistaken) party may under such circumstances insist on the conclusion of the contract provided that substantial harm is not caused.[14]

In summary, the avoidance of a contract by reason of mistake requires a) the *existence of a contract*; b) a *misapprehension* of the correct situation, circumstance or quality of a good or service (actual mistake) by one or both parties, in respect of a fundamental characteristic of the good or service; c) a *causal link*, namely that the contract would not have been concluded under those conditions had these been known to the ignorant party; and d) *apparent importance*, in the sense that it must be clear to the non-mistaken party that had the other party been aware of the truth it would not have agreed to the contract or its terms.

8.3 FRAUD

The type of *fraud* envisaged under article 134 CC overlaps to some degree with the concept of fraud under articles 354–361 of the Qatari Criminal Code, but here its application concerns whether or not the defrauded party would have accepted the offer had it known about the issue concealed under the fraud.[15] It is quite possible, therefore that a particular instance of fraud under the Criminal Code may not justify rendering the underlying contract void because the offeree would have accepted anyway.[16] While a claim of fraud will typically also be accompanied by the pleading of a mistake (as overlapping grounds), the former, if successful, allows not only the avoidance of the contract but also a possible claim for damages arising out of the tort of fraud.[17] This is particularly so where the defrauded party incurred costs in reliance on the other party's fraudulent representations.[18] The Court of Cassation has stipulated that contractual fraud may be achieved by using fraudulent or negative methods, and thus, to deliberately mislead the other contracting party which is ignorant of the fraudulent act. This requires that the defrauding party, its deputy or one of its partners must have participated or furthered the mistake,

---

[14] Art 132 CC.
[15] Other special types of fraud affecting contractual relations exist. Art 61 of Law No 14 of 2004 on the Promulgation of Labor Law stipulates that dismissal (and effectively termination of contract) of the employee is permitted where the latter assumes a false identity, alleges a nationality other than his or submits false certificates or document. See also Court of Cassation Judgment 2/2011.
[16] For the position in classical Islamic law, see A El-Khalek, 'The Regulatory Framework of the Defect of Fraud in Islamic Law', (1986) 3 Arab LQ 237.
[17] This overlap between a tort and fraudulent contracting was noted in Court of Cassation Judgment 36/2016.
[18] See Arts 199–219 CC.

which was difficult to discover and the fraud must relate to an essential element of the contract.[19]

Again, the starting point for an examination of fraud under article 134 CC is good faith. Good faith dictates that unless the law otherwise requires some element of due diligence (by the buyer), the seller is under an obligation to be truthful about the quality of the goods or services offered. Good faith under Qatari law (and its Islamic legal tradition)[20] equally commands that representation is fraudulent where the reasonable person in the position of the buyer would have been able to perceive the deception. An expert mechanic inspecting a car cannot claim to have been deceived as to the condition of the car's engine by the seller's representation. In a case where a car sold had been modified by the manufacturer for the GCC environment, the buyer argued that had he known about the modification he would not have agreed to buy the car. The Court of Cassation, after taking advice from an expert that the modifications were in conformity with GCC specifications, held that the seller had not defrauded the buyer.[21] The Court of Cassation has emphasised that context and the parties' personal attributes are important. Hence, in a case where one party convinced others through advertisements to purchase a company depicted as successful, which was riddled with debts, such representation was found to encompass an intention to enter into a fraudulent transaction.[22] Fraud under article 134(1) CC should be understood as the intentional misrepresentation of facts that are fundamental to the consent of the offeree.[23] Hence, so-called *promotional puffs* that are employed in order to accentuate or exaggerate the quality of a good or service do not constitute misrepresentation because they do not concern fundamental elements of the service or good.

While contractual misrepresentation typically concerns *active* deception on the part of the seller, paragraph 2 of article 134 CC equally encompasses *passive* deception. In the latter case, the seller either conceals or is otherwise silent about the fundamental qualities of a good or service, or is untruthful about such qualities when asked by the buyer. If the buyer does not possess sufficient expertise or is unable to inspect the goods or services and relies in

---

[19] Court of Cassation Judgment 242/2016.
[20] See N Majeed, 'Good Faith and Due Process: Lessons from the Shari'ah', (2004) 20 Arbitration International 97.
[21] Court of Cassation Judgment 242/2016.
[22] Court of Cassation Judgment 42/2016.
[23] Art 7 of the Consumer Law specifies that the supplier shall be prohibited from describing, advertising or displaying the commodity in a manner that involves false or deceptive information.

good faith on the seller's representation, the latter's silence, even if not asked (by a non-expert buyer) is assumed to be fraudulent with the intention of deceiving the buyer (so called subterfuge). In such circumstances, the seller is acting in bad faith and hence may not contest that he would have truthfully responded to the buyer had the latter asked. In one case, the appellants sold a company under the claim that it generated significant returns. They provided false information about the number of employees and did not disclose that they were trading under the company's name. They equally omitted to disclose that the company had been fined as a result. One of the appellants, moreover, upon completion of the sale, removed the funds from the company's account and failed to pay outstanding company debts. The Court of Cassation had no problem finding fraud under article 134 CC. Deception, it held, was both active (lying, misrepresentation) and passive, namely through silence, when requested by the other party to provide specific information.[24]

Article 135(1) CC requires that voidance of a contract on the basis of fraud demands proof that the deceit is attributable to the defrauding party or someone else validly acting on its behalf, or in whose interest the contract was concluded. If it is not satisfied that the deceit is not attributable to the defrauding party, the contract may not be voided.[25] Even so, if it is established that the defrauding party was, or should necessarily have been, aware of the fraudulent misrepresentation, the defrauded party may claim the voidance of the contract.[26] In one case the applicant alleged that the date on the contract, which itself was in the form of a photocopied document, was fraudulent. The Court of Cassation demanded that in order to successfully prove fraud the applicant was obliged to produce the non-fraudulent contract in writing, whether in the form of the original or a certified photocopy.[27]

The prohibition of fraud constitutes a public policy norm. The parties to a contract do not possess authority to validate fraudulent conduct. Hence, while contracting parties may validly agree to exempt each other from contractual liability, this is not possible in two notable cases: fraud and severe fault, according to article 259 CC.[28]

---

[24] Court of Cassation Judgment 29/2016.
[25] See to this effect, Court of Cassation Judgment 196/2010, which relied on Art 4 of Law No 14 Concerning the Land Registration System. The Court held that despite the existence of fraud on the part of the seller, the underlying purchase agreement between buyer and seller was not tainted by fraud and hence was not voidable.
[26] Art 135(2) CC. See also Art 136 CC, which stipulates that in respect of a contract or a gift, voidance thereof may be requested if consent to its terms was given as a result of fraud, even if caused by a third party.
[27] Court of Cassation Judgment 89/2011.
[28] See Court of Cassation Judgment 74/2011.

The existence of fraud has an impact on the parties' rights and obligations. In accordance with article 462 CC, the seller's obligation to guarantee hidden defects lapses with the passage of one year from the delivery of the thing sold, even if the defect is not discovered until after that, unless the seller accepts a longer warranty period. However, if the seller deliberately conceals fraud, the warranty does not lapse until 15 years have passed since the sale took place.[29]

8.4 THREAT OR COERCION

The terms 'threat', 'duress' and 'coercion' are used inter-changeably and carry the same legal meaning for the purposes of article 137 CC. Article 137(1) CC defines these as the 'unlawful instillment of justifiable fear'. Fear is justified, in order to avoid the underlying contract, where the affected party was 'confronted by circumstances that led him reasonably to believe that a grievous and imminent danger to life, limb, honor or property threatened him or others'.[30] Even though coercion seems self-evident this is not the case. The coercive act must be *unlawful* in nature.[31] This is clearly spelt out in article 137(1) CC. As a result, actions that might otherwise appear to be coercive, yet lack illegality, do not justify avoidance of the contract by the claimant.[32] By way of illustration, if the seller threatens a prospective buyer that he will sell the house to another person unless the buyer accepts the offer in two days, this is not unlawful; a purchase under such a 'threat' would not subsequently justify the invalidity of the agreement.

Besides the unlawful character of the threat, paragraph 1 of article 137 CC requires that the threat, moreover, instil justifiable fear upon the threatened party. *Unlawfulness* and *justifiable fear* are not conjunctive but must exist simultaneously. As a result, an unlawful threat that does not instil unjustifiable fear on the threatened person, and who subsequently goes on to adopt the contract, may not invoke the threat to avoid the contract. It is, therefore, important to ascertain how and if the coerced party was subject to a justifiable

---

[29] Court of Appeal Judgment 339/2018.
[30] Art 137(2) CC.
[31] That is exactly why the text in Arts 241, 245 and 251 CC indicates that forcing the debtor to carry out its obligation in kind does not entail coercion because this does not compromise the debtor's dignity nor does it stifle its freedom in contravention of the law. See to this effect, Court of Cassation Judgment 80/2015.
[32] Exceptionally, where the law requires good faith for the validity of an act or transaction the existence of illegality is irrelevant. Art 946(2) CC makes it clear that acquisition of property by means of coercion [irrespective of illegality] is always presumed to be in bad faith and hence it is invalid. See Art 948 CC concerning the transfer of property in the event the possessor acquired it in bad faith.

fear. The test put forth by paragraph 3 of article 137 CC clearly seems to be
a subjective one. It stipulates that in determining the effect of the threat,
account shall be taken of the 'gender, age, knowledge, ignorance, or health
of the affected party, as well as any other circumstance that might have aggra-
vated the duress'. The coerced party may invalidate the contract where the
threat was such that he or she would not have agreed to the suggested terms
had the threat not been present. The existence of such a causal link is para-
mount as is the case with all the other types of defective consent.

Finally, just like the other forms of defective consent, the threat must be
attributable to the other party, or a representative thereof, or a person acting in
its interest.[33] A threat is not typically attributable to the principal if undertaken
by the agent in its personal capacity and acting ultra vires in respect of the
powers and instructions provided by the principal.[34] The courts have absolute
authority to examine all evidence alleging the existence of threats,[35] and in
any event, the claimant must provide proof of its claim.[36]

8.5 EXPLOITATION

Article 140 CC sets out a fourth ground that may give rise to defective consent,
namely exploitation. This is a wide ground that is also known as 'undue influence' under civil law systems. Article 140 CC stipulates that exploitation arises
where a contracting party exploits its counterpart out of 'need, obvious frivolity, visible vulnerability, or sudden heat of passion, or his moral influence over
the other person causes that other person to conclude a contract … and such
contract contains an excessive imbalance between the obligations he must
perform and the material or moral benefits he shall obtain from the contract'.
Given that disparity in the value of mutual performances is common in all
types of transactions (e.g. consumer transactions), article 140 CC targets only
those obligations that are *excessively imbalanced*. It is necessary, however, that
such excessive contractual imbalance be the direct result of undue influence
or exploitation, as defined in article 140 CC. This gives rise to a double test
of both procedural and substantive fairness. The test for exploitation seems to
be subjective and based on the circumstances of the exploited person. Given
that the underlying principle aims to prevent and invalidate excessive (gross)
disparities, the intention of the other party (the exploiter) is irrelevant. Hence,

[33] Art 138 CC.
[34] See Chapter 4 for an analysis of the law of agency.
[35] Court of Cassation Judgment 394/2015.
[36] Court of Cassation Judgment 260/2019, where the claimant failed to prove that its settlement
agreement was the result of coercion.

if a party to a contract is subject to a grossly disparate set of obligations, even if this was not intended by its counterpart, the very fact of such disparity suffices to invalidate consent.

Where the courts encounter such disparity, they are entitled to modify or invalidate the contract altogether. If the court decides to intrude and modify the contract it shall adapt the parties' respective obligations in a manner whereby the gross disparity is alleviated.[37] This is an exceptional mechanism that is consistent with transnational practice[38] and finds support also in situations of *force majeure*.[39] The same principle applies *mutatis mutandis* in respect of donations made but in respect of which the donor was the subject of exploitation or undue influence.[40]

Unlike the previous three types of defect (mistake, threat or coercion), whereupon general limitation periods apply, article 142 CC introduces a limitation period specifically designed to address exploitation. Paragraph 1 of article 142 CC contemplates that actions concerning exploitation expire a year after the conclusion of the impugned contract, save where the defect continues, in which case the one-year limitation period commences from the date such defect disappears.[41]

8.6 INJUSTICE

This is an innovation of the CC. Article 143 CC stipulates that injustice not resulting from mistake, fraud, duress or exploitation shall have no effect on the contract – that is, it may not be voided – except in special circumstances determined by the law. Although such *injustice* is not defined, we have a pretty good idea what it consists of.[42] For one thing, it may not result from any of the aforementioned defects of consent. Second, article 144(1) CC makes it clear that what is at stake is *excessive* injustice harming a limited number of

---

[37] Art 140 CC.
[38] See Art 3.2.7 UNIDROIT Principles of International Commercial Contracts (PICC), which refers to the authority of courts to adapt obligations in contracts giving rise to 'gross disparity'.
[39] See Art 6.2.3(4)(b) PICC; Art 171(2) CC.
[40] Art 141 CC.
[41] Art 142(2) CC. Under no circumstances can this period be longer than fifteen years, in accordance with Art 142(3) CC.
[42] In other legal systems, injustice (in the sense of grossly imbalanced obligations) is usually classified as an unfair term, over which the courts are granted authority to either adapt or invalidate. See, for example, Art 3(1) of EU Directive 93/13 on Unfair Terms in Consumer Contracts, which stipulates that a standard term in a consumer contract causing a 'significant imbalance to the parties' rights and obligations' and which is to the detriment of the consumer is considered unfair. It is the opinion of the authors that in the Qatari CC this is treated as a defect of consent.

entities, namely the state, any public juridical entity, incompetent or partially incompetent persons,[43] or the Authority for Endowments (*Waqf*). Hence, with the exception of persons under guardianship, article 143 CC targets contracts involving a state entity. Contracts between a public and a private entity are known as administrative contracts[44] and are typically regulated by administrative law, with jurisdiction conferred to the administrative circuit of the court of first instance.[45] It must be emphasised that article 144 CC does not aim to regulate administrative contracts as a whole, but only those aspects of such contracts that produce excessive injustice. Paragraph 2 of article 144 CC quantifies injustice as excessive where 'it exceeds one-fifth at the time of concluding the contract'. Just like the effects of exploitation on the exploited party, paragraph 1 of article 144 CC allows the courts to amend the injured or other party's obligations in order to redress the injustice incurred. In addition to this remedy, the non-injured party may request termination of the contract with a view to avoiding amendment to its obligations.[46]

While the device of injustice under articles 143ff CC is laudable it is not free from contention. For one thing, the Court of Cassation has emphasised that: 'it is not permissible for a judge to rescind or amend a valid contract on the ground that the revocation or modification is required by the rules of justice. Justice completes the will of the contracting parties, but does not abrogate it'.[47] Moreover, the remedy envisaged in article 144(1) CC may amount to an expropriation under an applicable bilateral investment treaty (BIT),[48] or a breach of contract on the part of the state where the governing law of the underlying agreement is not Qatari law. It may also be in conflict with

---

43 See Chapter 4.
44 Administrative contracts are regulated by Law No 24/2015 on the Regulation of Tenders and Auctions, known as the Procurement Law.
    The Court of Cassation in Judgment 49/2008 defined administrative contracts as 'contracts concluded between a legal person of public law and related to the operation of a public service and which include exceptional and unusual conditions [clause *exorbitante*] that are distinct from the ambit of private law'; iterated in Court of Cassation Judgment 118/2008. See also Court of Cassation Judgment 100/2016, which further stipulated that a contract is not of an administrative nature, unless related to the management or organization of a public facility and the administration has demonstrated its intention to adopt public law by including in the contract exceptional and unusual conditions.
45 Disputes arising from administrative contracts confer jurisdiction upon the administrative circuit, in accordance with Art 3(5) of Law No 7/2007 on the Settlement of Administrative Disputes; public housing disputes are not considered administrative disputes. See Court of Cassation Judgment 28/2010.
46 Art 145 CC.
47 Court of Cassation Judgment 122/2013; equally, Court of Cassation Judgment 109/2015.
48 See, for example, Art 5 of the 2017 Qatar-Singapore BIT, which sets forth the classic formulation of expropriation.

other provisions of Qatari law, in which case the courts will have to undertake a conflict of rules determination. Given the limited range of circumstances that can potentially fall under articles 143 and 144 CC, it is advisable that such matters be dealt by administrative law and that if the civil law is to be applied, recourse should be had to the ordinary defects of consent. In trying to address some, but certainly not all, of these concerns, article 146 CC stipulates that contracts concluded by auction and tender may not be subject to injustice claims if concluded in accordance with the law. Equally, article 147(1) CC provides a limitation period of one year.

8.7 EFFECTS OF DEFECTIVE CONSENT

Defects of consent arising out of mistake, fraud, threats, exploitation and injustice should be distinguished from contracts suffering from illegality. Defective consent renders a contract *voidable*, as opposed to void.[49] The key difference is that a contract suffering from defective consent may be cured by the parties or the court (i.e. through adaptation of the parties' mutual obligations), whereas a void contract cannot be salvaged. This distinction is fundamental in the civil law tradition and is reflected in article 158 CC, which stipulates that voidable contracts are deemed to be effective unless revoked. When revoked they are deemed by the law to be void *ab initio*. The law rightly considers that the parties to contracts, or their guardians, possess sufficient acumen and judgment by which to decide if despite the existence of defective consent, the terms of the contract are still favorable to their personal interests; save where it is in the interests of justice not to do so, or if the law says otherwise.[50]

Articles 159 and 160 CC recognise two particular rights available to injured parties, namely, a) the right to *revoke* the contract and b) the right to *authorise* the contract despite the defect. Both of these rights are conferred on the injured party. Article 160 CC makes it clear that where an injured party authorises the operationalisation of an otherwise voidable contract, the authorisation does not extend to the underlying defect.[51] Hence, while the defect persists, the contract remains alive. Given the inclination to render voidable contracts functional (where this is agreeable to the injured party), as opposed to the mechanism concerning void contracts, article 162 CC is not oblivious to the expectations of the other party (concerned party). Paragraph 1 of article 162 CC allows the concerned party to notify the injured party to declare its intention to either

---

[49]   On void contracts, see Art 163 CC.
[50]   Art 159(2) CC.
[51]   See to this effect, Court of Appeal Judgment 166/2019.

authorise or revoke the contract. This should be done within three months from the date of the notice. Where the period of the notice expires without a declaration of authorisation or revocation of the contract by the injured party, such omission is deemed to constitute authorisation, provided notice is served to the injured party in person.[52] In equal measure, article 161(1) CC reinforces the salvation of otherwise voidable contracts by prescribing a limitation period of one year from the date the defect arose within which to revoke the contract. If the injured party fails to do so, the general presumption applies and the contract is considered as being live.[53]

According to article 166 CC, where any provision of the contract is voidable, such provision alone shall be revoked, unless it is evident that the contract would not have been concluded without such provision, in which event the contract shall be revoked in full. Moreover, article 167 CC goes on to say that where a voidable contract contains the elements of another contract, the voidable contract shall be deemed valid to the extent of the other contract, whose elements are available if the intention of the contracting parties indicates that they wish to conclude such other contract. In this manner, the CC attempts to salvage parts or the entirety of voidable agreements, although this may not always be feasible or desirable by one or more of the parties.

---

[52] Art 162(3) CC.
[53] But see also possible extensions to this time limit in Art 161(2) and (3) CC.

9

Prohibited Contracts

In Chapter 8, we discussed the defects of consent, whereas here we shall dive deeper into the effects of defects in general. Before doing so, we need to lay the foundations by which to evaluate the legal impact of each defect on civil and commercial contracts. It will be recalled that under the civil law tradition, contracts are predicated on three general pillars, namely: (i) consent, consisting of offer, acceptance and intention to be legally bound; (ii) subject-matter and (iii) cause. In addition, there might, but not necessarily, exist two further requirements (special pillars), namely: (iv) form[1] and (v) delivery.[2]

---

[1] According to the Court of Cassation Judgment 20/2007, form is a fundamental pillar for the formation of any sale contract concerning retail stores. Thus, the law requires such sale contract to be notarised in an official document and issued by the concerned public body, that is, the Documentation Department under the Ministry of Justice. The contracting parties are prohibited from agreeing to circumvent this pillar and any contrary agreement is deemed null and void (absolute nullity). Moreover, contracting parties cannot elect to authorise (affirm) the sale contract because it is invalid. However, once the contracting parties complete the statutory requirement of 'form', then the sale contract becomes legally binding because all its pillars have otherwise materialised.

[2] According to the Court of Cassation Judgment 274/2015, delivery is a fundamental pillar for the formation of any sale contract concerning the sale of real-estate (immovable properties). The registration of conveyed property with the concerned public body, that is, the Real-Estate Registration Department under the Ministry of Justice, is a regulatory requirement for the finalisation of the conveyance but *is not* a pillar for the formation of the sale contract. This means that any sale contract of real-estate whereby the seller *does not* deliver the property to the buyer is invalid (absolute nullity) and the mere formality of completing the registration process *does not* authorise (affirm) this void contract. Thus, the seller is obligated by law to deliver the sold real-estate to the buyer and the buyer is obligated to make payment to the seller. Once this has materialised the sale contract becomes valid and produces full legal effects; see also G Mahgoub Ali, *The General Theory of Obligation*: Part One – *Sources of Obligation in Qatari Law* (Doha Modern Printing Press, 2016) 302.

As a rule of thumb, when one of these pillars is tainted with a defect, then the contract will be at risk of being challenged on any of the following grounds: (i) absolute nullity or (ii) relative nullity. Absolute nullity indicates that the contract is invalid from its inception and henceforth does not produce any civil obligations on the parties[3] (in common law jurisdictions, this is known as voidity). Relative nullity, on the other hand, indicates that the contract is valid from its inception but contains a defect that enables the innocent party to either revoke (rescind) or authorise (affirm) the contract (in common law jurisdictions, this is known as voidability). In this particular scenario, if the innocent party elects to revoke a voidable contract, then nullity will cast its shadow on the contract from its inception and not the day it was deemed invalid, that is retroactive impact.

9.2 ABSOLUTE NULLITY (VOID CONTRACTS)

According to article 163 CC:[4]

> An invalid contract shall have no effect, and every concerned party may hold to such invalidity. The court may ex officio rule on such invalidity. An invalid contract may not be corrected by authorisation thereof or by lapse of time. An invalidity suit shall prescribe after a period of 15 years has elapsed from the date of the conclusion of the contract.

The Qatari legislator posits the general rule that void contracts are invalid from their inception and do not give rise to civil obligations or liabilities. The party[5] that acknowledges or upholds such absolute nullity does not require a court order to establish that its void contract is invalid, because absolute nullity manifests itself automatically. Moreover, courts may declare a contract null and void without any pertinent claim by the parties.[6] Unlike relative nullity (voidable contracts) where the innocent party may revoke or authorise the

---

[3] Court of Cassation Judgment 221/2014, where it was held that void contracts invalidated by absolute nullity *do not* exist from their inception and the act of authorisation does not rectify them.

[4] Qatar Law No. 22 of 2004.

[5] We have to pay attention to the term 'concerned party' in Art 163 CC, which refers to (i) the contractual parties themselves; (ii) their general successors, that is, heirs through inheritance and donees; and (iii) their special successors, that is, individuals who gain either personal rights or rights in rem or both through an assignment agreement. For general successors, one should refer to Art 175 CC, whereas for special successors Art 176 CC.

[6] According to the Court of Cassation Judgment 74/2010, a void contract cannot be relied on as a legal ground for any civil obligation. It is not legally binding and cannot be authorised by any party. Every concerned party is entitled to uphold its nullity, and the courts are under obligation to make such declaration without a nullity lawsuit.

contract's defect, absolute nullity (void contracts) cannot be authorised by the innocent party; equally, it does not arise simply because of the 'lapse of time'.[7] The statute of limitations for contractual disputes is fifteen years from the contract's effective date, thus any nullity claim filed after the lapse of fifteen years will automatically fail.

9.2.1 Defective Effects on Consent

In general, contracts tainted with an obstacle error[8] are deemed void and absolutely null. As discussed in Chapter 8, articles 130–133 CC shed light on two types of obstacle errors, namely: (i) common or identical errors and (ii) unilateral errors. Common or identical errors materialise when both parties were under the same errant belief, for example error about the mere existence of the subject-matter. Unilateral errors exist where only one of the parties was acting under an errant belief and the other was aware of the error (bad faith) or could have easily detected such error prior to concluding the contract. The existence of an errant belief is a matter of fact that negates an intention to be bound; it does not encompass therefore misspelling or typing errors, that is indifferent errors.

The only exception to the general rule whereby an obstacle error invalidates consent is 'good faith', because even though errant consent may invalidate the contract, the other party retains the right to substitute the errant subject-matter with one that meets the errant party's intention.[9]

9.2.2 The Effect of a Defect on the Contract's Subject-Matter

Defective subject-matters are chiefly concerned with illegality and/or contravention of public policy. In the civil law tradition, the subject-matter is composed of two elements: (i) the subject of the contract[10] and (ii) the subject of the obligation.[11] The subject of the contract encompasses the underlying

---

[7] Lapse of time means the time granted by law to the innocent party to either revoke or authorise a 'voidable contract', which is not applicable to 'void contracts'. Readers should consult Section 3 of this chapter.

[8] According to the Court of Cassation Judgment 87/2011, an obstacle error as stipulated in Art 130 CC allows the concerned party to seek a declaration of absolute nullity from the court either because (i) of common error; or (ii) a unilateral error where one party was aware of the error or could easily detect it. Courts of substance, namely the court of first instance and the court of appeal have sole jurisdiction to adjudicate on errors of error.

[9] A Faraj Yousef, *Restatement and Commentary of the Kuwaiti Civil Code: Comparative Law Study with the Egyptian Civil Code* (Modern Academic Office 2014) vol 1, at 386.

[10] Arts 149 and 154 CC regulate the subject of the contract.

[11] Arts 148, 150, 151, 152 and 153 CC regulate the subject of the obligation.

transaction that is central to the parties' agreement. The subject of the obligation, on the other hand, means the specific actions or omissions required to
perform the underlying obligations. Examples of the 'subject of the contract'
include but are not limited to: (i) sales contracts, where the transaction consists in the transfer of ownership of the sold goods or services in exchange for a
fee (price) and (ii) lease contracts, entailing the right to use specific property
in exchange for a rental fee. The two elements of the subject-matter complement each other in relation to a potential defect in the contract.[12]

A defect in the subject-matter renders the contract void (absolute nullity).
It can be construed from the CC that a three-step test in order to establish a
defect in the subject-matter is as follows: (i) is the subject-matter in existence or
likely to exist in the future? (ii) is the subject-matter identified in the contract
or past commercial practices? (iii) is the subject-matter permitted by law?[13]

9.2.2.1 Existence of Subject-Matter

The Qatari legislator permitted agreements concerning a subject-matter that
either exists or which is likely to exist at some point in the future. However,
the law prohibits agreement on a subject-matter that is impossible to exist at
any time (absolute impossibility). If the subject-matter perishes following the
conclusion of the contract, the ensuing absolute nullity will impact the contract and render it invalid. Furthermore, if the cause of perish was the result
of *force majeure*, the contract will be terminated from the day the intervening
event occurred and not from the contract's effective date. Moreover, if the
obligor has caused or contributed to the perish of sold goods, then the obligee
is entitled to a remedy, that is compensatory performance. The law strictly
prohibits agreement on a subject-matter involving hereditary wills because it
contravenes Qatar's public policy.[14]

9.2.2.2 Identification of Subject-Matter

The subject-matter must be identifiable either explicitly in the contract or
construed from the contract itself, in addition to the intention of the contracting parties or their past commercial practices. For example, a sale must

---

[12] Mahgoub (n 2) 268–269.
[13] Mahgoub (n 2) 270.
[14] Qatar applies Islamic inheritance law as stipulated in the Family Law (Qatar Law No. 22 of
2006), where the gross inheritance must be divided among all heirs after deducting (i) the
deceased person's debts; and (ii) gifts to non-heirs up-to one-third of the net inheritance if
there is a will (donation agreement) to prove such gifts. There are certain exceptions and
conditions, but this will not be discussed here as it falls outside the scope of this book.

contain a description of the goods, quantity, quality, price per item and delivery details (incoterms). If any of the above elements is missing, the court may adapt the contract through a construction based on the parties' prior commercial conduct. If subject-matter cannot be identified, the contract is invalid.[15]

9.2.2.3 Legality of Subject-Matter

The legality of the subject-matter is straightforward. Contracts must not be illicit or attempt to contravene public policy.[16] If such a defect materialises, then no civil obligation is established and thus the contract becomes null and void. This outcome is consistent with article 151 CC whereby: 'a contract shall be void if the subject matter of the obligation breaches public order[17] or morality'.

9.2.3 *The Impact of Defects on Cause*

A simple method to differentiate between the contract's subject-matter and its cause is by using the 'what' and 'why' questions; the subject-matter is the answer to 'what is the civil obligation which the obligor has to perform?' The

---

[15] According to the Court of Cassation Judgment 163/2011, subject-matter must not be explicitly identifiable in a contract as long as there is sufficient information allowing its identification from the parties' intention at the time of concluding the contract.

[16] According to the Court of Cassation Judgment 348/2015, any civil obligation contravening public policy is strictly invalid (absolute nullity) pursuant to Arts 151 and 155 CC. The Court of Cassation has the jurisdiction to define the legal principle of public policy. Henceforth, public policy is defined as a collection of essential principles which fosters the political system [as established by the constitution], social fabric, economic rules and moral values, and thus collectively create the main pillars of society and achieve public interest. Even if the legal principle of public policy is codified in any legislation, its meaning must not be limited to the legislative text because it has a wider implication that makes it independent of any legislative text. If any legislation contains a general rule that either commands or prohibits a certain action (or omission of action) due to its association with public policy, compliance with this general rule is mandatory to protect public interest and any deviation contrary to the general rule is strictly prohibited. Thus, any contractual agreement that contravenes public policy is invalid and the nullity in this regard is absolute and the parties must be reinstated to the position they were before the void contract was concluded. If restoration of the contracting parties' condition is impossible, then courts have discretion to award damages (i.e. compensation) to the concerned party.

[17] Public order is synonymous with 'public policy'. According to Mahgoub (n 2) 281, public order is defined as a collection of rules, which serves as a societal pillar in the fields of politics, economy and social issues. Public morality, on the other hand, is a set of rules that reflects the acceptable mainstream morals in a society at a specific point in time. Public morality serves as a pillar to protect society from corruption and differs from one society to another. As a result, it is best described as a set of relative rules not absolute.

cause is the answer to 'why is the obligor liable to perform a civil obligation?'[18] Qatari law has adopted the modern theory of cause under the civil law tradition, which requires the assessment of two factors, namely: (i) direct cause and (ii) impulsive motive. Direct cause deals with intrinsic matters, which can be derived directly from the contract itself. Thus, 'direct cause' is considered an objective assessment by legal scholars. On the other hand, impulsive motive deals with extrinsic matters, which although not stated in the contract could be derived from either the intention of the parties at the time of concluding the contract or the foreseeability of an unlawful cause. Unlike direct cause, the impulsive motive is considered a subjective assessment because it looks at the behaviour of the contracting parties.[19]

Article 155 CC dictates that:

> A contract shall be revoked where the obligation of a contracting party is *without good cause*[20] or *unlawful*.
>
> In the determination of good cause, the motive for concluding the contract shall be taken into account if the other contracting party was aware or must have been aware thereof.

The Qatari legislator aims to cast absolute nullity on all contracts which: (i) do not have a 'good cause', that is the existence of direct cause and/or (ii) 'unlawful' cause, that is illegal impulsive motive. The main objective here is that 'good cause' serves as a protection for innocent parties concluding a contract lacking a valid cause. On the other hand, the strict prohibition of 'unlawful cause' is meant to protect society at large from contracts which are unlawful or contravene public policy.[21]

According to the Court of Cassation, the general rule for 'will' (الإرادة) is legality.[22] The contracting parties' will is respected by law and is not nullified

---

[18] Mahgoub (n 2) 288.

[19] Mahgoub (n 2) 296.

[20] See Court of Cassation Judgment 107/2008, where it was held that if a contract includes an explicit provision on its cause, this does not necessarily mean that the written cause is true. The cause may be challenged before the courts, where claimants have the burden to show that a civil obligation is *without good cause*. In general, only *written* evidence is admissible in order to challenge the cause of a *written* contract. However, an exception was granted to commercial contracts, where non-written evidence is admissible (e.g. testimonies on accepted commercial practices).

[21] According to the Court of Cassation Judgment 40/2009, when a contract is nullified because it contravened public policy, then the respondent cannot acquire good title (i.e. ownership) of properties received as contractual damages because the sale contract in dispute does not legally exist. Thus, granting compensation for the loss of ownership of those properties, which the defendants never owned in the first place, is impermissible.

[22] Court of Cassation Judgments 87/2010 and 32/2014.

unless the civil obligation that arises from such will is either illicit or in conflict with public policy (this is applicable for both the subject-matter and cause of the contract in question). Also, the contracting parties' will must not conflict with a statutory requirement (whether commanding or prohibitive).

9.3 RELATIVE NULLITY (VOIDABLE CONTRACTS)

As discussed earlier, most of the defects which tarnish consent will cast relative nullity on a contract in order to protect the innocent party and allow it to either authorise or revoke the contract. that is the contract was valid from its inception and legally binding on the parties but its defect rendered it voidable. Such defects include threat or coercion, exploitation, fraud[23] and injustice.[24] Article 158 of CC states that:

'A voidable contract shall be effective unless revoked. Where revoked, such contract shall be deemed void ab initio'.

Article 159 of the CC goes on to explain that:

'Where the law recognises the right of one of the contracting parties to revoke the contract, the other party cannot avail himself of this right. Where the right of revocation is available and the holder thereof requests its enforcement, the court shall so enforce it, unless the law provides otherwise'.

The law stipulates that voidable contracts are binding and have full legal effect until the innocent party elects to either authorise or revoke the contract in question. If the voidable contract is revoked, nullity will be deemed from the contract's effective date. The courts do not have the discretion to revoke or authorise a voidable contract without a request from the innocent party; unlike void contracts, where the courts possess such discretion to annul.

---

[23] Court of Cassation Judgment 112/2008, holding that pursuant to Arts 134 & 135 CC deceit that leads an innocent party to fraud can be manifested with either positive or negative action from the counter-party. Positive action exists when the counter-party or its representative intentionally deceives the innocent party to induce it to enter into a contract, whereas the negative action (i.e. omission of action) arises where the counter-party or its representative hides an essential fact that the innocent party was unaware of at the time of concluding the contract. Henceforth, the innocent party is legally entitled to authorise or revoke the voidable contract following a declaration that it would not have concluded it had it been aware of the fraudulent action.

[24] Court of Cassation Judgment 46/2009, where the court concluded that fraud tarnishing consent must arise from deceitful actions and means, which mislead the innocent party that subsequently becomes unable to make an informed decision. A mere lie does not amount to fraud unless it is proven that the innocent party could not *reasonably* figure out the truth. If the innocent party could figure it out, then there is no fraud.

Moreover, the obligees and special successors cannot file a claim to revoke or authorise a voidable contract.[25]

Article 160 CC further states that:

> 'Where a voidable contract is authorised by the party holding the right of revocation, whether express or implied, such right shall not be applicable to the defect, the cause of such authorisation'.

The law makes it crystal clear that once the innocent party authorises a voidable contract, whether explicitly or implicitly, the contract is rectified for good and any future claim on the same grounds (i.e. defect) will not be admissible. Furthermore, the authorisation of a voidable contract by the innocent party is considered a waiver of its right to uphold relative nullity that can be exercised unilaterally in bilateral agreements.

Article 161 C goes on to emphasise that:

> 'Unless the law provides otherwise, the right to demand the revocation of a contract shall be prescribed if not invoked within three years from the date on which the right arose.
>
> Prescription shall run: in the case of legal incapacity, from the date of the cessation of such incapacity; in the case of error or fraudulent misrepresentation, from the date on which the error or misrepresentation is discovered; in the case of coercion, from the date it has ceased.
>
> In all cases, the right to demand the revocation of a contract as a result of error, fraudulent representation or coercion shall lapse after a period of fifteen years has elapsed from the date of the conclusion of the contract'.

The law here regulates statutory limitations for voidable contracts. The innocent party may elect to authorise or revoke a voidable contract within three years from the date on which: (i) legal capacity is either gained in case of a minor that reaches the age of consent (i.e. eighteen years old in most jurisdictions) or recovered in the case of an intoxicated adult; (ii) fraud is discovered and (iii) coercion or exploitation ceases to exist. However, a claim will not be admissible after the lapse of fifteen years from the date of concluding the voidable contract. Thus, the statutory limitation materialises when the due date of one of the above periods elapses first (either 3 or 15 years).

Article 162 CC states that:

> 'Any concerned party may notify the party holding the right of revocation to declare its intention to authorise or revoke such contract no later than three months from the date of such notice.

---

[25] Faraj Yousef (n 9) 482.

A notice shall not be effective unless given during the time limit before the right of revocation lapses.

Where the period of the notice expires without a declaration of authorisation or revocation of the contract having been made, such omission shall be deemed authorisation of the contract, provided that the notice is given to such party in person'.

As mentioned earlier, voidable contracts are vulnerable to revocation and thus the law permits any concerned party to notify the innocent party in writing to seek a declaration of its stance on the defect. The innocent party may declare its intention to either authorise or revoke the contract within three months from the date of serving the written notice. If no declaration is made by the innocent party within the prescribed period, its silence will be deemed an authorisation of the voidable contract and henceforth the risk of annulment is lifted. The law here emphasises that the written notice must be delivered *in person* to the innocent party as a prerequisite for the commencement of the three-month period.

9.4 EFFECTS OF NULLITY

Article 164 CC makes it clear that:

Where a contract is void or annulled, the contracting parties shall be reinstated to the position they were in prior to the conclusion of the contract. Where such reinstatement is impossible, damages equivalent to any loss incurred may be awarded.

Where, however, a contract concluded by a person without legal capacity or with deficient capacity is invalid or annulled by reason of such lack of capacity or deficient capacity, such person shall only be liable to refund any profits he realised from the performance of the contract'.

The effect of nullity on void contracts and 'revoked' voidable contracts is the same. These contracts *do not* have any binding effect on the parties and thus cease to exist. The law aims here to reinstate the contracting parties to the position they were in prior to concluding the annulled contract (the legal principle of restitution). As a result, each contracting party is liable to return to its counter-party(ies) any money owed in relation to the annulled contract. However, when such reinstatement is impossible or the counter-party(ies) have acted in 'good faith', the concerned parties are entitled to seek damages (i.e. compensation) for the loss suffered.

The second paragraph of article 164 CC sheds light on an important issue related to minors and other individuals who lacked legal capacity at the time of concluding the contract due to illness, intoxication, etc. These innocent parties have the right to either authorise or revoke a voidable contract to which they previously consented once the legal capacity is gained or restored. Nevertheless, the law requires the implementation of the rules of 'unjust enrichment'.[26] Hence, the innocent party should refund its counter-party(ies) in order to achieve restitution. Minors and individuals who lacked legal capacity are liable to refund only the money they used and which *added value* to their life. Thus, any wasted money spent foolishly/recklessly prior to gaining legal capacity is exempted by law from liability to refund one's counter-party(ies). The law intends to protect and *not punish* individuals who lacked the legal capacity for their past actions.

Article 165 CC makes it clear that:

> 'The invalidity of title-transferring contracts shall not be effective against a special successor that may receive a right in kind from either contracting party, provided that such successor received such right as indemnity in good faith.
>
> A special successor shall be considered a bona fide party if, at the time of transfer thereto, this successor was not aware of the reason for revoking the contract of its predecessor, and could not have known of such reason if the successor exercised prudent and reasonable judgement'.

The law protects third parties acquiring a good title of property (applicable for both real-estate and chattels) through a sales agreement or donation (i.e. gift) concluded with a party to an annulled contract. The third party must have acted in 'good faith' at the time of concluding the deal and must not have been aware or could not reasonably foresee that the property in question was not owned by such party. Thus, the test of 'good faith' and 'reasonableness' will be applied to verify if the third party is eligible for legal protection. Article 166 CC states that:

> 'Where any provision of the contract is invalid or voidable, such provision only shall be revoked, unless it is evident that the contract would not have been concluded without such provision, in which event the contract shall be revoked in full'.

The Qatari legislator has adopted the legal principle of 'reduction of contract'[27] to avoid nullifying the whole contract if only a specific provision/clause is voidable or invalid. However, if the voidable or invalid clause is fundamental to the contract as a whole, then the contract cannot be saved and the inevitable fate of absolute nullity will materialise. The claimants in any contractual dispute have

---

[26] Faraj Yousef (n 9) 497.

[27] A reduction of contracts operates in a similar manner to severability clauses in common law contracts.

the burden to show that the offending provisions/clauses are indivisible from the whole contract; otherwise, the court will rule in favour of invalidating the offending provisions/clauses and thus retain the remaining provisions of the contract. It is worth noting that the court is not permitted to save the contract from absolute nullity if the parties collectively *did not intend* to save it; an exception is possible if there is *an explicit statutory requirement* to do otherwise. Henceforth, the court will reinforce the application of the law.[28]

Article 167 CC states that:

> 'Where a void or voidable contract contains the elements of another contract, the contract shall be deemed valid to the extent of the other contract, whose elements are available if the intention of the contracting parties indicates that they wish to conclude such other contract'.

The Qatari legislator has adopted the legal principle of 'conversion of contract', whereby the remaining enforceable provisions of an annulled contract may create a new valid contract. There are certain conditions which must be met for the conversion to take place. The first is that conversion is only available to void contracts (absolute nullity) but not voidable contracts (relative nullity) because the latter may be reduced by the courts rather than converted. The second condition demands that annulled contracts must include all the elements of the newly converted contract without adding new elements. The third and last condition is related to the will and intention of the contracting parties, that is the court must determine the willingness of the parties to enter into the newly converted contract if they were aware of the defect that annulled their original contract. If the parties collectively insisted that they *did not* intend to enter into the converted contract, the courts cannot force such conversion.[29]

Article 168 CC states that:

> 'Where a contract is invalid or revoked due to an error committed by either party; the other party or any third party may claim indemnity for any damage that may arise from such invalidity or revocation.
>
> Indemnity shall not be applicable if the party suffering damage due to such invalidity or revocation may have contributed to such damage, or knew or should have known of the cause of such damage.
>
> The provisions of this Article shall be subject to the provisions of Article 117 of this Law'.

The law permits any concerned party that was negatively impacted by the annulment of a contract to have recourse to damages (indemnity/compensation) for

---

[28] Mahgoub (n 2) 327–329.
[29] Mahgoub (n 2) 329–331.

any loss sustained. However, it is worth highlighting that these damages cannot be sought under the contract because once the contract is annulled it has no legal effect. Such damages can be sought under the law of delict (i.e. torts in the common law tradition).[30] The courts will apply the rules of negligence to determine damages. Paragraph 2 of article 168 CC prohibits the claimant from receiving any damages if it contributed to the defect that caused the annulment of the original contract. This is contrary to the general rule of 'contributory negligence' whereby the party entitled to damages will receive a reduced compensation that reflects its contribution to the negligence.

9.5 NULLITY OF SPECIAL CONTRACTS

9.5.1 *Sales Contract*

Article 95 CL[31] states that:

> 'Where at the time of contract the two contracting parties note the possibility of damage to an item, the item may be sold and the Buyer shall not get his money back if the sale item is in fact damaged. The sale shall be void if the Seller was confident that such damage would definitely occur'.

The contracting parties are permitted under the Commercial Law to conclude a sales contract where the subject-matter (i.e. sold goods) is foreseen to be damaged; however, if such probability materialises after concluding the deal, then the buyer is not entitled to seek refund from the seller because it was aware of such risk and accepted it from the outset. Nevertheless, if the seller was confident that the subject-matter would become damaged, then it is prohibited from proceeding with such a sale transaction and any sales contract that results from such action will be deemed invalid (absolute nullity) due to unilateral error.

Article 247 CL states that:

> 'Any agreement concluded at the time of the mortgage decision or after the decision shall be invalid. In the event of failure to pay the debt at maturity, the mortgagee shall have the right to own the mortgaged property or sell the same without reference to the procedures set out in Articles 241 to 243 herein.

---

[30] See Court of Cassation Judgment 125/2008, granting damages to a concerned party who suffered loss due to nullification of a contract. Such damages are governed by the law of delict. Equally, Court of Cassation Judgment 60/2012, awarding damages to be awarded to the counterparty negatively impacted due to nullifying the contract must be determined in accordance to the rules of 'enrichment without cause'; that is, the calculation of damages must take into account two factors, namely (i) the profit gained from the invalid contract; and (ii) the loss suffered from the such contract, with the lesser value of the two granted by the court.

[31] Qatar Law No 27 of 2006.

However, after the debt or an instalment thereof becomes payable the creditor may agree with his debtor that the mortgaged property or part thereof may be credited against the debt, and the court may order that the mortgagee owns the mortgaged property or part thereof in payment of the debt provided that its market value is estimated by an expert'.

Article 247 CL prohibits property owners (real-estate or chattels) from selling their property if such property was used as collateral to secure the payment of a debt, namely a mortgage transaction. The Qatari legislator aims to protect creditors and maintain a legal stability of transactions. Thus, any attempt to sell one's encumbered estate is invalid due to the defect of illegality on both subject-matter and cause (i.e. absolute nullity of the sales contract).[32]

Article 459 CL goes on to emphasise that:

'Obligations of minors and their equivalent, who are not authorised to transfer, arising from their signatures on bills of exchange as drawers, endorsers or in any other capacity, shall be null and void for them only.

They may adhere to this nullification in respect of any holder of a bill of exchange, even where the latter has acted in good faith'.

The law here sheds light on the consent of minors or individuals who lack legal capacity to authorise commercial instruments such as cheques. As discussed earlier, relative nullity is an inevitable outcome of this defect and the commercial instrument in question will become voidable. Once the legal capacity is gained or restored, the issuer of this commercial instrument may authorise or revoke it against the holder, even if the latter has acted in good faith.

---

[32] Another example of strict prohibition of selling a property under mortgage is stipulated in Qatar Court of Cassation Judgment 221/2014, where the court held that Art 10 of the Housing Law (Qatar Law no. 2 of 2007), which replaced the obsolete Public Housing Law (Qatar Law no. 1 of 1964), obligates the beneficiary to abstain from selling the block of land or the residential property granted by the government for a period of fifteen (15) years from the date of handing the property to the beneficiary, in addition to making a full payment of the housing loan. This prohibition includes, but not limited, to the conveyance of all rights in rem of the property to third-party(ies). The exception to this general rule is where the beneficiary after the lapse of fifteen (15) years has submitted sufficient guarantee to Qatar Development Bank (creditor for the housing loan) and sought its consent to proceed with such conveyance. Any contrary agreement is invalid (absolute nullity) and the effect of such defect applies not only to the beneficiary but also to its general and special successors. The prohibition contained in this general rule is aimed to protect public interest, where the government intends to (i) provide housing to citizens with limited income; and (ii) prevent [misusing/abusing] the housing system for trading purposes. Void contracts cannot be affirmed because absolute nullity tarnishes them from their inception, even if the contracting parties agree to proceed with the real-estate registration requirements at a later stage after meeting all statuary conditions. The real-estate registration requirements are essential elements for a valid conveyance not a pending condition that can wait. In Judgment 62/2013, the Court of Cassation held that selling a mortgaged real-estate is strictly prohibited by law in accordance with Arts 1085 and 1080 CC. Any contrary agreement concluded contravenes public policy and thus is null and void (absolute nullity).

The Court of Cassation has ruled that sales contracts contravening public policy are null and void. In the case at hand the appellant was a foreign broker who practised brokerage (a regulated commercial activity) in Qatar without a Qatari partner holding 51% equity ownership, which is strictly prohibited.[33] The Court stipulated that the appellant cannot rely on an invalid contract to seek damages. A similar case concluded that a commercial contract between a foreign national who operated a private school in Qatar (school principal) and the Qatari partner was invalid because it violated public policy in accordance with paragraph 9 of article 5 CL.[34] The law requires any foreign national who intends to operate any authorised commercial activity in Qatar to meet two main criteria, namely: (i) involve a Qatari partner who owns 51% of the business equity and (ii) obtain a valid licence from the competent public authority. The appellant in this particular case concluded a contract with a Qatari national who acted as a 'sham' partner in the business. The foreign school principal received the full revenue of the business and was liable for all its losses, whereas the Qatari partner received a lump sum of QAR 400,000 per annum in exchange for this partnership. The Qatari partner did not get involved in the business and had no role in managing the venture. Even though the foreign school principal had a valid licence issued by the Ministry of Education to manage the private school, the mere fact of the 'sham' partnership violated Qatar's public policy. Thus, the contract was deemed void from its inception and produced no legally binding effects.

9.5.2 *Lease Contracts*

Lease contracts and their associated defects are regulated, in addition to the CC, by specialised legislation. Article 12 of the Property Leasing Law[35] states that:

> 'The existing lease shall form part of the title of a new owner even if such lease is not specifically dated on a date preceding the conveyance of such title, unless it is proven that the lease is null or void'.

If a real-estate owner decides to sell rented property to a third party, the lease becomes a right in *rem* that is attached to the sold property in favour of the lessee, who has a valid lease contract that goes beyond the conveyance effective date. Unless the lease contract is void or revoked by an innocent party (voidable contract), the existing lease at the time of conveyance of such title has no effect.

---

[33] Court of Cassation Judgment 102/2010.
[34] Court of Cassation Judgment 60/2012.
[35] Qatar Law No. 4 of 2008.

9.5.3 *Labour Contracts*

Just like leases, labour agreements are subject to specialised legislation. Article 4 of the Labour Law (LL)[36] states that:

'The rights prescribed by this Law represent the minimum rights of workers. Therefore, any conditions contrary to the provisions of this Law, even if made prior to its effectiveness, shall be [null] and void unless they are more advantageous to the worker. Any release, compromise or waiver of the entitlements prescribed herein for the worker shall be deemed [as null][37] and void'.

In addition, article 43 LL stipulates that:

'Any condition stipulated in the employment contract, even if the employment contract precedes the enforcement date of this Law, shall be considered [as null] and void if it included an undertaking from the worker to work for life with the employer, or abstain from carrying out for life any other craft or profession that could be practised after leaving the employment.

If the nature of the work allows the worker to know the clients of the employer or the secrets of the business of the establishment, the employer may stipulate a condition that the worker shall not compete with him or participate in any competing project after expiry of the employment contract. Such stipulation shall be confined in its duration and place and type of the work to the extent necessary for protection of the lawful interests of the employer, and shall not exceed two years'.

The Labour Law emphasises that the prescribed rights granted to workers establish minimum rights, that is the 'floor'. Thus, any agreement between the parties aiming to circumvent these minimum rights, even if waived by the worker, is unlawful.[38] The defect here is related to illegality that tarnishes both subject-matter and the cause of the labour contract. For example, a worker who signs a contract subjecting him or her to life-time employment is unenforceable because 'life-time employment' is deemed slavery and servitude, both of which infringe international law and the Qatari constitutional order.

---

[36] Qatar Law No. 14 of 2004 as amended by Decree-Law No. 22 of 2007, Law No. 6 of 2009, Law No. 3 of 2014, Law No. 1 of 2015, Law No. 13 of 2017 and Decree-Law No. 18 of 2020.

[37] Missing words from the English translation of Art 4 LL as provided by Al Meezan online portal.

[38] According to the Court of Cassation's Judgment 92/2011, employees are prohibited from waiving their minimum statutory rights in accordance with Art 4 LL. The employee in this particular case signed a final settlement on 22 February 2007, waiving all occupational benefits. However, facts presented before the court showed that the worker continued to work for its employer many months after the signatory date. Thus, this final settlement was found to be unlawful and invalid (absolute nullity).

Such defect of illegality will render the contract null and void. that is absolute nullity. Furthermore, the law prohibits employers from attempting to *prevent* their workers from trading in the same profession after the expiration or termination of the labour contract *for life*. The law takes into consideration the employer's concern for protecting its trade secrets and hence allows them to restrict former employees from using knowledge acquired from their employment for a period that does not exceed two years from the expiry or termination of the labour contract. Furthermore, the employer must define in the same provision the place where the worker is prevented to trade against the former employer during the limited period of time. The law aims to strike a balance between the employers' legitimate concern while protecting the worker's rights from potential abuse.

Article 81 LL states that:

> 'The worker may not waive his right to annual leave. Any agreement to the contrary shall be [null] and void. If the employment contract ended, for any reason, before taking such leave, the worker shall be entitled to a cash alternative equivalent to his payment for the due leave days'.

Another example related to the defect of illegality on both subject-matter and cause in labour contracts arises when the contract is subjected to a term that deprives employees of the entitlement to a paid annual leave. Such deprivation may amount to modern-day slavery and servitude. Thus, the law prohibits any agreement in this regard and deems it null and void, i.e. absolute nullity. Employees are entitled to claim for a compensation for any unutilised paid annual leave.

The Court of Cassation held that workers who practice a profession without obtaining the proper licence from the competent public body may not file a claim for contractual breach because such worker has violated Qatar's public policy, and thus the labour contract in question is null and void from its inception (absolute nullity).[39] The contracting parties cannot elect to authorise or settle it by themselves. The appellant in this particular case was a nurse who practised nursing in Qatar without obtaining a proper licence from the Ministry of Public Health. This illegality tarnished the cause and/or subject-matter of the labour contract and no associated claim for contractual damages was available.

---

[39] Court of Cassation Judgment 22/2011.

10

Performance and Damages

10.1 INTRODUCTION

We briefly mentioned in Chapter 2 that the main source of contractual obligations under Qatari contract law arises from (i) the contract itself; (ii) the intention of the parties at the time of forming the contract; and lastly (iii) the relevant laws regulating contractual affairs. Here, we need to highlight the fact that obligations,[1] in general, under the civil law are comprised of three tiers:[2] (i) civil obligations; (ii) natural obligations; and (iii) moral duties. Understanding these is vital to one's appreciation of the contractual performance. Civil obligations include statutory and contractual undertakings, such as the sale of goods and services. Civil obligations also include civil-wrongdoings, which are governed by the law of delict under the CC. Civil-wrongdoings are concerned with personal injury, negligence, defamation, mental distress, etc. All civil obligations are enforceable.

Natural obligations were originally treated as civil obligations, but due to prescription, they became unenforceable. The third and last tier comprises moral duties such as charity works and 'informal' gifts or donations, etc. It is important to note that civil obligations are predicated on two pillars, namely: (i) liability and (ii) debt. Liability represents the legal dimension of obligations and arises by virtue of contract and/or law. Debt, on the other hand, represents the financial value of an obligation. When liability fails by reason

---

[1] Obligations are legal bonds (in Latin *'vinculum iuris'*) between one or more parties (such as obligors and obligees, creditor and debtor, etc.), who undertake to act or refrain from acting as per the terms and conditions of their agreement.

[2] This classification is common in the civil law tradition, which generally recognizes three types of obligations, namely: imperfect obligations [moral duties], natural obligations, and civil or perfect obligations. See K Shaw Spaht and H Alston Johnson II, 'Private Law: Obligations' (1976) 37 Louisiana L Rev 332.

of prescription, civil obligations are automatically converted into natural obligations and are no longer enforceable. Thus, natural obligations comprise a single pillar, namely debt.

10.2 COMPULSORY PERFORMANCE (INCLUDING DAMAGES)

The civil law of obligations regulates the implementation of the 'three-tier' system as illustrated in Figure 10.1, whereby only civil obligations are enforceable, unlike natural obligations and moral duties, which although not enforced are nonetheless recognised. Qatari legislators have followed the civil law system in dividing the performance of obligations into two types: (i) specific performance and (ii) compensatory performance (damages). Article 241 CC states that:

(i) Where the obligor fails to perform his obligations voluntarily, such obligation shall be enforced.

(ii) However, where the obligation is natural, it may not be enforced.

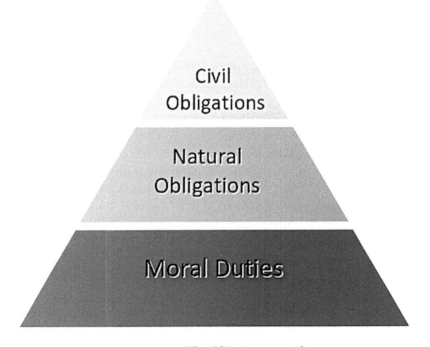

FIGURE 10.1 The obligations pyramid

Article 241 CC emphasises the importance of the general rule whereby [civil] obligations must be performed by the obligor voluntarily. However, where the obligor fails to fulfil its [civil] obligation, the courts will enforce the performance. It is worth noting that compulsory performance dictates that the obligor must fulfil its civil obligations with 'reasonable care'. The test of reasonableness here does not require the obligor to achieve a specific objective unless the parties agreed during the negotiation and prior to finalising the contract that the obligor must achieve such a specific objective. In such cases, the court must respect the parties' intentions.

10.2.1 *Determination of Natural Obligations*

Article 242 CC stipulates that:

> In the absence of an express provision, the court shall determine whether an obligation is natural or not. In all cases, a natural obligation shall not breach public order.

The law here grants the courts *discretion* to decide the applicable classification to a particular obligation (whether natural or moral duty), where no explicit statutory provision exists. As a rule of thumb, natural obligations should never breach public order. The role of the judge in this particular scenario is closer to that of a legislator because of the unlimited discretion conferred upon the courts. The judge should consider the spirit of the law, natural law principles and jurisprudence. In this respect, the courts must apply a 'three-step' test to verify if an obligation is natural or a mere moral duty. The first step is meant to determine whether the obligation in question is a demoted 'civil obligation' due to prescription or a moral duty transformed into a natural obligation. Step two asks whether there exists a 'sense' of obligation to perform the duty in question by the obligor. Finally the last step, asks whether the said obligation or duty is in compliance with public order.[3]

Article 243 CC goes on to state that:

> An obligor may not recover any voluntary payment made by him in the performance of a natural obligation, nor shall such payment be considered a voluntary contribution.

Although natural obligations are unenforceable, any voluntary fulfilment thereof is deemed as non-recoverable payment of a debt. The obligor cannot

---

3 A Farag Yousuf, *Restatement and Commentary of the Kuwaiti Civil Code: Comparative Law Study with the Egyptian Civil Code* (Modern Academic Office 2014) vol. 2, at 780–781.

claim that such payment is a contribution or a donation because he or she owed that amount of money (or payment in kind) to the obligee:

In this vein, article 244 CC claims that:

> a natural obligation may, depending on the circumstances, be sufficient to found a civil obligation.

The Qatari legislator here provides a circumstance where a natural obligation is elevated to a civil obligation, namely when the obligor *promises* to fulfil the said obligation to the obligee. Such a promise or undertaking may be enforceable because it is within the realm of public order for obligors to pay their debts to obligees. Thus, the aim here is to protect the stability of economic transactions.

It is worth noting that when an obligor voluntarily fulfils a natural obligation, a subsequent 'set-off[4] between the natural obligation with another civil obligation *is prohibited*. Moreover, natural obligations cannot be guaranteed by a third party because a guarantee, as a matter of principle, is only available to civil obligations. Last but not least, if an obligor (a natural person) voluntarily fulfils its natural obligation at the death-bed, such fulfilment will be deemed as a contribution or 'informal' donation to the obligee; unless the obligee proves that the fulfilment in question concerned a debt created by a natural obligation, which is recognised by law.[5]

10.2.2 *Specific Performance*

The general rule for the enforcement of civil obligations is 'specific performance', that is, the law here expects obligors to voluntarily[6] comply with the

---

[4] The principle of 'set-off' is regulated by Arts 390 to 397 CC. The Court of Cassation, in Judgment 181/2011 has interpreted set-off as competing or opposing civil obligations (debts) arising from a contractual relationship. If the contracting parties have a commercial relationship and/or previous trade transactions, which resulted in such competing debts, then each party is a creditor to the other party in one transaction but at the same time, the said party is a debtor to the other in another transaction (simultaneously). The parties in this case may 'set-off' these debts when they settle the payments.

[5] Yousuf (n 3), at 782–785.

[6] See Court of Cassation Judgments 80 & 104/2015, in its interpretation of Arts 241(1), 245, 251 and 255 CC. It pointed out that when the court enforces compulsory performance of a civil obligation against the obligor, this action must not be understood as coercing the obligor; specific performance has a condition that must be met at all times, namely 'feasibility'. If specific performance is no longer feasible for any reason, the court will switch its course to compensatory performance. The Court of Cassation elaborated that the obligors' dignity and rights are protected by law and that the obligees' contractual right to request specific performance is limited to the obligor's resources. The rule is that the court may enforce specific performance

undertakings they made to their obligee(s) and perform the specific task to the satisfaction of the obligee(s). The 'conditional' exception to this general rule is the payment of compensation (in cash or in-kind) either in full or part in exchange for non-performance or partial performance by the obligor. Article 245 CC states that:

(i) Upon the obligor being notified, the obligation shall be enforced in kind, as soon as possible.

(ii) However, where enforcement in kind is extremely onerous to the obligor, the court may, at the request of the obligor, limit the right of the obligee to indemnity, provided that he suffers no serious prejudice thereby.

Paragraph 1 of article 245 CC clearly states that the obligee must *notify* the obligor *in writing* to fulfil its civil obligation by performing the contractual undertakings as agreed between the contracting parties. If the obligor does not set a deadline for performance, the obligor is expected to fulfil its obligation *within a reasonable time*. However, in paragraph 2 of the same article, if specific performance by the obligor is likely to produce an adverse impact, compensatory performance is permitted to mitigate that risk. As mentioned earlier, compensatory performance is a 'conditional' exception subject to: (i) serving a 'written notice' to the obligor with or without a deadline and (ii) specific performance is likely to cause *a severe adverse effect* to the obligor. Specific performance requires a balance between the interests of both contracting parties and hence specific performance *will not* be imposed where it is likely to result in great harm to the obligor(s); a minor harm to the obligor(s) is, however, acceptable.

Civil law jurisprudence has emphasised that specific performance relies on four elements:

i.   It must be feasible;
ii. the obligee must demand specific performance, or the obligor must elect to perform its civil obligation in this particular manner;
iii. specific performance must not adversely impact the obligor; and

on the obligor only when such performance *does not* require the obligor's intervention. Thus, the court may step-in and fill that gap by ruling in favour of the obligee, in which case its decision will be deemed as a replacement of the obligor's specific performance. However, when specific performance requires the obligor's intervention, the court may: (i) impose monetary penalties on the obligor in order to induce him/her to perform in-kind, provided that the obligee has requested specific performance; or (ii) grant compensatory performance to the obligee, if either the obligee does not request specific performance or the obligor refuses to intervene and perform in-kind.

iv. a written notification must be served by the obligee to the obligor *on or before* the expiration of a specified or an agreed deadline, if such deadline exists from the outset, or within 'reasonable time' as mandated by the law or accepted commercial practice.[7]

10.2.2.1 Transfer of Ownership

Article 246 CC states that:

> The obligation to transfer title or any other right in kind shall automatically transfer such right, provided that the subject-matter of the obligation is a self-identified thing held by the obligor and subject to the rules in connection with registration.

Here the law provides rules governing the transfer of title and ownership of property (both real-estate and chattels) as part of fulfilling a civil obligation as a means of specific performance. If a contractual undertaking between obligee and obligor states that during the lifetime of the agreement, ownership of certain objects will be transferred from the obligor to the obligee, then once this condition materialises, the transfer of 'title and ownership' to the obligee is instantaneous by virtue of contract and law, with the exception of the statutory requirement to register such a property. Thus, there is a 'grace period' between the specific performance for a property that is intended to be transferred to the obligee and the time when 'title and ownership' passes from the obligor to the obligee after registration. Two conditions are required in order for the obligee to claim title and ownership of an object:

i.   The said object must be owned by the obligor at the time of forming the binding contract with the obligee, or the title and ownership must have been acquired by the obligor during the lifetime of the contract and

ii. the said object must not contain a right *in rem* over which third parties have a right to in 'good faith', such as a mortgage or easement.[8]

Article 247 CC states that:

(i) Where the obligation relates to the transfer of a right in kind to a thing identifiable only by its kind, such right shall not be transferred until such thing is apportioned.

---

[7] Yousuf, above (n 3), at 787.
[8] Ibid, at 793.

(ii) Where the obligor fails to perform his obligation, the obligee may, with the permission of the court, or without its permission in the case of an emergency, obtain a thing of the same kind at the expense of the obligor. The obligee may also demand the value of the thing, without prejudice in either event to his right to indemnity.

The law stipulates that if the civil obligation requires the transfer of a particular object to the obligee, then the mere transfer of another object, even if similar, will not suffice. Specific performance of such civil obligation is mandatory and a monetary compensation is not acceptable as a general rule. If the obligor refuses to perform as the law requires, then the obligee must serve a written notice to the obligor and remind him or her to fulfil this civil obligation. If the obligor responds in writing confirming its refusal to perform, the law permits the obligee to file a claim to the court for compensatory performance (indemnity) from the obligor for the full damage; or even claim it directly from the obligor without judicial determination in the case of an emergency. Compensatory performance constitutes a valid exception in this case, not because specific performance is impossible but because of the confirmed refusal of the obligor to perform its contractual undertaking.

If the civil obligation pertains to the transfer of a defined amount of cash (debt) from the obligor to the obligee, then specific performance is compulsory too, and the court shall freeze the obligor's bank accounts if the latter fails to pay.[9]

10.2.2.2 Reasonableness Test and Statutory Duty of Care

Article 248 CC stipulates that:

> the obligation to transfer a right in kind [pertaining] to a thing shall include the obligation to maintain such thing in safe custody until it is delivered.

The law requires the obligor to exercise a statutory duty of care while fulfilling its civil obligation as a matter of specific performance. For example, the merchant must provide a duty of care while delivering or handing a good sold to the buyer. This duty of care does not render the merchant responsible for factors beyond its control. The appropriate test rests on the exercise of prudence and is hence a test of reasonableness. As already mentioned, the statutory duty of care required for specific performance is reasonableness, henceforth it does not require the obligor to achieve a specific target unless the parties agreed on

---

[9] Ibid, at 800.

such contractual condition beforehand. The law does not permit the parties to decrease the bar of reasonableness to a level whereby the obligor is exempted from fraud and gross negligence. Obligors are always liable if fraud or gross negligence materialises.

Article 249 CC states that:

(i) Where the obligor undertakes delivery of a thing but fails to do so after having been notified, he shall be liable for any loss caused by such failure, even where the liability for such loss lies with the obligee prior to the notification.

(ii) The obligor shall, however, not be liable for the loss even where he was notified, provided that he proves that the thing would also have been lost in the possession of the obligee if it had been delivered to the obligee, unless the obligor accepts liability for *force majeure* or unforeseen incident.

(iii) Where a thing that has been stolen is lost or damaged in any manner whatsoever, the thief shall be liable for such loss or damage.

The law makes it crystal clear that if the obligor promises to deliver a good but fails to deliver it even after being served with a written notice by the obligee, the liability of safeguarding this good falls. This is true even if such liability was contractually borne by the obligee. The obligor may escape from this burden by proving that the good in dispute is likely to perish under the possession of the obligee, as is the case with the delivery of food, which is susceptible to expiration. The only exception to this rule is *force majeure*. The burden of proof rests with the obligor. The third paragraph of article 249 CC sheds light on the fate of stolen goods, whereby the defence of *force majeure* in respect of goods that perished while in the custody of the obligor is impermissible. The obligor who is aware that a sold item was stolen (bad faith) *remains liable* for its safeguard *at all times* because this is a matter of public order.

10.2.2.3 Performance In-kind Directly by the Obligor

Article 250 CC states that:

Where the terms of the agreement or the nature of the debt requires performance of the obligation by the obligor himself, the obligee may reject payment by any third party.

The law here enforces the will of the parties at the time a contract was formed by upholding the obligee's right to refuse specific performance from a third party rather than the obligor. This rule is very important where specific performance is expected from the obligor and there is no explicit provision of 'assignment' in whole or part to a subcontractor. This protection ensures that the obligor will not assign the contract to a third party that is less experienced in order to reduce costs. The obligee must be aware of the potential assignment and its consent is mandatory in this scenario.

Article 251 CC goes on to say that:

> (i) Where the obligor fails to perform his obligation, the obligee may apply to the court for permission to enforce the obligation at the expense of the obligor, if such enforcement is possible. (ii) In the event of an emergency, the obligee may enforce the obligation at the expense of the obligor without permission from the court.

The law confers upon the obligee the right to demand specific performance for a civil obligation when the obligor fails to fulfil its contractual duty through a court order. Alternatively, in the event of an emergency, the obligee may perform the duty on behalf of the obligor and charge it to the obligor's account. It is worth noting that allowing the obligee to perform the duty on the obligor's expense is controversial in civil law because the law does not require the obligee to notify the obligor prior to performing the duty. Notification in the civil law serves the purpose of reminding the breaching party of its obligation, and in case of non-compliance, the notification may be used as evidence against the breaching party before the courts.

It is also important to distinguish between civil obligations requiring specific performance by the obligor personally from those where a substitute is permissible through assignment to a third party. Substitution is impermissible where the obligor is an artist or a person with unique skills hired to perform a specific job, thus, the obligee will be entitled to seek compensatory performance.

Article 252 CC allows the courts to close the parties' performance gap. It states that: 'the court judgment shall be considered as performance if the nature of the obligation so permits'. In certain circumstances where a contracting party to a civil obligation refuses to acknowledge its consent to it, the court steps in to fill that gap. If a mortgagor pays all instalments as per the mortgage agreement, albeit the mortgagee refuses to acknowledge receipt of the final instalments or take the necessary regulatory steps to free that property in question, the court may rule in favour of the mortgagor after reviewing all the evidence and remove the mortgage from said property. The same rule applies to cases where one contracting party denies the validity of its signature on a written contract to avoid specific performance. In this case, the other contracting party may seek court permission to validate the agreement and enforce specific performance.

Reasonable care in the discharge of contractual obligations is a key requirement. This is clearly articulated in article 253 CC, which goes on to say that:

(i) Where the obligor is required to maintain or manage a thing or
     to act carefully in the performance of his obligation, he shall have
     performed his obligation if he uses reasonable care, even where
     the intended purpose is not achieved unless the law or agreement
     provides otherwise.
(ii) At all times, the obligor shall be liable for any fraud or gross negligence
     committed by him.

As discussed earlier, the law demands from the obligor to act reasonably at
all times while performing its contractual obligations and the duty of care
imposed on the obligor does not require achieving a specific target or objective unless the law or the contract demands otherwise. Thus, the test of reasonableness applies. If the obligor commits fraud or gross negligence, the obligee
will be entitled to damages for this civil wrongdoing.

When the obligor promises to refrain from doing something and fails to
uphold or fulfil such a promise, the obligee has the right to obtain a court
order to enforce the contractual condition between the parties. For example,
if an employee breaches a promise preventing him from working for a com-
petitor, the former employer may obtain a court order to enforce the specific
performance in addition to seeking indemnity for the breach of the condition.
This position is aptly illustrated in article 254 CC, which states that:

> where the obligor undertakes not to do something and then breaches such
> obligation, the obligee may petition the court to remedy such breach at the
> expense of the obligor, without prejudice to the obligee's right to indemnity.

10.2.2.4 Disciplinary Penalties

Where the execution of a specific performance becomes futile, article 255 CC
allows the courts to impose a disciplinary penalty. This unique remedy is set
out as follows:

(i) 'Where the performance of an obligation in kind is not possible or
     appropriate unless the obligor executes it, the obligee may obtain a
     judgment to require the obligor to perform such obligation or other-
     wise to pay a disciplinary penalty.
(ii) Where the court believes that the amount of the penalty is insufficient
     to force the obligor to perform the obligation, the court may increase
     the amount as necessary.

(iii) In the event of performance in kind, or where the obligor insists on rejecting the performance, the court may determine the amount of indemnity against the obligor's non-performance or delay in performance, taking into account the damages suffered by the obligee'.

The first paragraph sheds light again on the importance of using the 'disciplinary penalty' as a means of inducing a specific performance, where the contractual undertaking so demands. The obligee may obtain a court order to impose a disciplinary penalty on the obligor until the specific performance is achieved. The obligee is permitted to charge a 'disciplinary penalty'[10] (on a specified rate) to enforce performance in-kind on the obligor, solely to the extent that such disciplinary penalty is either explicitly provided in the contract or exists implicitly in the law. Last but not least, in contrast to the common law, penalties are prohibited in the civil law tradition of contracts; however, 'liquidated damages' are permitted.

The second paragraph stipulates that the court at its discretion may increase the disciplinary penalty if it deems it insufficient to force the obligor to perform the civil obligation in dispute. The disciplinary penalty does not amount to compensatory performance nor indemnity; rather, it is *an interim penalty* until a final judgement is rendered by the court. Hence, time is crucial, because specific performance is subject to time limitations, for example a completion date for handing over a project to the client as specified by the contract.

The third paragraph mandates that if such deadline has elapsed without specific performance being achieved due to the obligor's refusal to perform, the court will order compensatory performance (damages) for partial performance or non-performance, which may include indirect and consequential losses (also known as collateral damages), such as loss of profit or revenues.

---

[10] As of the time of writing this book, our research did not indicate that the Qatari Court of Cassation has interpreted or established a legal principle concerning disciplinary penalties in civil and commercial contracts. As persuasive authority we looked at case law from the Kuwaiti Court of Cassation. In particular, in Judgment 908/2013 the Kuwaiti Court decided that disciplinary penalties are indirect means by which to force the obligor to perform the civil obligations in-kind. Thus, the magnitude of disciplinary penalties may not be proportional to the actual loss suffered by the obligee. The court has the discretion to either increase or decrease the disciplinary penalties as necessary and such decision is a temporary measure until the obligor declares that it will not perform in-kind. Alternatively, if the court decides that specific performance is no longer feasible it will not enforce the disciplinary penalties, but will determine the applicable compensatory performance (damages) for either partial performance or non-performance.

10.2.3 *Compensatory Performance (Damages)*

In the civil law tradition, preference is granted to specific performance over compensatory performance (damages) because of the inherent public interest in honouring civil obligations by performance in-kind. In this vein, article 256 CC states that:

> Where the obligor fails to perform the obligation in kind or delays such performance, he shall indemnify any damages suffered by the obligee, unless such non-performance or delay therein was due to a cause beyond his control.

As discussed earlier, the obligee has the right to claim for compensatory performance from the obligor, that is, indemnity or damages as a last resort if specific performance is not feasible. The obligor's liability for non-performance or delay in performance remains at all time unless the obligor proves that the breach was the result of *force majeure*.

Article 257 CC complements article 256 CC by stating that:

> The court may decrease the amount of indemnity or reject any request for indemnity where the negligence of the obligee contributed to or aggravated the damage.

This provision gives rise to the delict of 'contributory negligence' whereby the obligee's breach of the statutory duty of care [with a valid causation] has contributed to the overall negligence by the obligor. Thus, the court will apply the principle of set-off;[11] that is, the court may decrease damages due to the obligee's contributory negligence.

Article 258 CC makes the case that the parties may well agree that the obligor shall bear liability in respect of unforeseen events, or those otherwise described as *force majeure*.[12] The Qatari legislator permits the contracting parties to agree beforehand that *force majeure* will not offer relief to the obligor.[13] The obligor may use the defence of coercion to prove being forced to accept such a strict condition during the negotiation phase, which may help relieve him from such obligation. The burden of proof of 'coercion' will be on the obligor.

---

[11] See Art 390 CC.

[12] Court of Cassation Judgment 257/2018. See also Court of Cassation Judgment 13/2010, where it was held that impossibility beyond the control of the obligor arises where the event in question is unpredictable and impossible to avoid and the implementation of the commitment under the contract was impossible for everyone in the debtor's position. See also Court of Cassation Judgment 51/2008 regarding the burden of proof.

[13] The Court of Cassation in its Judgment 114/2009 emphasised the sanctity of party autonomy in consonance with the parties' agreement. This clearly applies to the contractual regulation of *force majeure*.

10.2.3.1 Limitation Clauses

The parties may well agree in their agreement to limit each other's liability. Such limitation of liability is acceptable under article 259 CC, which also complements article 258 CC, by stating that:

(i)   'The parties may agree to discharge the obligor from any liability arising from his failure or delay to perform his contractual obligation, except for his fraud or gross negligence.

(ii) The parties may also agree to discharge the obligor from liability for fraud or gross negligence committed by persons employed by the obligor to perform his obligation.

(iii) Any agreement concluded prior to the liability for the unlawful act arising shall be revoked and the obligor shall be discharged from such liability in whole or in part'.

The parties are allowed during the negotiation of the contract to limit or waive their right to claim damages against certain liabilities. However, such 'damage limitation clauses' *shall not exempt* any party from 'civil wrongdoing' liabilities, which include but are not limited to fraud and gross negligence. The only exception to this rule is that the parties are permitted to exempt the obligor from the liability of fraud and/or gross negligence arising from work performed by its subcontractor. The third and last paragraph of this article emphasises that any agreement to limit or discharge statutory liability concerning 'unlawful acts, that is, delicts' is strictly prohibited by law. Statutory obligations include implied warranties for goods and services protecting consumers against defective products. If a contracting party forces such agreement, the contract will be considered null and void and the obligor will no longer be liable for performing the contractual obligations, whether in whole or in part.

10.2.3.2 Notifications

Notifications are a central part of the civil law tradition and this is true of the Qatari CC. Article 260 CC states that:

Indemnity shall not be payable until the obligor is notified, unless the parties agree or the law provides otherwise.

The law here demands the obligee to notify the obligor in writing on or before the contractual deadline for specific performance in order to be entitled at a later stage to claim for compensatory performance. The only applicable exception is where the law or the obligor waives its right to receive a notification prior to initiating any legal action by the obligee to claim for damages arising from non-performance or partial performance or delay in performance.

The form of notification is equally important. Article 261 CC states that: 'an obligor may be notified by a warning or by any other official paper in lieu of the warning. A notice may be given by registered mail or by any other means as agreed'. The parties may agree on the form of written notification in case of a potential breach. The notification may take the form of (i) a court statement of claim or (ii) written notice signed by the obligee and delivered by registered mail to the obligor's address as mentioned in the contract. It is worth noting that there is no general rule mandated by law to regulate the acceptable forms of notification.

The CC sets out when notification is mandated. This is specified in article 262 CC, which states that:

'A notice shall not be necessary in any of the following cases:

   (i) Where it is agreed that the obligor be considered notified immedi-
        ately upon the maturity of the debt;
  (ii) Where the performance of the obligation in kind is not possible or
        futile due to the act of the obligor[14];
 (iii) Where the obligation is an indemnity arising from any unlawful act;
  (iv) Where the obligation requires the return of a thing that the obligor
        knows to have been stolen, or the delivery to the obligor of a thing to
        which he knowingly has no right;
   (v) Where the obligor expressly states in writing that he shall not perform
        his obligation'.

The law here provides conditions in circumstances where notification to the obligor will serve no purpose and thus not required as a prerequisite to initiate a legal action against the obligor and claim for compensatory performance. These conditions include a contractual agreement between the parties whereby the breaching party is automatically considered as having been noti-fied as soon as the deadline to perform in kind elapses. Another scenario arises where the obligor is not cooperative and refuses to perform the civil obliga-tion in kind, in which case the obligee's notification is futile. A third situation arises where notification is useless because the indemnity in question arose

---

[14] See Court of Cassation Judgment 261/2014, where it was held that tendering a written notification
      to the obligor – in this particular case the seller of 10 blocks of land – who breached a sales contract
      to enforce performance in-kind is not possible or futile due to his acts. The seller sold the property
      in 1977 and received full payment from the buyer in the tune of QAR 1.1 million. The seller later
      registered the sold property under his name with the Real Estate Registration System (Ministry of
      Justice) during 1982 and re-sold it to third parties. Thus, the tendering of a written notification to
      the seller prior to initiating a legal action by the buyer or his heirs was deemed not to be required.

from a civil wrongdoing (delict) or statutory obligation, both of which are protected by law. Thus, the claimant need not serve a notification by which to commence legal proceedings. Furthermore, the law here emphasises the principle enunciated in article 249(3) CC as explained above. Lastly, when an obligor expresses its non-compliance in writing to the obligee and refuses to perform in-kind then notification by the obligee is not necessary.

10.2.3.3 Estimation of Damages and Collateral Damages

The parties are generally at liberty to agree on the extent of applicable damages. Article 263 CC states that:

(i) 'The court shall calculate the indemnity unless such calculation is provided in the contract or by the law.
(ii) Indemnity shall cover damages incurred by the obligee, including loss of profit, provided that such damages or loss of profit are a natural consequence of the obligor's failure or delay to perform the obligation. Damages shall be deemed consequential if they were reasonably foreseeable or within the contemplation of the parties at the time of the conclusion of the contract.
(iii) However, if the source of obligation is contractual, an obligor who *did not* commit fraud or gross error is only liable to indemnify damages which are reasonably foreseeable at the time of concluding the contract[15]'.

The courts possess discretion to calculate the value of compensatory performance (damages) where this is not specified in the contract or the law. Indemnity should include direct and indirect losses (also known as collateral damages) unless the parties waive their right to claim indirect and consequential losses. Indirect and consequential losses are required by law to be 'reasonably foreseeable or within the contemplation of the parties at the time of the conclusion of the contract'; thus, any claim for 'remote' indirect losses is impermissible.

10.2.3.4 Moral Damages

This is not free from controversy and indeed moral damages are not necessarily envisaged in all legal systems. Article 264 CC states that:

indemnity shall include moral damages and shall be governed by the provisions of Articles 202 and 203.

---

[15] Art 263(3) CC was mistakenly omitted in the English translation of the legislative text as published by Al-Meezan database, compared to the original Arabic text.

Qatari legislators adopted the approach of encompassing moral damages, which includes the delicts of mental distress and defamation. Moral damages will be discussed in more details under sub-section 10.2.3.8 of this chapter.

10.2.3.5 Liquidated Damages

Much like other developed jurisdictions, article 265 CC provides for the justification of liquidated damages, as follows:

> 'Where the obligation *is not for*[16] the payment of money, the parties may calculate the amount of indemnity in advance in the contract or in any subsequent agreement'.

Qatari legislators have permitted the parties to foresee and calculate indemnities for potential damages at the time of the contract in the form of a 'liquidated damage' clause subject to the condition that the obligation itself is unconcerned with the payment of money. The rationale behind the restriction of establishing indemnity for a payment of money is related to the Islamic prohibition of monetary interest (*riba*). Islam considers monetary interest as 'enrichment without cause', where the obligee will gain more money compared to the original amount of money borrowed by the obligor without performing anything justifying the extra profit. It is worth noting that Islamic opposition to 'monetary interest' does not take into account the economic principle of 'inflation', where the economic value of the original amount of borrowed money today will not be the same after the passage of time when the money has been repaid to the obligee.

10.2.3.6 Restitution

Restitution is a remedy that is recognised in most legal systems and in the common law it is also an equitable remedy. It is envisaged as a contractual remedy under article 266 CC as follows:

> No agreed indemnity shall be payable if the obligor proves that the obligee has suffered no damages. The court may decrease the agreed amount of indemnity if the obligor proves that the calculation is exaggerated or if the obligation has been performed in part. Any agreement to the contrary shall be invalid.

---

[16] There is a mistake/discrepancy in the English translation of Art 265 CC as published by Al-Meezan database, compared to the original Arabic text.

Here the law emphasises the importance of 'restitution', which allows the courts to grant indemnity for non- or partial performance on the basis of 'fairness'. The law intends to place the injured party in the position before the occurrence of the breach. If the obligor proves that the obligee did not suffer losses, the obligee will not be entitled to indemnity, even if the contract mandates otherwise. Moreover, the court at its own discretion may increase or decrease the contractually liquidated damage based on evidence demonstrating that such indemnity was exaggerated or inflated by the obligee at the time of the contract. Thus, any agreement contrary to public order is invalid. The burden of proof falls on the obligor, who must demand it in the statement of claim; otherwise, the court will not automatically grant it without request.

Article 267 CC goes on to say that: 'where the damages exceed the agreed amount of indemnity, the obligee may not claim a higher amount unless he proves the obligor's fraud or gross negligence'. The law here sets a clear rule that indemnity must be equal in value to the loss suffered by the obligee, unless the latter proves that the obligor committed fraud and/or gross negligence. In this particular circumstance, the obligee will be entitled to 'inflated' damages as a penalty for a conduct that breached public order.

Article 268 CC makes the point that: 'Where the obligation is the payment of money and the obligor fails to make such payment after being notified to do so and provided that the obligee proves he has incurred damages due to such non-payment, the court may order the obligor to pay indemnity, subject to the requirements of justice'. This article must be read in conjunction with article 265 CC because the civil obligation concerns borrowing/lending money, which encompasses an inherent prohibition of 'monetary interest' in order to be compatible with Islamic law. Article 268 CC deals with situations where the obligor is financially capable of returning the debt but chooses to either avoid or delay payment. If the obligee can prove that: (i) the obligor refused to pay the debt even after being notified in accordance with the parties' agreement and (ii) the obligee has suffered damages due to non-payment, such as by its reliance on the obligor's promise to pay another debt or civil obligation, the court is entitled to award damages (direct and indirect) to the obligee. Qatari legislators adopted this approach in order to mitigate the risk of obligors deliberately delaying payment of monetary debts by relying on the *riba* prohibition, at least at an individual level (not corporate level), which conflicts with public order and hinders economic growth.

10.2.3.7 Nature of Damages

In the civil law tradition, damages accruing from a contractual obligation[17] or liability arise where (i) an obligor breaches either an 'explicit' term that is mandated by the contract or an 'implied' term that is mandated by applicable law (statute) or accepted commercial practices and (ii) the obligee has suffered an actual damage (not a possible damage) due to the action or omission of the obligor. If the mere contractual breach does not result in actual damage to the obligee, then a claim for damages under contract law is not admissible.[18] For example, if a seller under a sales contract was overdue at delivering the sold goods to the buyer, while the latter was not available at the time and place of the supposed delivery and did not even delegate a third party to collect the sold goods on its behalf, then the former does not have recourse to compensation because the buyer has contributed to the breach and did not suffer an actual damage from such a breach, that is, the over-due delivery by the seller.

The main objective of granting damages to a contractual obligation or liability is to indemnify and compensate obligees from an actual damage that was a direct result of the obligor's non- or partial performance. Thus, *causation*[19] between the contractual breach[20] and actual damage is a mandatory requirement. The

---

[17] Qatar Court of Cassation Judgment 36/2016, where it held that the general rules governing a contractual obligation (المسؤولية العقدية) differ from those governing a delictual obligation (المسؤولية التقصيرية). Damages which arise from a contractual obligation must be governed by the terms of the contract and relevant laws. If the parties to a dispute have a contractual relationship, then it is not permissible to apply the general rules of delict unless the contractual breach is deemed a criminal offence or the result of fraud or gross error. The main objective behind prohibiting the application of delictual rules to a contractual breach is the risk of diluting the enforceability of contractual terms, and thus weaken the legal instrument of contracts as a whole.

[18] Mohammad Hassan Qassim, *Civil Code – Sources of Obligations: Contracts* (Al-Halabi Legal Publications, 2018) vol 2, at 215–216.

[19] According to the Qatar Court of Cassation Judgment 390/2017, courts of substance (i.e. court of first instance and the court of appeal) possess discretion to determine: (i) the contractual breach; (ii) damages; and (iii) causation between the breach and damages, without supervision from the Court of Cassation as long as the outcome is supported by evidence filed with the court. Moreover, contractual remedies in the case of the obligor's non-performance or late performance may be granted in accordance with Arts 256 and 253 CC. Courts of substance *may not* award contractual remedies to the obligee, if the obligor managed to prove that *no damage occurred* in the first place. Furthermore, courts of substance may *reduce* contractual remedies if the obligor managed to prove that the estimated value of contractual remedies is either *disproportionate to the damage in dispute* (i.e. an exaggerated value) or *partial performance of the contractual obligation has already been fulfilled.*

[20] According to the Court of Cassation Judgment 122/2017, a breach constitutes non-performance of a contractual obligation by the obligor. Such contractual obligation can be construed from the contract, the intentions of the parties and the law.

general rule here is that obligees have the burden to prove that actual damage has occurred due to the contractual breach committed by the obligor(s). Courts of substance have the discretion to assess the evidence filed by the parties and decide on the contractual damages to be awarded, if any.[21]

10.2.3.8 Types of Damages

Damages in contract law comprise two main types, namely: (i) material damages and (ii) moral damages. The former is defined as damages which harm the obligee's economic estate such as property, money, shares and bodily injury.[22] Thus, material damages can be easily identified and quantified. On the other hand, moral damages are defined as harm to the obligee's non-economic estate, such as reputation and mental status. Hence, moral damages are intangible and difficult to quantify. Unlike the common law which limits contractual damages to one's economic assets and thus excludes bodily injury,[23] the civil law tradition permits contractual damages to encompass both economic and non-economic claims.[24] The legislative text makes a clear reference to material damages[25] by emphasising that: 'indemnity shall

---

[21] According to the Court of Cassation Judgment 95/2016, the estimation of damages falls within the discretion of the courts of substance, which may rely on the available evidence as the basis for their ruling. Estimation of damages must be based on sound justification, where a proportionality between the damage in dispute and value of remedies to be awarded is established. Remedies shall not exceed nor fall short of the actual harm suffered by the obligee (i.e. rules of fairness apply here); equally to the same effect, Court of Cassation Judgments 46/2008 and 37/2014.

[22] According to Qassim, above (n 18), at 222, bodily injury claims are considered material damage rather than moral damage. Qassim provides an example of a transportation contract where the obligor has a legal duty to transfer passengers from point A to point B while complying with applicable health and safety standards. If the obligee suffers a bodily injury as a direct result of the obligor's breach, a claim for a material damage under the transportation contract is permissible.

[23] In common law systems, bodily injury and non-economic claims fall under the ambit of tort law such as the torts of personal injury, mental distress and defamation.

[24] Contractual and delictual damages overlap in civil law systems, whereas in the common law there is a clear divide between damages under contracts and torts. The reason behind the overlap in the civil law tradition is that the law of delict did not develop into an autonomous discipline in the same way as tort law in the common law world. According to Qassim, above (n 18), at 222, 'Moral damages as a contractual remedy is no longer a controversial topic among systems scholars in civil law. Even if moral damages are better visualised as a delictual remedy under negligence, judges have the discretion to award moral damages in contractual disputes. There is a consensus in the civil law jurisprudence that moral damages in contractual disputes may be granted without material damages, if the court determines that the contracting party's interest was moral (non-economic) not necessarily material (economic). Thus, the general rules which apply to material damages can be applied in the same manner to moral damages'.

[25] Art 263 CC.

cover [material] *damages incurred* by the obligee, including loss of profit' and moral damages[26] ('indemnity shall include *moral* damages'). As discussed earlier, material damages consist of two elements: (i) direct losses and (ii) consequential or indirect losses (collateral damages), that is, loss of profit. The latter must be foreseeable by the contracting parties at the time of concluding the contract; otherwise, the court may not grant indemnity for consequential losses (collateral damages). The contracting parties may exclude consequential losses (collateral damages) by using a limitation clause in the contract, which the courts must respect. In all cases, causation between the contractual breach and actual damage is a mandatory requirement that is referenced in the statutory text as 'a *natural consequence* of the obligor's failure or delay to perform the obligation'.[27]

Moral damages are governed by articles 202 and 203 CC,[28] whereby the general successors of a deceased obligee who suffered the aftermath of the obligee's death arising from the contractual obligation may claim for moral damages up to the obligee's second kin.[29] The court may not grant moral damages to all applicable second kins but the judge has discretion to indemnify only those who suffered a 'real' pain for the loss of the deceased obligee.[30] As persuasive authority, the Egyptian Court of Cassation held that the legislative text in articles 121 and 122 Egyptian CC [equivalent to articles 263 and 264 Qatari CC] does not limit moral damages to the obligee's death but these may be extended to cover the obligee's severe injury if he/she remains alive. Thus, indemnity may be granted to the obligee's general successors or relatives up to the second kin.[31] Finally, the Qatari legislator has followed the Egyptian CC and mandated in article 203 CC that moral damages cannot be assigned

---

[26] Art 264 CC.

[27] Art 263 CC.

[28] According to the Qatari Court of Cassation Judgment 89/2016, courts of substance shall take into consideration moral damages alongside material damages when determining indemnities. Moral damages include disputes related to defamation and mental distress among others. Courts of substance shall not underestimate moral damages to avoid aggregating the pain of the injured person. Indemnity must be: (i) monetary in form; and (ii) sufficient in value to fully rectify the injured party for both material and moral damages. Similarly, the Court of Cassation in Judgment 124/2016, held that despite the award of moral damages only, courts of substance had not clearly construed the elements on which moral damages were estimated. Furthermore, there was no valid justification for the ruling to exclude material damages, even if they were adjudicated in previous rulings [i.e. different claims]. The general rule for damages is to encompass both material and moral elements.

[29] Second degree kinship includes a living spouse, parents, grandparents, children, grandchildren and siblings, that is, brothers and sisters. Qassim, above (n 18), at 227.

[30] Qassim, ibid, at 228.

[31] Egyptian Court of Cassation Judgment 755/1959.

or transferred to third parties (general or special successors) unless one of the following conditions materialises: (i) moral damages are stipulated either by contract or law or (ii) the obligee has filed a claim for moral damages before the obligee passes away.[32]

10.2.3.9 Conditions for a Valid Claim of Damages

Contractual damages must be (i) certain; (ii) direct and (iii) foreseeable. Certainty entails that the damage must be actual, not just possible, that is, either a damage has already occurred or will inevitably occur in the near future. Let us assume a procurement contract to supply a factory with raw materials needed for a manufacturing process. When the supplier fails to deliver the raw material on time to the factory, the contractual damage may not occur immediately because it is reasonably expected that factories should have a sufficient stock of raw materials in their warehouse to keep their production process healthy for a limited period of time. Thus, contractual damages arising from the supplier's failure to perform its obligation under the procurement contract are deemed to be inevitable in the near future, once the factory runs out of stocked raw materials. Courts of substance have the discretion to either: (i) determine 'provisional' contractual damages from the evidence available while permitting the oblige to seek 'final' contractual damages at a later stage or (ii) grant a stay to the litigation proceedings (i.e. postpone the adjudication of the case) until the contractual damage materialises, at which time the court will determine the final damages and applicable compensation.[33]

The second condition here is directness. When the Qatari legislator demands that contractual damages must be direct, this condition refers to causation between the contractual and the claimed damage. As discussed earlier, the law does not grant a remedy to an obligee merely because a breach has occurred. An obligor is liable to indemnify the obligee for direct damages only (including both direct losses and consequential losses). Indirect damages are not recoverable because the legislator expects prudent obligees to exercise a reasonable effort to avoid the risk of indirect damages; thus, its occurrence is deemed as an error made by the obligee.[34] A famous example of indirect damages was illustrated by the French jurist Robert Joseph Pothier, who is credited with the narration of a story where a farmer purchased an ill cow and then put it in the same barn with other healthy cows without isolation. The healthy

---

[32] Qassim, (n 18), at 230.
[33] Ibid, at 231–232.
[34] Ibid, at 235.

cows became infected with the same disease as the purchased ill cow, and consequently all the cows died. The farmer became unable to seed his land and thus lost the potential profit of the land's harvest. As a result, the farmer could not pay his debts and all his estates were sold in auction, which yielded a low-value outcome. The seller of the ill cow may not be held liable for all the damages. The buyer has a legal recourse to seek remedies for direct damages, that is, the death of his healthy cows, if the buyer can prove to the court that an error or fraud has occurred at the time of concluding the sales contract and the buyer could not reasonably avoid the death of his cows. However, for the loss of potential harvest profit and default payment of his debts (collateral damages), the seller is not liable for the indirect losses because the buyer could have: (i) procured new cows in order to seed his land; (ii) arranged for other farming tools or methods to seed his land without the need for cows, so he will not miss the harvest season or (iii) even renegotiated the postponement of the default payments of his debts with its creditors to avoid the aftermath of selling his estate in an auction.[35]

The third and last condition is foreseeability. In civil law systems, foreseeability is a mandatory condition for contractual remedies only – that is, delictual remedies may be awarded for direct damages whether these damages are foreseeable or unforeseeable. The general rule of limiting obligors' liability to foreseeable direct damages is based on the legal principle of 'good faith'; that is, the obligor must have acted in good faith while performing its civil obligations under the contract in dispute. The exception to this general rule materialises in circumstances where the obligor committed fraud or gross error[36] (acting in bad faith), in which case contractual liability extends to unforeseeable damages as well as damages pursuant to paragraph 3 of article 263 CC. The main objective for enforcing foreseeability as a condition for contractual damages is the law's expectation that while negotiating a potential contract obligors should demonstrate prudence and assess the potential risk of non-performance or partial performance of their civil obligations. Moreover, this objective aligns with the principles of fairness (known as equity in the common law), because an obligor acting in good faith must not be liable for damages that are more severe or which 'go above and beyond' the original civil obligation itself.[37]

---

[35] Ibid.

[36] In the civil law tradition, fraud in contractual obligations is deemed an 'intentional' wrongdoing because the obligor intended to avoid performing its obligation. On the other hand, gross error is deemed an 'unintentional' wrongdoing, but is treated in a similar manner to intentional wrongdoings. Thus, an obligor may commit a gross error without intending to do so and henceforth becomes liable to pay damages to the obligee. Qassim, ibid, at 248 and 251.

[37] Qassim, ibid, at 240.

One controversial question arising from the requirement of foreseeing contractual damages concerns whether the obligor must have foreseen the 'cause' of the harm, its 'value' or both. Let us assume a situation where a passenger loses luggage handed to an airline company for safekeeping during a flight from point A to point B and the luggage contained precious items, whose value the airline company could not possibly foresee. Is the airline liable to indemnify the cost of the lost precious items? French jurisprudence (not unanimously it has to be said) tends to suggest that the cause of harm alone is sufficient to establish liability for foreseeable damages even if the true value of the harm was not foreseeable. Thus, by making reference to the above example, French courts may award contractual damages to the passenger for the loss of precious items. Nevertheless, Egyptian jurisprudence requires the foreseeability of both cause and value of contractual damages. According to the Egyptian Cassation Court, a foreseeable harm materialises when a prudent person facing circumstances similar to those of the obligor at the time of concluding the contract would be able to foresee (i.e. the court here applies the reasonableness test).[38] The same Court elaborated that it is not sufficient to foresee the cause of harm only, since foreseeability of the value of such harm is a mandatory element in order to establish liability.[39]

10.3 PERFORMANCE IN ACCORDANCE WITH SPECIAL LAWS

10.3.1 *Performance in Sales Contracts*

Articles 102 to 124 of the Qatari Commercial Law uphold specific performance between seller and buyer as the default method for fulfilling civil obligations and discharging contractual liabilities under a sales contract. Compensatory performance (damages) is the exception to the general rule. The seller is obligated to safeguard the sold merchandise, while the goods are kept under its possession. The point whereupon 'title and risk' may pass from seller to buyer depends on the agreed delivery arrangements. In commercial practice, such obligation may pass temporarily to a third party hired by either the buyer or seller to collect the sold goods from the seller and deliver to the buyer. If the goods perish or become defective before collected or delivered to the buyer, the loss must be borne by the seller, unless the seller can prove that this unfortunate result: (i) was unforeseeable and (ii) occurred beyond the seller's control (i.e. *force majeure*). In this case, the buyer will be entitled to cancel

---

[38] Egyptian Court of Cassation Judgment 145/1973.
[39] Qassim, (n 18), at 243–244.

the transaction and receive a refund. However, if the seller takes reasonable precautionary measures to protect the sold goods and notifies the buyer of its conditions for collection or delivery, the loss must be borne by the buyer. If the said defect(s) does not render the sold goods 'seriously' defective and consequently reduce its economic value, the buyer will be entitled to either cancel the transaction [and get a refund] or accept the merchandise with a 'reasonable' discounted price.

10.3.1.1 Delivery and Incoterms Clauses

In general, most sale and purchase agreements nowadays contain specific clauses, which deal with 'incoterms' and specify which party bears the obligation for the collection/delivery of the sold good. In the absence of such clauses, the law fills this gap by conferring this obligation on the seller for exportation and the fulfilment of such a duty will not suffice until the sold goods are delivered to the buyer.[40] When the parties agree to outsource delivery to a third party, such as a courier, the law[41] stipulates that if the contractual terms and conditions of such delivery mature once the sold items reach the courier, both title and risk pass from seller to buyer at that particular moment. Moreover, if the buyer requests the seller to deliver the sold goods to a shipping address that is not specified in the sale contract, the buyer bears the risk of loss or damage of such delivery unless the seller does not follow the buyer's shipping instructions without reasonable justifications; that is, the necessity to deviate from the buyer's shipping instructions for safety or regulatory compliance.[42] If the sold goods are paid in instalments, the title thereof does not pass to the buyer during the delivery process. However, the risk passes to the buyer during delivery and hence if the goods perish while in the possession of the buyer, the buyer is liable.

In sales contracts, the type of commodity sold determines the rules regarding delivery, especially where the underlying contract is silent about the deadline of delivery. In circumstances concerning perishable goods, article 108 CL states that delivery should take place: (i) before the items perish and (ii) before the end of a season as mandated by acknowledged commercial practices. However, if the buyer specifies the delivery deadline in the sales contract, the seller is expected to comply and deliver the items within the deadline,

---

[40] It is worth highlighting that Qatari law has regulated 'Incoterms' pertinent to maritime transactions in Arts 142 to 163 of the Commercial Law.

[41] Art 105 CL.

[42] Art 106 CL.

taking into consideration relevant commercial customs and practices. In case the seller fails to fulfil its contractual obligation and delivery to the buyer did not materialise, the buyer must *notify the seller in writing* of its intention to enforce the terms and conditions of the sale agreement *within three days from the delivery deadline*; otherwise, the sales contract will be unenforceable. Once this condition is met, the buyer will have recourse to the courts, or in urgent situations without the court's permission, to procure the sale items from a different vendor and charge all relevant costs to the seller.[43] This requires 'good faith' on the part of the buyer. If the sale agreement states that the seller shall deliver the sold items in batches and fails to meet the delivery requirements, the buyer may request the revocation of the non-performed obligations. In order to revoke the entire sales contract, the buyer must prove an 'adverse effect' from the seller's performance even for the delivered items.

Once the sales contract is revoked either in whole or in part, the buyer may claim compensatory performance (damages) from the seller. The buyer has the right to claim monetary compensation for the difference between the market price for the sold items effective on the delivery deadline and the agreed price as per the sales contract.[44] This monetary compensation does not prejudice the buyer's right to seek other damages from the court as a result of the seller's failure to perform the contractual obligations, that is, specific performance.

10.3.1.2 Inspection of Sold Goods

The law obligates the buyer to inspect the delivered goods[45] once under its possession in accordance with commercial custom. The buyer must immediately notify the seller in writing about any defects discovered during the inspection process; otherwise, the buyer is deemed to have waived its right to return the defective goods. If the buyer fails to notify the seller in writing of its findings (whether during the course of normal examination of the goods or as soon as the defects are discovered), the buyer may risk losing its right to seek compensation from the seller.

10.3.1.3 Payments and Financial Securities

With regard to payment, buyers are obligated by law to make such payment at the time of delivery, that is, when title and risk pass to the buyer, or at a

---

[43] Art 109 CL.
[44] Art 110 CL.
[45] Art 114 CL.

specific due date as stipulated under the sales contract or established by commercial custom. The place for making the payment is the buyer's residence, especially in cross-border transactions.[46] If the buyer suspects that the seller does not possess good 'title' to the sold goods, the law grants the buyer the right to withhold payment until such claims are resolved, unless the sales contract prohibits such withholding. The same right is granted to the buyer if it detects defects in the sold goods.[47] However, the seller may still demand that payment be made by the buyer subject to a guarantee or a financial security on the sold goods, that is, a third-party guarantor who shall indemnify the buyer in case the sold items do not have a good title or contain defects.[48] The law grants the seller the right to withhold delivery of the sold goods if it was agreed that payment (partial or full) be made *immediately* to the seller until the money is collected. Even if the buyer provides the seller with a mortgage or a financial security to secure payment, the seller still has the right to maintain temporary possession of the sold goods until payment is made; save if the sales contract granted the buyer a 'grace period' for payment.[49] The seller is allowed to prolong the possession of the sold goods if it becomes aware that: (i) the buyer has declared bankruptcy; (ii) the buyer's financial security has weakened due to its action or even without the intervention from the buyer's side but through its failure to take the necessary action to rectify such weakness, or (iii) because of the buyer's failure to provide the seller with the required guarantees or financial security as per the terms and conditions of the sales contract. In this scenario, if the sold goods perish while in the possession of the seller, any loss will be borne by the buyer unless the goods perished through conduct attributed to the seller.[50]

10.3.1.4 Damages in Sales Contracts

Sellers are entitled to compensatory performance from buyers who fail to perform under the sales contract. This is generally fixed at the price difference (delta) between the market price at the effective due date for payment and the agreed sale price between the parties, subject to notification in writing. Buyers may make payment for the sold goods or services *on or before* the due date of the payments.[51] It is worth highlighting that the sales contract or the established

[46] Art 116 CL.
[47] Art 117 CL.
[48] Ibid.
[49] Art 118 CL.
[50] Art 119 CL.
[51] Arts 120 and 121 CL.

commercial customs and practices can determine the deducted amount from the price against payment made *before* the due date, that is, an early payment. If the sales contract or customs are silent about the time and place, or the place of performance, time and place are deduced from the circumstances of the conclusion of the underlying transaction. The sold goods must be delivered to the buyer as soon as possible without delay unless reasonable logistical requirements must first be met.[52] The default rule here is that delivery cost shall be borne by the seller unless the sales contract shifts this obligation to the buyer. Finally, if the buyer refuses to collect or receive the sold goods, the seller is entitled to keep them temporarily in a warehouse until disposed, whether by direct negotiation with potential buyers or through an auction after notifying the buyer in writing of the contractual breach. The seller also has the right to determine a reasonable time and place to dispose the goods rejected by the buyer. If the sold goods are perishable, the seller can dispose them without notifying the buyer.[53] Moreover, if the sold goods have a known market price (price index), they may be sold at that price through a broker. The sale proceeds of such disposal process shall be deposited in the court's account. The law grants the seller the right (without prejudice) to reduce the price and/or deduct all expenses incurred in this commercial transaction.[54]

10.3.2 *Performance in Lease Contracts*

Performance in lease contracts embodies the same priorities as civil contracts in general, that is, specific performance first, then compensatory performance (damages), if the latter is not feasible – subject to notification in writing with the exception of urgent situations. According to articles 4 to 14 of the Lease Property Law ('**LPL**'), specific performance for lease agreements is a straightforward process, whereby the lessor is obliged to ensure that the leased property is readily available for hand over to the lessee on the effective date of the lease agreement, free of possession. The possession of such leased property must remain with the lessee as long as the lease agreement is valid. On the other hand, the lessee is obliged to pay rent as agreed in the lease contract, whether on a monthly rate (which is most common in residential properties), biannually or annually.[55] The lessor has a duty to maintain the leased

---

[52] Art 122 CL.
[53] Art 124 CL.
[54] Ibid.
[55] See Court of Cassation Judgment 108/2015, which held that the lessee's civil obligation to pay due rent as agreed in the lease contract depended on the applicable law for such contract, that is, the CC or LPL. If the lease contract is subject to the LPL, Art 11 thereof dictates that

property and repair any damage brought to its attention by the lessee, such as electrical, plumbing or structural, as well as arrange for the completion of any other works needed to keep the leased property's condition suitable for residential renting. The lessee must notify the lessor in writing and within a reasonable time about all repairs. If the lessor fails or refuses to fix and maintain the property, the lessee is entitled to report to the Leasing Committee and seek permission to repair the property from the lessee's account and deduct it from the rent (i.e. set-off the maintenance costs against due rent payments). It is also worth highlighting that in practice most tenants end up paying for property repairs from their own pocket without exercising their right to seek support from the Leasing Committee due to the bureaucracy of the application process.

The law permits the lessee to carry out 'emergency or necessary maintenance' on the leased property even without consent from the lessor in order to preserve and keep the 'habitational condition' of the said property. In this case, the lessee is entitled to: (i) deduct repair costs from the rent; (ii) extend the duration of the contract, that is, the term in exchange for the money paid toward repairs; or (iii) terminate the lease contract. However, the law deems the lessee's right in this circumstance waived if the lessee occupies the leased property for thirty days from the date such maintenance works were undertaken without resorting to the Leasing Committee. The sole exception to this is where the lessee provides reasonable justification for such delay. The law prohibits the lessee to make any changes, especially structural changes to the premises, without obtaining written consent from the lessor and use the leased property for a different purpose other than the purpose stipulated in the contract. If the lessee breaches these statutory obligations, then the lessee is obligated to restore the leased property to its original condition at its own expense,

the lessee is obliged to: (i) pay the lessor on the due date and no longer than seven days from the due date in full; and (ii) collect a written receipt from the lessor to prove that the rent was paid on-time. In case the lessor refuses to accept the rent or provide a receipt, the lessee is obligated by law to: (i) notify the lessor in writing that the rent is due within seven days and if the lessor does not accept the rent, then the money will be deposited to the Leasing Committee; and (ii) deposit such rent within seven days of the lessor's refusal to the treasury of the Leasing Committee. When the lessee performs the required action mandated by law, the rent is deemed to have been paid on the due date by virtue of such deposit. However, where the lease contract is regulated by the CC, the lessee's obligation to pay the rent is prescribed by Art 607 CC. The lessee does not have a positive obligation to notify the lessor in writing about payment nor to deposit the rent. Nevertheless, the lessor has the civil obligation to request such payment of due rent and collect it from the lessee's place of domicile unless there is agreement or accepted commercial practice dictating otherwise. If the lessor fails to take the proper action of requesting and collecting the rent from the lessee, the lessee is not in breach of the lease contract but remains in debt to the lessor until the rent is paid in full.

in addition to monetary compensation to the lessor.[56] Furthermore, the lessee may not sublease or assign all or part of the lease to third parties, except with the written consent of the lessor.[57] Moreover, the lessee is obligated to pay all utility bills during the term of the lease contract, unless the rent rate is inclusive of such utility charges.

10.4 ENRICHMENT WITHOUT CAUSE

Enrichment without cause in the civil law system[58] is a legal principle that falls outside the ambit of contract law and, in general, its rules cannot be applied to disputes arising from contracts.[59] However, courts may apply it to disputes in which contractual obligations cease to exist such as disputes arising from (i) nullity of contracts[60] or (ii) prescription of commercial instruments,

---

[56] See Court of Cassation Judgment 32/2015, which held that according to Art 8 LPL, the lessee is prohibited from making any significant change to the leased property without seeking prior written consent from the lessor. The law has already prescribed the remedy of such statutory breach, whereby the lessor is entitled to demand that the lessee remove all changes made to the leased property and reinstate it to its original condition, with all costs of such modification borne by the lessee. The lessor may be entitled to seek compensatory performance (damages), in addition to making all the required changes to the leased property. The Court emphasised that such a breach *is not* a sufficient reason to evict the lessee from the leased property.

[57] According to the Court of Cassation Judgment 98/2015, under the terms of Arts 14 and 19 of the Leasing Property Law, the lessor is entitled to evict the lessee once he or she subleases the leased property to third parties without written consent. The Court emphasised that even if the lessee attempts to rectify the breach after its occurrence, such rectification does not suffice to remedy the situation. In this particular case, the lessee was a legal person (company) that subleased the leased shop to another legal person without the lessor's consent. Both the lessee and the sub-lessee had different commercial registration numbers. After the lessor sought legal action against the lessee, the lessee submitted documents showing that the sub-lessee had been acquired by the lessee. However, the court did not accept such manoeuvre because the acquisition was a disguised attempt to rectify the breach of subleasing to third parties without consent.

[58] The common law doctrine of 'unjust enrichment' is the equivalent counter-part to the civil legal principle of 'enrichment without cause'.

[59] According to Court of Cassation Judgment 443/2017 and its interpretation of Art 220 CC, where the parties have *a valid contractual relationship*, then a claim of 'enrichment without cause' and in particular its application of 'receipt of undue payment' is *inadmissible*. The rationale here is that the contract [as a lawful cause] is the only legal ground which defines the rights and obligations between the contracting parties and thus determines any damage that may be awarded to rectify a breach.

[60] According to Court of Cassation Judgment 60/2012, a nullified contract pursuant to Art 163(1) and 164(1) CC *does not* create any legally binding effect between the parties who intended to form it. Thus, the nullification process has a retroactive effect and the parties must be reinstated to their original position at the time of concluding the nullified contract. If such reinstatement is impossible, then the court may grant damages on the ground of 'enrichment without cause' to the impoverished party, that is, the lesser value of either enrichment or impoverishment.

for example cheques.[61] The most disputed application of enrichment without cause is the 'receipt of undue payment'.[62] Damages awarded pursuant to article 220 CC is *the lesser value* of either enrichment or impoverishment. Enrichment without cause aims to provide fairness and restitution to the parties in dispute when one party gains at the expense of its counterpart without lawful cause to justify it.

10.5 DETRIMENTAL RELIANCE ON A PROMISE

The last topic discussed in this chapter concerns detrimental reliance on a 'promise', which is recognised in the vast majority of civil law jurisdictions. This arises where one contracting party (a 'promisee') has acted in 'good faith' and relied on a promise made by its counterparty (a 'promisor') before the former becomes aware that this particular promise is legally *unenforceable*. It depends on the criticality of such promise whether unenforceability tarnishes the contract in whole or part (i.e. severability). Unlike the common law tradition which requires valid contracts to comply with the doctrine of 'consideration' and its *rigid* requirement of 'bargaining', the civil law tradition *does not require bargaining (i.e. an exchange of promises)* between the contracting parties under the *flexible* legal principle of 'cause'. Thus, a unilateral promise that is made by the promisor without seeking in exchange an obligation to perform or abstain from a specific act by the promisee may form a legally binding contract under the civil law tradition, as is the case with donation contracts and gifts.

French legal theory did not adopt 'detrimental reliance on a promise', which effectively mirrors the common law doctrine of promissory estoppel, because of the consensus that 'the command of the [French Civil Code] that contracts be performed in good faith has been read broadly and extended to pre-contractual negotiations. Taken together with the vast scope of rights,

---

[61] According to Court of Cassation Judgments 55/2012, 94/2013, 139/2014, and 62/2019, pursuant to Arts 599 and 602(1) CL, prescription of commercial instruments (e.g. cheques) of one year from the date of issuing the commercial instrument *does not* bar the issuer of claiming damages on the ground of 'enrichment without cause'. The holder who cashed the cheque without lawful cause is obligated by law to refund the issuer. Prescription of 'receipt of undue payment' as an application of 'enrichment without cause' pursuant to Art 228 CC is 'three years from the date on which the claimant became aware of its right to recover such prepayment, or after a period of fifteen years from the date on which such right arose, whichever occurs first'. The court elaborated by saying that the law aims to provide stability and trust in commercial instruments even after the prescription, so issuers will feel protected and claim for partial or full refund against a partial or non-performance by the holder.

[62] Receipt of undue payment is regulated by Arts 222–228 CC.

French law is well equipped without promissory estoppel'.[63] Egyptian legal theory maintains that 'detrimental reliance does not fall within the definition of cause'.[64] It is evident that the Qatari position, chiefly through case law, does not deviate from the Egyptian and French approaches. As discussed earlier, in Judgment 125/2008 the Qatari Court of Cassation granted damages to a concerned party suffering loss due to the nullification[65] of a contract with retroactive effect on the contracting parties. Such damages are governed by the law of delict. Hence, Qatari jurisprudence did not see the need to adopt the legal principle of detrimental reliance. Instead, it relied on the law of delict to award damages (i.e. the rules of negligence were applied).

In a similar ruling, the Qatar Court of Cassation held that the courts may grant damages to a contracting party that suffered harm from the annulment of a contract, *not on* the basis of a contractual obligation but in accordance with article 164(1) CC.[66] In another case, the Qatari Court of Cassation concluded that upon annulment a contract shall not be used as a legal basis to claim for contractual damages.[67] Damages in this context arise from civil wrongdoings that are governed by the law of delict (rules of negligence). Delictual damages require the materialisation of three conditions, namely (i) breach of the statutory duty of care; (ii) injury; and (iii) causation between the breach of the statutory duty of care and the subsequent injury in dispute.

---

[63] D V Synder, 'Comparative Law in Action: Promissory Estoppel, the Civil Law, and the Mixed Jurisdiction' (1998) 15 Arizona Journal of International and Comparative Law 695, at 705.

[64] Synder, above (n 63) at 722.

[65] It is worth highlighting that unlike nullity of contracts which produces retroactive effect and bars claims for contractual damages, contracts may be terminated where a significant contractual obligation is not performed, even following notification. Thus, claims for contractual damages arising from terminated contracts are admissible for the period covering the lifetime of the contract. The Qatari Court of Cassation in Judgment 99/2016 held that contractual damages arising from the unilateral termination of an indefinite employment contract by the employer without making any justification was limited to the employee's wage during the notice period pursuant to Art 49 LL. In judgment 335/2016 the Qatar Court of Cassation held that contractual damages could be sought against unilateral termination or non-renewal of a commercial agency contract (i.e. 'exclusive' sale of goods and/or services). Such claims were found to be admissible pursuant to Arts 300, 301 and 304 CL. On the other hand, contractual damages sought against unilateral termination or non-renewal of a distribution contract (i.e. 'non-exclusive' sale of goods and/or services) *are not* admissible because 'exclusivity' is a fundamental requirement for a valid contractual damages claim.

[66] Court of Cassation Judgment 32/2014.

[67] Court of Cassation Judgment 100/2016.

11

Termination and Rescission of Contracts

11.1 INTRODUCTION

This chapter deals with a single, yet complex and over-arching topic, namely termination of the life of a contract. When a contract is terminated it no longer demands obligations from the parties, although the parties may be liable for damages or restitution. As will be shown, the CC distinguishes between two types of termination: termination proper and rescission. Given that termination produces significant consequences for the parties, the CC sets out general and subject-specific rules. General rules include those on *force majeure*, impossibility of fulfilment, discharge, set-off, novation and the effects of the death of one of the parties to a contract (among others). Subject-specific rules concern the likelihood of termination in respect of particular contracts, such as leases, deposits, employment and others. The chapter goes on to show that, exceptionally, termination or rescission is automatic, while in the majority of cases one of the parties, typically the debtor, must apply to the courts for termination or rescission.

11.2 RESCISSION AND TERMINATION IN THE CIVIL CODE

11.2.1 *The General Rule*

The termination of a contract by one of the parties is a remedy afforded by the law, in addition to other remedies, such as damages or specific performance.[1] Termination arises as a result of three possible grounds: a) convenience of

---

[1] Specific performance is rare, but it is stipulated in Art 468 CC, concerning the failure of the purchaser to pay by the agreed date. Termination is conjunctive to the remedy of specific performance in this case.

one of the parties;[2] b) breach (or default)[3] or c) impossibility to perform.[4] Termination is a unilateral act, save where it is mutually agreed, whose purpose is to release the terminating party from its own obligations under the contract. In most cases,[5] it is clearly an extreme act and hence the civil law typically sets strict conditions for its exercise by any of the parties or the courts,[6] as well as alternative or additional remedies.[7] As will be shown in the next section, notice is a *sine qua non* requirement of the law relating to termination.

An important distinction is necessary from the outset. The CC distinguishes between *rescission* and *termination* in respect of how the obligations in certain contracts may be extinguished; this might be confusing. Rescission is not the same as termination. It is largely equivalent to the notion of rescission at common law, which is a self-help remedy whose effect is to void the contract *ab initio* (i.e. discharge of obligations retrospectively),[8] whereas termination [or rescission as termination] serves to discharge the parties' obligations prospectively. The general rule concerning termination is found in article 183 CC. This provision, however, is concerned only with termination sought by the innocent party for the breach of contract by its counterpart.[9] Article 183(1) CC stipulates that breach of contract by one of the parties entitles the other party to demand performance or rescission.[10] Rescission under such circumstances is automatic.[11] Equally, as will be shown in a subsequent section, *force majeure* under article 188 CC serves to rescind the contract between the parties.

[2] See, for example, Art 707 CC (known also as 'termination at will, or termination of convenience'), in which case, however, the terminating party will compensate the other party for any expenses incurred until such time, anticipated profit or other. See Court of Cassation Judgment 222/2016, which relied on Art 707 CC, recognizing the employer's right to terminate the contract, subject to payment of compensation for work accomplished, damages for losses as well as moral damages, where applicable.

[3] As contemplated in Art 183 CC, discussed in more detail below.

[4] Arts 187 and 188 CC.

[5] But not always. Art 291 CC refers to situations whereby 'an obligation shall persist for a fixed time if its validity or termination depends on a definite future event'. See Court of Cassation Judgment 154/2012.

[6] See Court of Cassation Judgment 122/2013, where it was emphasized that 'it is not permissible for a judge to rescind or amend a valid contract on the ground that the revocation or modification is required by rules of justice. Justice completes the will of the contracting parties, but does not abrogate it'.

[7] For example, mutual, or unilateral withholding of performance until performance is made by the other party. See Art 191 CC.

[8] *Long v Lloyd* [1958] EWCA Civ 3 (Eng).

[9] Court of Cassation Judgment 219/2011, noting that Art 183 CC is not a peremptory norm.

[10] See Court of Cassation Judgment 8/2012, which stated that in addition to rescission the claimant may also demand compensation; equally Court of Cassation Judgment 371/2014, where it held that: 'The contract is considered to include the rescinding condition, even if it is free of it'.

[11] Art 184(1) CC.

Another type of termination is recognised by article 189 CC. This is known as *ekalah* and refers to the mutual termination of the contract by the parties.[12] Hence, the difference between articles 183 and 189 CC is that under article 189 CC, the parties may decide to amicably put an end to their contract even if there is no breach by one of them. This mutual termination is considered an agreement that is distinct from the contract that the parties seek to terminate. In order for this new agreement (i.e. the termination agreement) to come into force, fresh offer and acceptance are necessary, as well a fresh subject-matter Indeed, the subject-matter of such an agreement is the termination itself. However, if any of the contracting parties has received a benefit from a third party relating to the contract which the parties are seeking to terminate, the mutual termination shall be considered a new contract for this third party. This is because of restitution. For example, if one party sells the subject-matter of the contract to a third party, while the original contract is terminated by a mutual agreement, the termination is considered a new contract for the third party. As a result, the price must be paid to the original owner if it has not so been paid. But if the price is already paid, the party who received payment must return it back to the other party to fulfil its restitution obligation. Yet, the contract with the third party remains valid in accordance with article 190 CC. The CC does not differentiate between termination under the terms of articles 184 and 189 CC when determining the retrospective discharge of the parties from their obligations. Moreover, articles 183 and 189 CC apply equally to all types of bilateral agreements.

It should be emphasised that restitution is always required[13] whether termination takes place through the court (article 183 CC) or by mutual agreement (article 185 CC). In both cases, the parties are discharged from their obligations retrospectively.[14] Article 190 CC distinguishes between rescission and termination by providing that: 'in terms of its correlative effects, rescission shall be deemed termination of the contract between the contracting parties and a new

---

[12] A specific application of *ekalah* is illustrated by explicit or implicit automatic termination clauses in contracts. The Court of Cassation, for example, has decreed that if a company is subject to a fixed term mentioned in its contract and that term has expired, then the company must be terminated by the force of law starting from the date of the expiry of the term fixed in the contract. This does not prevent any of the partners from obtaining a judgment ordering the termination of the company for the renaming partners. Judgment 114/2012.

[13] Court of Cassation Judgment 219/2011.

[14] See Court of Cassation Judgment 91/2015. The Court noted that the effect of termination is that the 'contracting parties return to the state they were in before the contract, so the buyer returns the sold object and its fruits if it has received it, and the seller returns the price and interest received'; the Court of Cassation has held in the event of time-based contracts or regularly renewable contracts, such as lease contracts, that they cannot be subjected to retroactive effect. This is because of their nature as well as because of the reciprocity of obligations, which makes it impossible to turn back the part executed thereof. Court of Cassation Judgment 28/2010.

contract in favour of third parties'. Article 185 CC, which departs from the civil law tradition,[15] stipulates that upon rescission the parties shall be:

> 'reinstated to the position they were prior to the date of the conclusion of the contract ... [and] if reinstatement is impossible the courts may grant indemnity'.

The Court of Cassation has made a notable exception to the general rule in article 185 CC. It has emphasised that a term contract or a continuous and periodic contract of implementation is inherently unamenable to the idea of retroactive effect; rather, the retroactive effect of the annulment does not apply to the past except in respect of immediate contracts.[16]

According to paragraph 2 of article 183 CC, the courts may determine an appropriate period of grace for the obligor to perform its obligations and will reject an application for termination if the impugned obligation is relatively insignificant compared to the overall corpus of obligations incumbent on the obligor (fundamental non-performance). The parties may mutually agree, in express language, that failure to perform automatically terminates the contract, without the need to seek approval from the courts.[17]

Party autonomy generally confers upon the parties the right to terminate the contract upon its conclusion, provided that the subject matter of the contract still exists and is in the possession of either party.[18] Where the subject matter is lost, damaged, or otherwise disposed of in part in favour of a third party, the contract may be rescinded to the extent of the remaining part, in accordance with article 189(2) CC. Moreover, *bona fide* special successors to a contract susceptible to rescission remain unaffected.[19]

When a contract is terminated, it ceases to be a valid basis upon which to make a request for compensation. This is quite apart from claims arising out of breach of contract. The absence of a contract upon termination excludes the possibility of a contractual breach. If the basis of the pertinent claim is a fault of the debtors, the correct legal basis for any post-termination claim is tort.[20]

---

[15] See Art 7.3.5 and Art 7.3.7 UNIDROIT PICC. Restitution 'of whatever has been supplied under the contract' is possible under the PICC, in accordance with Art 7.3.6, but in respect of contracts to be performed at only one time; hence excluding contracts to be performed over a period of time.

[16] Court of Cassation Judgment 53/2012.

[17] Art 184(1) and (2) CC. Such an eventuality was expressly stated in the contract in Court of Cassation Judgment 219/2011.

[18] Art 189(1) CC.

[19] Art 186 CC.

[20] Court of Cassation Judgment 100/2016.

11.2.2 *Notice to Terminate*

Article 183(1) CC requires that formal notice be given to the non-performing party (obligor) in order to fulfil its performance before going on to terminate or rescind the contract. Notice is a quintessential element of the civil law tradition concerning termination[21] because of the cooperative nature of contracts and the prevalence of good faith therein. Article 184(3) CC rightly specifies that a formal notice is always required, even if the parties agree otherwise, save for commercial transactions where it is assumed that the parties possess sufficient experience and are operating at arm's length. Exceptionally, notice is *not* required in the sale of movables where the buyer fails to make payment by the agreed date and unless the parties have agreed otherwise.[22] The Court of Cassation has equally iterated that the parties to a lease may validly agree that no notice is required in the event of persistent non-payment of the agreed fee.[23]

What is not *prima facie* clear from a reading of articles 183 and 184 CC is whether automatic termination clauses in contracts governed under Qatari law are binding as such, or whether a further application to the courts is required. The case law of the Court of Cassation concurs in favour of party autonomy on this issue and the Court does not demand further recourse to the courts.[24] In a notable case decided by the English High Court, where the contract was governed by Qatari law, appropriate notice was the key issue.[25] The High Court delved deep into, among others, the legislative history of the notice requirements underlying the CC. The parties had agreed that in the event of default on the part of the contractor, Qatar Foundation (QF) would issue a notice of default with details of such default. If the contractor did not commence work in a manner consistent with the terms of the agreement, QF could then issue a notice of termination.[26] The contractor argued that Qatari law required an application to the courts for termination on the ground of breach. The High Court did not find anything in articles 183 and 184 CC, or the judgments of the Court of Cassation, that specifically precludes the parties from agreeing to automatic termination clauses without recourse to the courts.[27]

---

[21] Notice requirements apply in respect of all types of contractual terminations, as explained in this chapter. See, for example, Arts 744 and 746 CC regarding deposit contracts; Art 778 CC concerning insurance.

[22] Art 471 CC.

[23] Court of Cassation Judgment 110/2007. But see Court of Cassation Judgment 86/2009 and the discussion below in the sub-section dealing with the termination of lease agreements.

[24] Court of Cassation Judgment 219/2011, noting, however, that a prerequisite for automatic termination clauses is that they be clearly and unequivocally stated in the parties' agreement.

[25] *Obrascon Huarte Lain SA et al v Qatar Foundation*, [2019] EWHC 2539 (Comm).

[26] Ibid, para 5.

[27] Ibid, paras 73–75.

11.2.3 *Termination on the Basis of Anticipated Breach*

The CC does not specifically address the legality of termination on the basis of an anticipated breach. Such a right should be deemed and exercised mutatis mutandis in accordance with articles 183–84 and 187 CC. There are several reasons for this. Firstly, the obligor's impossibility to perform must certainly also operate in the interests of the obligee. If the obligor does not seek to terminate a work that is impossible to conclude, then surely the obligee has the right to terminate before the scheduled delivery. Secondly, there is nothing in the CC that expressly or implicitly prevents the parties from agreeing to terminate in the event of an anticipated breach. Thirdly, termination on this basis is a general principle of the law of contracts.

11.3 UNILATERAL DISPOSITION

Article 192 CC regulates the so-called unilateral disposition. It recognises that as a general rule unilateral acts do not create, amend or terminate an existing obligation, save if the law provides otherwise. There are several instances in this chapter whereby the CC recognises that certain unilateral acts either justify termination by the other party (e.g. non-payment of debt upon the agreed date) or otherwise (in limited circumstances) terminate a contract in and by themselves.

11.4 DISCHARGE

Article 400 CC regulates when the debtor may be discharged from its obligation by a unilateral act of the creditor. It enunciates that an obligation expires when the debtor fulfils or performs its obligation to the creditor (obligor). Discharge shall be effective when the creditor becomes aware of the performance. In the event that the obligation is only partially or poorly performed, the creditor may reject that such performance shall discharge the debtor from its obligation. In this case, the original obligation and all its terms, securities and remedies shall become effective once again.[28] In many cases, however, the creditor may refuse discharging the debtor on arbitrary grounds. In case 152/2018, an employee argued that his employer refused to pay the lawful end-of-service gratuity in respect of the period from 1979 to 2006. The employer had apparently secured a signed statement from the employee that the end-of-service gratuity had been paid, but the employee provided sufficient proof that the employer withheld its performance (i.e. to pay the end-of-service gratuity)

---

[28] Art 400(2) CC.

until the employee signed the statement. The Court of Cassation was satisfied that discharge was not evident from the employee's signed statement and was thus entitled to his end-of-service gratuity.[29]

11.5 TERMINATION BY REASON OF DEATH

The admonition in article 39(1) CC whereby legal personality ceases upon death is not particularly useful. As a general rule, although the death of the offeror terminates the offer,[30] once the contract has been made the death of one of the parties thereto does not automatically terminate the said contract. In some cases, the CC specifically articulates automatic termination, subject to the parties' approval, in the event of the death of one of the parties,[31] but not in others.[32] The death of the landlord or the trustee (of a *waqf*) does not terminate the contract, as the contract can clearly be inherited by its heir. In the case of a lease agreement, neither the death of the tenant nor the landlord terminates the contract, save where the tenant's heirs can demonstrate that continuation of the lease has 'become more burdensome than their resources can bear or that the lease exceeds their needs'.[33] Where the deceased tenant leased the property for its personal or business affairs, its heirs or the landlord may seek to terminate the lease.[34]

With respect to employment contracts, these terminate upon the death of the contractor if 'its personal qualifications or capabilities are taken into consideration upon making the contract', otherwise the contract shall not terminate automatically.[35] This no doubt covers situations where the contractor was an employee of a corporation or other legal person, in which case its death does not terminate the contract. Article 705 CC goes on to say that the employer may demand termination of the contract where the contractor's personal skills are significant and the employer has no desire to see the work incomplete in the event of the contractor's death. In this case, termination is possible 'if no adequate securities to perform the work properly are available in the heirs of the contractor'.

---

[29] Court of Cassation Judgment 152/2018.
[30] Art 71 CC. Equally, in accordance with Art 74 CC, acceptance shall be terminated by the offeree's death if this occurs before the acceptance reaches the notice of the offeror.
[31] Art 681 CC, according to which lending shall terminate on the death of the borrower.
[32] For example, in accordance with Art 98(2) CC, the promisor's death shall not preclude the conclusion of the promised contract if accepted by the promisee and its acceptance reaches the promisor within the time limit prescribed by the promise.
[33] Art 633 CC. See also Arts 659 and 668 CC.
[34] Art 634 CC.
[35] Art 705 CC.

It is clear that the law views several types of agreements as being capable of survival well after the original parties' demise. This is, however, only possible if the original parties so agreed and provided that their heirs or surviving third parties have equally agreed to substitute the rights and obligations of the deceased.[36] In this sense, the death of the insured (person) does not automatically terminate the insurance agreement. The rights and obligations arising from such contract pass to the insured person's heirs, subject to the consent of the insurer.[37] Alternatively, either the insurer or the heir may terminate the agreement by notice to the other party.[38]

11.6 LIMITATIONS

Limitation or prescription is a definitive period of time stipulated in the law upon the expiration of which the creditor's right to claim performance of an outstanding obligation is deemed to have expired. The general prescription period is fifteen years in accordance with article 403 CC.[39] A five-year prescription period applies to claims by certain classes of professionals, such as doctors,[40] tax claims,[41] certain insurance claims[42] and guarantees.[43] One-year prescription periods apply to claims of traders, craftsmen and those in the hospitality industry against their clients.[44]

The period of prescription shall commence from the date the aforementioned creditors supplied their initial (first) service or delivery,[45] or the date the debt matured.[46] The calculation of prescription periods shall be in days and not hours in accordance with article 409 CC. Where a reason exists to suspend the calculation of a period of limitation (e.g. in accordance with article 413 CC) for certain heirs, such suspension shall not apply to other heirs in respect of whom the suspensive reason does not apply.[47]

---

[36] For example, Art 681 CC concerning lending; Art 705 CC (contractors); Art 747 CC (deposits).
[37] Art 795(1) CC.
[38] Art 795(2) and (3) CC.
[39] See Court of Cassation Judgment 63/2016, relating to a loan agreement entered into by a bank.
[40] Art 405 CC. See Court of Cassation Judgment 225/2011.
[41] Art 406(1) CC.
[42] Art 800 CC. See in this connection Cassation Court Judgments 145/2013 and 181/2014. It has been emphasized that claims under Art 800 CC are subject to a 'special tripartite statute of limitations'. Court of Cassation Judgment 141/2015. The statute of limitation begins when the debt becomes payable. See Court of Cassation Judgment 36/2005.
[43] Court of Cassation Judgment 2/2010.
[44] Art 407(1) CC.
[45] Art 408(1). Paragraph 2 stipulates that where the claims in Arts 405 and 407 CC were incorporated in a deed, the claim arising thereof shall prescribe after fifteen years.
[46] Art 410(1) CC.
[47] Art 412 CC.

Prescription is not deemed to have commenced where the creditor lacks capacity unless represented by a competent agent.[48] Prescription shall not apply where a creditor is prevented from claiming his right, even if such prevention is moral and equally does not apply to the relationship between agent and principal.[49] An interesting case concerning article 411 CC arose in a case that reached the Court of Cassation in 2017.[50] There, an employee claimed end-of-service gratuity and damages against his employer for unfair dismissal. More than a year had elapsed since the termination of the employment contract, however, and according to article 10 of the Labour Law, such claims are admissible only if brought within a year from termination. The employee argued that his late claim was the result of his fear that he would forfeit his residency (moral claim) he to bring a suit and hence he waited until finding new employment. The Court of Cassation dismissed the employee's claim, arguing that the moral reasons offered by him were insufficient to justify delaying the suit against the employer.

Prescription may be suspended in several ways. The first is articulated in article 413 CC, whereby this may be achieved by requesting the courts to accept one's right in bankruptcy or distribution, and any other procedure available to the creditor. The second is enunciated in article 414(1) CC, which allows suspension if the debtor expressly or implicitly acknowledges the creditor's right.[51] Where the period of prescription is interrupted, a new period shall begin from 'the time of expiry of the effect arising from the cause of such interruption and such new period shall be the same as the original period'. Where the right has become *res judicata* and the prescription has been interrupted by acknowledgement of the debtor, the new period of prescription shall be fifteen years unless the pertinent judgment provides otherwise.[52]

Article 418 CC makes an important departure from general party autonomy. It provides that prescription may not be waived before the pertinent right is established, nor are the parties free to mutually agree on their own prescription periods, nor waive statutory prescriptions in respect of an established right.[53]

---

[48] Art 411(2) CC.
[49] Art 411(1) CC. See Court of Cassation Judgment 167/2012.
[50] Court of Cassation Judgment 86/2017.
[51] Para 2 of Art 414 CC explains when this is implicit.
[52] Art 415(1) and (2) CC.
[53] See Court of Cassation Judgment 284/2014.

11.7 TERMINATION BASED ON THE TYPE OF CONTRACT

The CC, while providing a general framework for termination/rescission, introduces special provisions for the termination of particular types of contracts, in respect of which there is a desire to distinguish from general contracts. Some, but not all, of these will be analysed in the following subsections.

11.7.1 *Termination of Lease Contracts*

The lease shall terminate upon the expiry of its term without notice to vacate[54] unless it is agreed to extend the lease for a fixed or other terms if no specific date is stated.[55] Notice is generally required even where the lessor is the State.[56] The Court of Cassation has emphasised that notice to evict is a legal act unilaterally issued which includes a desire by its issuer, based on its intention to terminate the contract. 'It shall include an unequivocal expression of such desire. For the effect of such notice to be realized it is sufficient that it generally indicates the intention behind it, being an expression of the desire to consider the contract terminated at a specific date'.[57] The right not to be evicted and by extension, the prohibition against the termination of a residential lease constitutes a rule of public policy.[58] It has further been established that the sub-tenancy contract shall inevitably end upon termination of the principal lease contract, even if it is grounded on the conditions stipulated therein.[59]

The CC and Law No. 4 of 2008 Regarding Property Leasing spell out certain instances which entitle the tenant to terminate or demand the reduction in rent, in addition to a claim for damages. This occurs where: a) the condition of the leased property does not meet its intended use, in which case the tenant may also demand repairs;[60] b) the repairs cause any breach, partially

---

[54] Court of Cassation Judgment 19/2011; Court of Cassation Judgment 113/2012; Court of Cassation Judgment 58/2012, in accordance with Art 15 of Law No 4 of 2008 Regarding Property Leases; equally Court of Cassation Judgments 42/2013 and 258/2016.

[55] Art 625 CC. Art 588 CC spells out the period of notice required under the CC in order to make termination effective.

[56] Court of Cassation Judgment 28/2010.

[57] Court of Cassation Judgment 86/2009.

[58] Court of Cassation Judgment 32/2015.

[59] Court of Cassation Judgment 138/2010.

[60] Art 591(1) CC. See also Art 594(1) CC giving rise to a claim of repairs in conjunction with a right to terminate; Art 5 of Law No. 4 of 2008 Regarding Property Leasing empowers the tenant to terminate the contract when the lessor (landlord) fails to provide the tenant's leased premise in a useable condition. However, the lessee is required to notify the lessor. Law No 4 provides an option to the tenant to either terminate the lease contract or decrease the rent to such an amount that would provide a benefit.

or in whole, to the intended use, in which case the tenant may demand termination or a reduction in the rent.[61] If the tenant chooses to remain in the leased property until the repairs are completed, the right to termination is extinguished;[62] c) if the condition of the leased property endangers health, the tenant may demand termination even if such right was mutually waived.[63] The same applies in respect of leased property that is demolished;[64] d) where a third party claims a right that is in conflict with the rights of the tenant under the lease contract and the tenant is deprived of using the property, the tenant is entitled to terminate or seek a reduction in the rent, as well as indemnity;[65] e) termination is also possible in the event of considerable material interference by a third party, such that prevents the tenant from using the property;[66] f) the tenant is equally permitted to terminate where considerable deficiency in the use of the property is caused by the acts of a public authority, save if otherwise agreed between him and the landlord;[67] g) latent defects which the landlord knew or should have known give rise to a claim for repairs, termination or reduction of the fee [as well as damages];[68] h) the same is true where the leased property lacks the agreed specifications.[69]

The extinction effect of a termination ceases when the terminating tenant continues to occupy the leased property without objection by the landlord.[70] Moreover, where it has been agreed that the landlord may terminate the lease for personal reasons, the landlord shall so notify the tenant.[71]

The CC recognises an exceptional right of termination for the tenant where the lease is meaningless for the tenant, other than unforeseen circumstances under article 632 CC.[72] Article 635 CC allows the tenant to terminate the lease contract when required to change its place of residence. In equal measure, where a land tenant fails to cultivate the land due to illness or for any other reason, and if it is not possible that he or she be substituted by family members, either party may demand termination.[73]

---

[61] Art 595(2) CC.
[62] Art 595(3) CC.
[63] Art 591(2) CC.
[64] Art 596 CC.
[65] Art 599 CC.
[66] Art 600 CC.
[67] Art 602 CC.
[68] Art 604 CC. See also Art 608 CC to this effect.
[69] Art 606 CC.
[70] Art 626(1) CC. See Court of Cassation Judgment 134/2013, referring also to Art 588 CC.
[71] Art 631 CC.
[72] Court of Cassation Judgment 180/2011.
[73] Art 658 CC.

The Court of Cassation has maintained that expropriation of the leased property for the public benefit is considered a total destruction that results in the termination of the lease contract by virtue of the operation of law, specifically Law 13 of 1988.[74]

No doubt, the landlord (lessor) equally has a right to terminate the lease agreement. Article 19 of Law No 8/2008 states that the lessor may terminate the lease contract during the term of the contract if the lessee fails to pay rent on due dates without an excuse, as accepted by the Ministerial Committee for the Settlement of Rental Disputes. The parties may validly agree that in the event of persistent non-payment that termination by the landlord/lessor shall be automatic without a notice or obtaining a court ruling.[75] The lessor equally enjoys the right to terminate where it intends to elevate the building, subject to obtaining the required permits in accordance with article 19(6) of the Lease Law.[76]

11.7.2 *Termination of Employment Contracts*

Employment law is only briefly addressed by the CC, as is usual in the civil law tradition. The CC effectively addresses only the strictly contractual underpinnings of the employment relationship. It is Law No. 14 of 2004, On the Promulgation of Labour Law, which constitutes the more detailed legislation on employment. Under no circumstances does the CC allow the employer to unilaterally terminate its contract with the contractor[77] and as a general rule an employment agreement expires where the parties have agreed to a specific period of performance and such period has elapsed.[78]

There are, no doubt, situations where the contractor's (employee) performance falls below the parties' agreed expectations, which entails a breach of the employment contract. Article 688(1) CC enunciates the general principle whereby the employer may terminate its contract with the contractor in the event that the contractor's performance is defective, subject to a strict condition. The employer must notify the contractor to correct its performance (which is effectively a breach of the parties' contract) within a reasonable

---

[74] Court of Cassation Judgment 34/2011; equally, Court of Cassation Judgment 15/2012.
[75] Court of Cassation Judgment 110/2007.
[76] Court of Cassation Judgment 401/2015.
[77] There are a number of special circumstances where termination is never permitted, for example, following a labor accident whereby the employee has not fully recovered. See Court of Cassation Judgment 24/2010; see equally Court of Cassation Judgment 2/2011, discussing Art 51 of the Labour Law.
[78] Art 703 CC.

time.[79] Article 16 of the Labour Law provides that the employer may terminate the training contract before the end of its period where the trainee is proven to be unfit to learn the profession or breaches an essential obligation expressed in the contract. Article 39 of the Labour Law further provides that during the probation period, the employer may terminate the contract by giving a notice of one month where the employee breached the employment contract. The employee may also terminate the contract by giving a minimum of two months' written notice to the employer.[80]

Termination of employment requires sufficient notice under article 61 of the Labour Law;[81] otherwise, the terminating party is liable to compensation and disciplinary action.[82] Exceptionally, the employer may demand termination without notice or time limits if the correction or remedy (of the breach by the contractor) is impossible.[83] The same right to terminate arises where the contractor either delays the commencement or conclusion of the work to such a degree that this cannot possibly be delivered in the agreed period, or where its actions indicate its intention not to perform or otherwise make the performance impossible.[84] A notice is equally required where performance requires specific action within a prescribed timeframe and the employer has failed to act therein. Following the lapse of the prescribed timeframe, the employer may terminate the contract.[85] However, termination shall not be permitted where the contractor's defective performance has not significantly decreased the value of the work or its intended utility.[86]

11.7.3 *Termination of Insurance Contracts*

It should be pointed out that the Court of Appeal has iterated that in case of doubt, insurance contracts must be viewed as adhesion agreements under the terms of article 107 CC.[87] The CC distinguishes between termination and

---

[79] Failure to observe notice periods leads to an obligation to offer compensation for the periods where such notice was due, in accordance with Art 49 of the Labour Law. See Court of Cassation Judgment 38/2010.

[80] See Art 51 of the Labour Law for an enumeration of reasons under which the employer is entitled to terminate the contract.

[81] Court of Cassation Judgment 18/2010.

[82] Court of Cassation Judgment 212/2012.

[83] Art 688(2) CC.

[84] Art 689 CC. See Court of Cassation Judgment 36/2010.

[85] Art 692(2) CC.

[86] Art 688(3) CC.

[87] Court of Appeal Judgment 1272/2015. See also Arts 775 and 775 CC, which address void terms and conditions in insurance contracts, as well as a variation of the *contra preferentum* rule.

suspension of insurance contracts. Suspension exists where the insured person fails to pay the agreed premium despite being notified to do so.[88] Upon expiry of the suspension, the insurer may demand termination under paragraph 2 of article 789 CC. If during the suspension and prior to the termination the insured person pays in full the outstanding premiums and any accrued expenses, the insurance is reinstated.[89] Insurance contracts (regulated by law) whose duration exceeds five years terminate at the end of every five years by notifying the other party six months prior to its expiration.[90] Termination is also possible where the insurance premium involves considerations that increase the insured risk and these considerations cease to exist or are impaired.[91]

11.7.4 *Agency Contracts*

Agency and all forms of contracting through other entities are specifically discussed in detail in Chapter 4. Here it only suffices to state that an agency contract may be terminated unilaterally by either party, unless the agency is decided in favour of the agent, or if a third party has an interest in it. However, the termination of the agency at an inappropriate time or without an acceptable excuse gives rise to an obligation to compensate as one of the forms of abuse of rights.[92] This is in accordance with article 735 CC. Article 735 CC indicates that although the principal has the right to dismiss its agent at any time before the completion of the work, the agency ends with the agent's dismissal. However, as already stated, the legislator restricted this right where the agency was issued for the benefit of the agent. It is forbidden for the principal to terminate or restrict the agency without the consent of the one in whose favour the agency was issued, and the dismissal of the agent is not valid.[93]

11.8 SETTLEMENT

The notion of settlement envisaged in articles 354 ff CC aims to terminate an existing obligation. This may amount to the payment of an outstanding debt or the performance of a due obligation. When such performance or payment is made to the creditor, the obligation is deemed terminated. It is usual in the civil law of Qatar for the provisions of a settlement to be encompassed within

[88] Art 789(1) CC.
[89] Art 789 (4) CC.
[90] Art 778 CC.
[91] Art 758 CC.
[92] Court of Cassation Judgment 163/2016.
[93] Court of Cassation Judgment 51/2013.

the broader category of termination, because the settlement of debt serves to terminate the contract.

11.8.1 *Parties to the Settlement*

This may seem straightforward, but it is not. Article 250 CC expresses the general position that where the terms of an agreement require performance by the obligor itself, the obligee may validly reject performance by a third party. Article 354 CC is mindful of this general rule and stipulates that a debt may be satisfied by a third party against the will of the obligor only if such payment/performance meets the approval of the obligee. Where a third party pays a debt, it may have recourse against the debtor for reimbursement.[94] Even so, where a debt is paid against the will of the debtor/obligor, the latter may prevent recourse by the payer if it is able to demonstrate that the payer has an interest in objecting to such payment.[95] The third party (payer) substitutes the creditor, in accordance with article 357 CC, where: a) it was obliged to pay; b) it is a creditor itself; c) the payer pays the debt to retrieve a thing held as security and d) the payer has a special right of subrogation.[96]

Subrogation in the rights of the creditor is generally permitted under articles 359 and 360(2) CC but is naturally limited to the payment expected by the debtor. The rights of the new creditor following subrogation are only effective against third parties if the date of the agreement with the debtor, the loan agreement and the settlement are fixed.[97] Payment of a debt may be made to a person other than the creditor (and hence the debt is discharged), so long as the latter consents, or such payment is in the interests of the creditor.[98] This is a species of set-off, in the sense that the debtor sets off its debt to the creditor by paying another entity to which the creditor has a debt, or against which it expects to incur a debt or some other kind of financial relationship.

Payment is deemed to have been made where the debtor validly deposits the outstanding amount, provided it has offered to make such deposit and the creditor has accepted. If the latter has not so consented, the debtor may approach the courts for a judgment validating its deposit.[99] Where payment is in the form of an asset the debtor must notify the creditor of delivery thereof

---

[94] Art 356(1) CC.
[95] Art 356(2) CC.
[96] See also Art 358 CC.
[97] Art 358(1) CC.
[98] Art 363 CC.
[99] Art 365 CC. See also Art 366 CC, which allows unilateral deposit under particular circumstances, such as where the identity and domicile of the creditor is not known.

and apply to the court for permission to deposit the asset.[100] If the value of the asset while in deposit risks depreciation the debtor may seek approval from the court to sell it, in which case it is discharged from its obligation upon depositing the proceeds of the sale.[101] Where the debtor makes payment or performance and the creditor rejects or declares its intent to reject these, the debtor shall notify the creditor. Upon notification, 'the creditor shall bear the consequences of loss or damage to the relevant asset. In such event, the debtor shall be entitled to deposit such asset at the expense of the creditor and demand indemnity, as applicable'.[102]

11.8.2 *Object of Settlement*

The parties are free to resolve how to settle the debt of the debtor, but the general rule is that it must be paid immediately upon becoming final unless the courts or the law determine otherwise through periodic instalments.[103] Payment of the debt may not be higher than its value, nor lower and neither the debtor nor the creditor may be coerced into accepting alternative (or partial) payment, even if higher than the value of the debt.[104] Where an outstanding debt has incurred further expenses and compensation (for delay or other lawful reasons), and payment by the debtor is not sufficient to cover all three, article 372 CC provides that payment shall first be applied to expenses, next to compensation and finally to the debt itself. In the event of multiple debts by the same debtor to the same creditor, the debtor may designate which debt he wishes to settle unless the parties have agreed otherwise.[105] Any expenses associated with performance are borne by the debtor, unless otherwise provided.[106]

11.8.3 *Settlement with Agreed Consideration*

Discharge from an existing obligation may be achieved by the creditor's consent to be paid by a thing other than what was originally agreed. Such a settlement is accepted by article 379 CC and is known as a settlement with agreed consideration. This is because the new thing is given in consideration for the debt. Article 380 CC emphasises that the qualities of the transfer of the new

---

[100] Art 368 CC.
[101] Art 369 CC.
[102] Art 364 CC.
[103] Art 375 CC.
[104] Arts 370 and 371 CC.
[105] Art 373 CC.
[106] Art 377 CC.

thing apply to the settlement. If the title of the new thing was transferred to the creditor, the provisions of sale apply, including those concerning defects and guarantees.

11.8.4 *Novation*

The subject matter of novation is examined in detail in Chapter 13, to which the readers are directed. Novation is effectively the transfer of a debt by the debtor (novator) to a new creditor (novate), subject to the consent of the original creditor. The new party assumes the obligations of the original debtor and in this manner releases the original debtor from any obligation to perform. As a result, novation terminates the original contract, as well as any associated securities.[107]

11.8.5 *Assignment*

It should be pointed out that novation is different in its operation and effects as compared to the assignment. The Qatari CC distinguishes between a) the assignment of contractual rights by the assignor (rights holder) to a third party (assignee) and b) the assignment of debts by the debtor (assignor) to a new lender/creditor (assignee). Assignment of debt generally requires the consent of the original creditor, whereas assignment of rights simply warrants a notification to the debtor.[108] Chapter 13 of this book provides a fuller analysis of third parties to contracts.

11.8.6 *Set-Off*

Set-off is a mechanism whereby the debtor may discharge its debt to the creditor by offsetting it against a debt owed by the creditor to the debtor.[109] Article 390 CC stipulates that offset is possible even where the basis of each debt is different,[110] provided, however, that the subject matter of each debt is cash or fungible[111] things of the same quality and quantity and that both debts are free from any outstanding legal dispute. In many cases, the creditor will not accept the debtor's set-off offer and hence the debtor will apply to the courts

---

[107] Art 384 CC. Any securities placed by the original debtor to the obligation may be transferred to the new contract under the conditions specified in Art 385 CC.

[108] Court of Cassation Judgment 79/2012.

[109] See Court of Cassation Judgment 181/2011, where set off was construed as a competition of opposing civil obligations.

[110] See Court of Cassation Judgment 236/2013; Court of Appeal Judgment 450/2017.

[111] Fungible things are defined in Art 60(1) CC.

for a judgment to this effect. In this manner, set-off is a right prescribed by the CC. The courts, however, may not under any circumstances set-off a limited number of assets. These include, in accordance with article 392 CC, the following: a) a thing dispossessed without any right from its owner; b) a deposited or lent thing; c) a non-attachable right or d) an alimony debt.

It is also quite possible that the debtor's debt is larger than the debt of the creditor to the debtor, in which case discharge is partial.[112] While it is crucial that the asset destined for set-off is actually in the ownership of the debtor, if the debtor's ownership is conditional on the rights of third parties, such as where it is attached, then set-off is not possible.[113] Where the debt is prescribed at the time of set-off, such debt may still be set-off, 'provided that prescription shall not be effective at the time when set-off becomes possible'.[114]

The subrogation of the rights of the creditor to a transferee with the consent of the debtor should not be overlooked. In this case, if a set-off was possible prior to the transfer, such set-off may not be invoked against the transferee. In the event that the debtor had simply been notified of the transfer by the creditor, but had not assented, it may invoke the set-off against the transferee.[115]

11.8.7 *Combined Obligations*

Articles 398 and 399 CC contemplate the scenario of combined obligations. This arises where the same person is simultaneously both creditor and debtor in respect of a single debt. In such exceptional circumstances and to the extent of the overlap the debt expires. Where the grounds for the unity of the liability cease to exist, the debt and its attachments shall be renewed in respect of all the concerned parties.

11.9 FORCE MAJEURE

The Qatari CC distinguishes between various types of hardship, yet not all of these allow the debtor to terminate or rescind the contract or its effects.[116]

---

[112] Art 393 CC.
[113] Art 395 CC.
[114] Art 394 CC.
[115] Art 396 CC.
[116] A poignant example that does not neatly fall into the following subsections arose in a case where the parties had inserted an arbitration clause in their contract that designated as its seat a place that did not exist at the time of the contract. The Court of Appeal held that the possibility of its existence in the future is sufficient as long as it is not an absolute impossibility, and relative impossibility does not prevent the obligation from being established under Arts 148 and 149 CC. See Court of Appeal Judgment 523/2018.

Article 258 CC makes it clear that the parties may well agree that the obligor shall be liable for performance or indemnity in the event of *force majeure* or unforeseen incidents. Hence, in the first instance, the regulation of *force majeure* is a matter of agreement.[117] Nonetheless, even though rescission under articles 187 and 188 CC may be waived by the parties, this is not possible in the context of adhesion contracts.[118]

The CC distinguishes between *force majeure* arising in contracts binding on one party and in respect of contracts binding on both parties. *Force majeure* in contracts where an obligation burdens one party only is defined in article 187(1) CC as *impossibility* of performance 'beyond the control' of the obligor. Unlike the civil law tradition, this provision stipulates that *force majeure* in contracts imposing performance obligations on only one party serves to automatically terminate the contract and hence the obligation is deemed extinguished. Where the impossibility is partial, the debtor may enforce those part(s) of the obligation that can be performed by the obligor.[119]

In the event of contracts imposing obligations on both parties, where the obligor's obligation (but not also the obligee's) is extinguished by reason of *force majeure* (impossibility to perform critical obligations beyond the obligor's control), the contract is considered rescinded *ipso facto* for both parties. This is clearly stipulated in article 188(1) CC.[120] The Court of Cassation has held that the rescission of a contract by virtue of article 188(1) CC is possible only where the external cause has resulted in 'absolute impossibility to perform', in which case the burden of proof falls on the debtor.[121] It is for these reasons that the classical position on *force majeure* under Islamic law (qūwa qāhira) cannot, and in fact is not, sustained in the CC. The *Sharia* recognises any act of God or unforeseen condition as a ground for terminating the conduct,[122]

---

[117] The Court of Cassation in its Judgment 114/2009 emphasized the sanctity of party autonomy in consonance with the parties' agreement. This clearly applies to the contractual regulation of *force majeure*.

[118] See Chapter 7.

[119] Art 187(2) CC.

[120] This was duly noted by Court of the Cassation Judgment 257/2018. See also Court of Cassation Judgment 449/2017 where *force majeure* was referred to *obiter dicta* without much elaboration. In the case at hand, the Court argued that if the hacking of bank accounts was beyond the control of the bank (while at the same time not compounded by the account holder's negligence) then the unlawful removal of funds from bank accounts could amount to *force majeure*.

[121] Court of Cassation Judgment 257/2018. See also Court of Cassation Judgment 13/2010, where it was held that impossibility beyond the control of the obligor arises where the event in question is unpredictable and impossible to avoid and the implementation of the commitment under the contract was impossible for everyone in the debtor's position. See also Court of Cassation Judgment 51/2008 regarding the burden of proof.

[122] See S E Rayner, 'A Note on Force Majeure in Islamic Law' (1991) 6 Arab LQ 86.

which is not the case with the strict application of *force majeure*. Although it is not evident if qûwa qâhira was the inspiration behind article 171(2) CC (unforeseen circumstances), it is certainly compatible with that provision.

In 2007 the parties entered into a purchase contract of five units located on the 79th floor of a tower under construction. Delivery was due in 2010. In 2008, construction was suspended due to the economic crisis. Additionally, in 2015, the Civil Aviation Authority issued a decision by which to restrict the height of new buildings. Subsequently, the construction of floor 79 was halted and so delivery became impossible. The appellant sought remedy for both the delay and the non-performance. More specifically, the appellant requested the substitution of the contracted units by others on a different floor for a lower price. As regards the non-performance claim, the Court of Cassation held that the appellee had no obligation to substitute and since non-delivery was caused by an external event (i.e. the 2015 regulation), construction was beyond the appellee's control. This was thus a clear case of *force majeure* and there was no obligation to compensate.[123] The Court distinguished between the Civil Aviation Authority's sudden regulation and the economic crisis. The latter was deemed to be foreseeable and hence delay based on the economic crisis was held to constitute a breach of the contract warranting appropriate compensation.[124]

An event may be unforeseeable, yet not beyond the control of the obligor. In a case where a fire spread from one building to another in the presence of the fire brigade, the Court of Cassation held that while the destruction of the adjacent building was unforeseeable the prevention of the spread of the fire was avoidable.[125] The Court of Appeal has held that the basis of business is risk and speculation, and as a result, high prices and economic stagnation are not considered a sudden accident.[126]

Rescission, which is the consequence of *force majeure* is different to the termination stipulated in article 187(1) CC. Where the impossibility is partial, the obligee may either enforce the contract to the extent of such part of the obligation that can be performed or demand termination of the contract.[127] This is true also in respect of unilateral obligations that are susceptible to partial fulfilment under article 187(2) CC.

---

[123] Ibid. See also A A Abdullah, 'Coronavirus Pandemic and Contractual Justice: Legal Solutions and Realistic Approaches: A Study in Qatari Civil Law and Comparative Practices' (2020) 35 Arab LQ 1–20.

[124] Court of Cassation Judgment 257/2018.

[125] Court of Cassation Judgment 134/2015.

[126] Court of Appeal Judgment 257/2018.

[127] Art 188(2) CC.

At least one commentator has rightly argued that while article 188(1) CC refers to *force majeure*, the circumstances in which it is applied and its consequences are more akin to the English (and common law) concept of frustration.[128]

11.9.1 *Impossibility of Fulfilment*

The notion articulated in articles 187 and 188 CC is iterated in article 402 CC. This provision is known as impossibility of fulfilment. It states that obligations shall cease if the debtor can demonstrate that their fulfilment 'has become impossible due to a foreign cause beyond the control of the debtor'. It is clear that the impossibility must have arisen only after the obligation was assumed and that its effects are either permanent or at least indefinite. A similar provision regulating impossible fulfilment is found in article 704 CC, concerning construction contracts. It stipulates that where the agreed work is impossible to perform 'due to a foreign cause beyond the control of either party' the agreement shall terminate. In this case, the contractor is entitled to any costs incurred or wages, 'commensurate with the benefit obtained by the employer of such work'. In one particular case, the applicant had sought to reduce the lease price because of the global financial crisis. The Court of Cassation, in overturning the judgment of the lower court, emphasised that the applicant was required to show specifically how the crisis specifically affected him and his business.[129]

The difference between articles 187/188 CC and 402 CC seems to be their consequences. Whereas *force majeure* culminates in the rescission of the contract, impossibility of fulfilment does not expressly do so. As a result, the word 'cease' in article 402 CC must be construed as terminating the contract.

11.9.2 *Unforeseen Circumstances*

The CC takes into account the likelihood of 'unforeseen circumstances' as a factor for mitigating the parties' obligations. Article 171(2) CC specifically states that:

> Where, however, as a result of exceptional and unforeseeable events, the fulfilment of the contractual obligation, though not impossible, becomes

---

[128] Quinn Emmanuel LLP, 'Covid-19. A Comparison of the Issues Affecting Performance of Contractual Obligations under English and Qatari Law', available at: www.quinnemanuel.com/media/wxln23wu/client-alert-covid-19-issues-affecting-performance-of-contractual-obligations-in-construction-contracts-a-comparison-betwe_1-1.pdf, p 10.

[129] Court of Cassation Judgment 61/2011.

excessively onerous in such a way as to threaten the obligor with exorbitant loss, the judge may, according to the circumstances and after taking into consideration the interests of both parties, reduce the excessive obligation to a reasonable level.

Article 171(2) CC is clearly less drastic than article 188 CC. The event need only be unforeseen, but not beyond the control of the obligor. The Court of Cassation has held that the unforeseen event must arise once the fulfilment of the obligation becomes more exhausting. Once the unforeseen event takes place, the judge may balance between the parties' interests taking into consideration the current circumstances to reduce the gross imbalance of the debtor.[130] The event in question must be exceptional and unforeseen for the general public and not just for the obligor.[131] The Qatari Court of Cassation has emphasised that as businesses are required to anticipate and mitigate risk, they are presumed to anticipate future events[132] and as a result, the range of events classified as unforeseen are gradually decreasing. More significantly, the obligation under article 171(2) CC need not be impossible, but excessively onerous (so-called hardship). As a result, the courts are justified in adapting the parties' obligations to a reasonable level in order to alleviate the resultant hardship. These may include an adaptation to the value of obligations yet to be performed; granting additional time to the obligor, or even suspending certain obligations. Article 171(2) CC is a mandatory provision and may not be excluded even by agreement of the parties.

Particular manifestations of article 171(2) CC are scattered around the CC. One of these is articulated in article 632 CC, which concerns unforeseen circumstances in lease agreements. It stipulates that in the event of unforeseen circumstances making the continuation of a lease burdensome to one party, the courts may 'upon comparison of the interests of both parties, terminate the lease and fairly indemnify the other party'.[133] In one case where the lessee was unable to pay rent for a period of three years, the Court of Cassation relied on article 632 CC and released the lessee from an obligation to pay an entire year's worth of rental fees.[134] The Court of Cassation has demanded that where lower courts rely on article 632 CC, they must clarify and specify the precise nature and causes of the underlying unforeseen circumstances in

---

[130] Court of Cassation Judgment 257/2018.
[131] Quinn Emmanuel (n 128), at 11.
[132] Court of Cassation Judgment 257/2018.
[133] Art 632(1) CC.
[134] Court of Cassation Judgment 180/2011. The Court did not elaborate on the unforeseen circumstance applicable in the case at hand.

accordance with article 126 CCP, otherwise pertinent judgments will be set aside.[135] Where the landlord demands termination of the lease, the tenant shall not be forced to return the leased property until indemnity is paid in full or until sufficient security is provided, in accordance with paragraph 2 of article 632 CC. In one case where the Court of Cassation did not specifically refer to any particular provision in the CC, it went on to say that where an employee was ordinarily entitled by contract to a bonus, the employer is free from disbursing such bonus where there was a stagnation in its business that led to severe losses.[136]

Exceptionally, unforeseen circumstances may demand the termination of the contract. Article 680(1) CC states that the lender may terminate a contract, among others, in the event of an 'urgent unforeseen need at any time' during the life of the agreement.

---

[135] Court of Cassation Judgment 180/2011.
[136] Court of Cassation Judgment 246/2014.

12

Contracts and Third Parties

12.1 INTRODUCTION

This chapter will examine three distinct issues. The first concerns agreements whereby the creditor or debtor to an existing contract is substituted by a new (third) party. Two types of substitution are envisaged, namely, assignment of rights (assignment) and assignment of debt (novation). The second focus of the chapter is on the effects of contracts on *bona fide* third parties and how the law mitigates any adverse impact. The third is an innovation of the Qatari CC, examining agreements the sole object of which is to attract third parties. This chapter will not deal with the rights of successors (heirs) to a contract following the death of the contracting party.[1]

The cardinal rule of privity of contracts demands that persons who have not offered or accepted an offer – and an intention to be bound – cannot be made parties thereto. Hence, third parties may be bound to a contract in respect of which they are not original parties only through their unequivocal consent, as well as the consent of all existing parties.[2] Sometimes, such consent may be implicit whether by law or contract. The insurance carrier is entitled under its contract with the insured to pursue the latter's claim against a third-party causing loss to the insured. Here, the third party has not provided its consent, but the substitution of rights in the insurance contract between the insurance provider and the insured does not require the consent of third parties.[3] In

---

[1] See Arts 175 and 176 CC. See Court of Appeal Judgment 53/2019.
[2] See Court of Cassation Judgment 72/2011, which iterated this fundamental rule. In the case at hand, the claimant had contracted with the respondent through the latter's employee, who lacked capacity under the circumstances of the contract. The claimant was in bad faith about the employee's capacity. The Court held that the respondent was not liable for the acts of its employee (a third party).
[3] See Court of Appeal Judgments 255/2017 and 277/2017, where the Court reversed a first instance judgment rejecting the effects of a subsidiary warranty agreement. It explained that

other cases, a creditor may wish to assign its rights against a debtor to a third party, so that the third party substitutes the original creditor against the debtor. The Qatari CC regulates such matters extensively under the general principle that the consent of all parties is required.

12.2 ASSIGNMENT OF RIGHTS AND ASSIGNMENT OF DEBTS

An assignment of rights consists of a bilateral agreement between the assignor and the assignee, with sufficient notification given to the debtor. Assignment of obligations (also known as novation) clearly requires the approval of the creditor and hence the assignment of a debt necessarily encompasses an agreement between all three parties. The Qatari CC envisages both types of assignment; assignment of rights is regulated under articles 324–336 CC, while assignment of obligations is regulated by articles 337–353 CC. The pertinent structure in the CC is somewhat confusing. Despite the existence of assignment of rights and assignment of debts, as already described, which corresponds well to assignment (of rights) and novation (of obligations) under civil and common law principles,[4] the CC sets out two further sets of provisions on novation (articles 381ff CC) and assignment (articles 387–389 CC).

Where the nature of the contract or the conduct/silence of the parties permit an unequivocal inference that either party may substitute itself with another party (and hence transfer its contractual rights and obligations), the third party (assignee) becomes a party to that existing contract in substitution of the rights and obligations of the transferor/assignor.[5] The extensive sub-contracting inherent in the construction and energy sectors is generally predicated on express authority in the original contract, or is otherwise presumed as standard industry practice. Article 250 CC iterates the general position

a subsidiary warranty lawsuit is one in which the warranty applicant entrusts its guarantor to enter into an existing dispute between itself and a third party in order to hear the judgment ordering compensation of the damage that the warranty claimant suffers from the ruling in the original lawsuit.

4 In the common law, an assignment consists only in the transfer of the assignor's rights, whereas novation encompasses both rights and burdens. See *Burdana v Leeds Teaching Hospitals NHS Trust* [2017] EWCA Civ 1980. An agreement of novation must include all three parties, namely, debtor, creditor and new third party, all of which must provide their unequivocal consent. Moreover, the novator (original debtor) must be released from its obligation and there is a vesting of remedies.

5 There is a notable presumption against such inference. Art 33(2) CC clearly states that 'where the original debtor or the transferee notifies the creditor of such transfer and a reasonable time is fixed for acceptance thereof by the creditor, and such time expires without any declaration of acceptance by the creditor, such non-declaration shall be considered as a rejection of the transfer'.

by stating that 'where the terms of the agreement or the nature of the debt requires performance of the obligation by the obligor himself, the obligee may reject payment by any third party'. The agreement/consent of existing parties is therefore a *sine qua non* (fundamental) condition for the substitution of the debtor or creditor, wholly or partially, with another party.[6]

12.2.1 *Assignment of Rights*

Assignment consists in the transfer of existing contractual rights by one party (assignor) to another (assignee). This is achieved through a bilateral agreement between assignor and assignee under article 387 CC. In order to prevent harm to *bona fide* parties, the assignment is invalid if the assignee is insolvent at the time of the assignment.[7] Some commercial transactions can only be completed by assignment. Article 470 of Law No 27 of 2006 (Commercial Law) stipulates that when the drawer has inserted in a bill of exchange the words 'not to order' or an equivalent expression, the instrument can only be transferred according to the form, and with the effects, of an ordinary assignment.[8] Certain assets cannot be made the object of assignment, namely, real estate, movables subject to a mortgage or pledge and business enterprises.[9] It is suggested that while the CC does not permit the use of assignment as security, assignment of rights is often used as security, particularly where banks have no right to enforce the assigned rights, save in the event of default by the creditor.[10]

The Qatari CC generally allows such substitution, or subrogation (of rights) subject to several limitations.[11] In accordance with article 324 CC (assignment of rights) an obligee may transfer to a third party its rights against the obligor,

---

[6]   Art 338(1) CC; equally Art 340 CC.

[7]   Art 388 CC.

[8]   See equally Art 471 of the Commercial Law (CL) regarding endorsements on bills of exchange; in the event of bankruptcy, the group of creditors mentioned in Art 742 of the Commercial Law must assign their debts to a third party (assignee). The assignee may not participate in the company's deliberations on composition, nor vote thereon. Under Art 743 CL, such assignment may encompass a part of the securities provided that it is equivalent to no less than half of the debt.

[9]   S El-Serafy, 'Qatar: Assignment of Rights and Obligations under the Qatar Civil Code', available at www.tamimi.com/law-update-articles/qatar-assignment-of-rights-and-obligations-under-the-qatari-civil-code/

[10] Ibid.

[11] Limitations against transferring rights to third parties is not confined to contracts. Art 203 CC, for example, forbids the transfer of indemnity rights for moral damages to third parties, 'unless their value is fixed by law or by agreement, or if the obligee claims such indemnity before the court'.

unless the law, the agreement or the nature of the obligation otherwise requires. Where there is no applicable limitation on the transfer the consent of the obligor is not required, provided that the creditor's right/claim has been fully discharged by the third party, in accordance with article 358(1) CC. The assignment of the right whereby a third party is entitled to collect damages or a debt is recognised in article 356(1) CC. Paragraph 2 of this provision goes on to say that where a payment is made against the debtor's will, the latter may prevent recourse by the payer in connection with the debt, in full or in part, 'if the debtor proves that it has an interest in objecting to such payment'. As already stated, assignment of rights does not require consent of the debtor, save where the assignment agreement is made after the date of the payment of the debt.[12] The Qatari Court of Cassation has clarified that assignment of a right does not impose or create a new obligation on the assignee.[13]

Article 326 CC envisages assignment in respect of attached assets, whereby the liquidation of the assets would pass in the ownership of the third party. Article 326 CC stipulates that such transfer is effective against the obligor and the third party only where the obligor is notified of the subrogation and duly accepts and that moreover the transfer is fixed by a precise date.

Interestingly, article 396(1) CC explains that where assignment has taken place with reservation from the debtor, the latter may not hold the transferee/third party to any right of set-off available prior to the exercise of the transfer. In such cases, the debtor shall have a right of recourse against the transferor only. It is hence important to voice any reservations from the outset.[14]

12.2.2 *Novation or Assignment of Obligations*

A particular species of assignment is *novation*, which is regulated in articles 381ff CC and which is also known as assignment of debt. In practice, novation arises where the debtor (who now becomes the assignor) borrows from a third party (assignee) in order to pay its debt to the creditor. In such case, the original creditor is substituted by the new lender with the original creditor's consent. Such consent may not be required, 'provided that the loan agreement shall state that such money is designated to pay such debt and that, upon settlement, such money borrowed from the new creditor is applied to pay such debt'.[15] In all cases,

---

[12] Art 358(1) CC.
[13] Court of Cassation Judgment 49/2016. In the case at hand the question was whether the assignment encompassed also the arbitration clause in the original contract. The Court was adamant that under the particular circumstances it was not so encompassed.
[14] On set-off in the Qatari CC, see Chapter 12.
[15] Art 358(2) CC.

subrogation becomes effective only when the date in the relevant agreement is fixed, in accordance with article 358(3) CC. Novation overlaps with assignment to the degree that the parties to an existing contract agree to substitute either one with a new third party. The key difference with assignment is that one of the objectives of novation is to replace an existing obligation with a new one or add a new obligation to the underlying contract (whereas assignment concerns the transfer of rights). This may, or may not, include the introduction of a new party. Another difference is that assignment affects the parties' rights and duties from a particular point in time (the so-called point of assignment). Some commentators suggest that when securing a debt, such security is not automatically transferred under a novation agreement; in the event of assignment, however, the security is automatically transferred to the assignee.[16] A valid contract of assignment (between assignor, assignee and creditor) is deemed a renewal of the original debt obligation, albeit with a new debtor.[17]

Novation, in the sense of party substitution, is a tripartite agreement requiring the consent of debtor (novator), new creditor (novate) and original creditor.[18] Despite the use of the words 'replace' and 'substitute', both assignment and novation culminate in a new contract on the same terms as the original contract, albeit with a new set of parties. This is an important observation because it is not improbable that a novation agreement be supplemented by subsequent such agreements, particularly where the sub-contractor requests variation of its obligations. In such case, unless the subsequent novation agreements provide otherwise, all prior agreements remain in force.[19] In the context of Qatar, novation is prevalent in construction whereby the contractor enters into a sub-contracting agreement with a third party by which to conclude part of the work, requesting in the process that the third party acquires a demand guarantee (bonds) from a bank in favour of the contractor in the event it is in breach of its sub-contracting obligations.[20] The QFC Court, relying chiefly on English which it deemed as reflecting principles recognised internationally, including Qatar, has gone on to state that demand guarantees are not payable to the contract where fraud is involved (fraud exception).[21]

---

[16] El Serafi (n 9).
[17] Court of Cassation Judgment 195/2010.
[18] Art 381 CC.
[19] *Obayashi Qatar LLC and HBK Contracting Co WLL v Qatar First Bank LLC* [2020] QIC (F) 5, para 112.
[20] There are several cases of this nature before the QFC Court, which has clarified that the QFC Contract Regulations and the Qatari CC are very much identical in their treatment of demand guarantee bonds. See *Obayashi Qatar LLC and HBK Contracting Co WLL v Qatar First Bank LLC*, ibid, paras 52–56.
[21] Ibid, paras 9–100.

12.3 EFFECTS OF CONTRACTS ON THIRD PARTIES

The Qatari CC, just like its other civil law counterparts, imposes several limitations concerning the effects of contracts on *bona fide* third parties.[22] A sales contract disposing of property owned by a third party (without its consent) is invalid.[23] In addition to article 250 CC, explained above, article 63 CC sets out a fundamental rule, whereby the exercise of a right is deemed unlawful where, among others, its intended use is solely to cause damage to others, or if the exercise of the right 'may cause unusually gross damage to third parties'. This is an important observation, since anything below gross damage is permitted and is not considered an abuse of right. Where a contract is invalid or revoked due to a mistake of any of the parties to that contract, *bona fide* third parties suffering damage thereof may validly claim damages in tort and request the invalidity of the contract.[24]

Another fundamental rule is that assets that have come in the possession of a *bona fide* third party cannot be taken from such party by the operation of a contract to which it is not a party.[25] No doubt, if the object of the contract is lawfully in the hands of a third party, the underlying contract may be terminated or rescinded.[26]

---

[22] Although in this chapter we are concerned with effects arising from contracts, the CC is replete with provisions limiting any effect on third parties. See, for example, Art 1081(1) CC, which stipulates that a 'mortgage shall not be effective against third parties unless it is registered before the third party acquires any real right over the mortgaged real property without prejudice to the provisions of bankruptcy'. Confirmed by Court of Cassation Judgment 167/2016; see also Art 19 CL, concerning effects on *bona fide* third parties from the mismanagement of a minor's personal affairs; see also Art 65 CL concerning the assumption of commitments of the previous store owner by its successor.

[23] Court of Cassation Judgment 184/2016; see also Art 93 CL, stipulating that 'Where a trader sells movable property belonging to a third party, which comes within the remit of its business and delivers it to a buyer, then the buyer shall own the sale item if it has acted in good faith, but if the said item is a missing or stolen item then the real owner may recover it within five years from the time of loss or theft and the buyer may request the return of its payment'.

[24] Art 168(1) CC. See Court of Cassation Judgment 11/2015, where the parties had violated Art 2 of Law No. (13) of 2000 amended by Law No. 2 of 2005 Regulating the Investment of Non-Qatari Capital in Economic Activity, which requires that a Qatari partner hold 51% of shares. The contract was invalid between them but not against third parties; see equally, Court of Cassation Judgment 74/2010 to the same effect. There seems to be one notable exception to the principle enunciated in Judgment 11/2015. The Court of Cassation in Judgment 221/2014 held that a violation of Art 10 of Law No. 2 of 2007 establishing a system for popular housing did not create any legal effects 'between the contracting parties or third parties, on the heirs of the beneficiary'.

[25] Art 487 CC; see also Art 451(1) CC, concerning partial dispossession of goods encumbered with a lien in favour of a third party; see also Art 466(2) CC.

[26] Art 189(2) CC.

The Qatari CC imposes a general duty to provide information/notification to third parties, lest any action affecting third-party rights is deemed invalid. By way of illustration, article 82(2) CC sets out to protect the interests of *bona fide* third parties when dealing with the agent of the principal. Where the principal commits a mistake that leads a *bona fide* third party to believe that the agency upon which the agent contracted with this third party is still valid, the agent's agreement with the third party is enforceable against the principal.[27] Where an agency is predicated on an agreement and exceeds the authority of the agent under a discreet power of attorney deed, the authority under the agreement is valid against third parties if they have been so notified by the principal.[28] Another poignant illustration is offered by articles 514 and 515 CC. These maintain that until such time as a company has satisfied the pertinent publication procedures it (as a transacting legal persons) shall not be effective against third parties.[29] Even so, third parties may still derive, if they so wish, rights from a transaction with such unregistered company. In equal measure, although the absence of a written company contract renders the company invalid, such invalidity may not be invoked by the shareholders against *bona fide* third parties.[30] The Court of Cassation has consistently held that in order for the director of a limited liability company (LLC) to avoid liability through his or her own assets, the LLC designation must be clear to all those transacting with it. If such clarity/notification is missing, the director is liable against third parties.[31] Such formality/notification is apparent elsewhere, notably official registration of rights *in rem* over real property. Without appropriate registration such rights are not effective against third parties.[32]

We referred to subrogation of debt in the previous section. Article 347 CC stipulates that where the debtor transfers its debt under a transfer limited to the property in the custody of the transfer debtor and such property is lost prior to delivery thereof to the creditor, but not due to the fault of the transfer debtor, the transfer shall be terminated. However, 'where such property in custody is payable to a third party, the transfer shall be void'. In this manner,

---

[27] Court of Cassation Judgment 209/2015.
[28] In equal measure, although the agency contract may be terminated unilaterally by either party, this is not the case where the agency is decided in favour of the agent or if a third party has an interest in it. See Court of Cassation Judgment 163/2016.
[29] See Court of Cassation Judgment 55/2015. In the case at hand, the company's contract/articles of association were not drafted in Arabic and the partners had not fulfilled the pertinent registration obligations.
[30] Ibid.
[31] Court of Cassation Judgment 164/2010; iterated by Court of Appeal Judgment 36/2019.
[32] See Court of Cassation Judgment 123/2010, relying on Art 4, of Law No 14 of 1964, concerning Land Registration.

the third party's rights are not affected by the loss of the transferred property of the debtor.[33]

Article 385(1)(a) CC sets out yet another protective mechanism to prevent damage to third parties. It goes on to say that where an obligation is secured by securities in kind provided by the debtor and the creditor and debtor agree to transfer such securities, such transfer must cause no damage to third parties. A similar limitation is stipulated in respect of set-off (unilateral actions) that cause harm to a third party.[34]

12.4 CONTRACTS EXPLICITLY INTENDED TO CONFER RIGHTS ON THIRD PARTIES

Articles 177–182 CC set out the contours of a situation pertinent to third parties that is different from assignment or novation as discussed in previous sections. They envisage the creation of a contract with the aim, sole, or partial, of attracting a third party. Article 177 CC sets forth an important caveat in respect of such contracts. It stipulates that while contracts cannot create obligations binding upon third parties, contracts can in fact grant rights in favour of third parties. This is akin to the regime pertinent to minors whereby they are only bound to complex contracts through which they derive benefit.[35] The participation of the third party envisaged in article 177 CC, while ultimately requiring the approval of said third party, is effectively tantamount to an open offer conferring rights but not obligations. The original parties may stipulate particular obligations among themselves in favour of the third party, provided that the instigator of said obligations 'has a material or moral interest in such obligations'.[36] Article 179(2) CC makes it clear that the third-party beneficiary may be a prospective person, or a person not particularly identified in such stipulation if such person can be identified at the time of performing the relevant obligation. In any event, the stipulation in favour of the third party is required in order to prove the latter's right.[37] Given that the type of contracts envisaged in articles 177ff CC are geared towards favouring a third party, the stipulating party may well demand of its other contracting party to confer the relevant right on the third party. The original contract may, however, just as well indicate that such a demand is limited to the

---

[33] See to the same effect, Art 348 CC, which concerns subrogation of debt under wrongful possession.

[34] Art 395(1) CC; see also Art 397 CC to the same effect, concerning set-off against securities held by the debtor.

[35] See, for example, Art 115(1) CC; for further analysis, see Chapter 4 on capacity.

[36] Art 179(1) CC.

[37] Art 180(1) CC.

beneficiary.[38] In the latter case, the right is not yet established until such time as the pertinent offer is made by both parties to the original contract.

Clearly, the third party's participation is onerous to the existing parties, and this is clearly spelt out in article 178 CC. Hence, if a person contracts with another for the purpose of committing a third party, any obligation committed in the original contract must be performed.[39] Hence, if the third party, for whose benefit the original contract was made, rejects the benefit offered, 'the person who made the undertaking shall be liable to indemnify the other contracting party against any damage due to the breach of such undertaking, unless the party who made the undertaking fulfils the obligation itself, provided that this party can do so without causing any damage to the other contracting party'.[40] Although article 177 CC speaks of rights (only) being conferred on third parties, it is evident that once the third party consents to the offer, the relevant contracting party is discharged from its own undertaking to the other contracting party. In this case, the 'third party shall be bound by such undertaking from the time of acceptance thereof, unless it is indicated expressly or by implication that the consent is retroactive from the date of the agreement between the contracting parties'.[41]

The benefit stipulated in favour of the beneficiary/third party may be revoked by the stipulating party, following notification to the beneficiary, unless the revocation is contrary to the spirit of the underlying contract.[42] Revocation does not discharge the obligor towards the stipulating party, unless otherwise agreed or otherwise implied by the terms of the contract, and the stipulator may proceed to substitute the former beneficiary with a new one, or retain for himself the benefit of the stipulation.[43]

12.5 RESPONSIBILITY FOR ACTS OF THIRD PARTIES

Just like other civil codes, the Qatari CC envisages the liability of the guardian or employer for those acts of minors or employees, respectively, that cause harm to others. This type of liability is regulated under articles 208ff CC. In such cases the guardian and employer are third parties to the unlawful act caused by the minor or employee, respectively; albeit because of their particular relationship the law demands that they exercise heightened due diligence

---

[38] Art 180(2) CC.
[39] Art 178(1) CC.
[40] Art 178(2) CC.
[41] Art 178(3) CC.
[42] Art 182(1) CC.
[43] Arts 182(2) and (3) CC.

to prevent unlawful conduct. Articles 208ff CC are primarily concerned with the law of tort and hence fall beyond the purview of this book.

Even so, there is at least one context in which this body of law is relevant to the construction of contractual obligations. This concerns the so-called collateral damage or consequential loss, which consists of damage/loss caused while performing an existing contractual obligation (e.g. while erecting a building the builders damage the owner's car). It is not clear from the CC whether collateral damage is explicitly recognised as a contractual remedy. If not, the injured party may rely on articles 208ff CC.

12.6 VOIDANCE OF A CONTRACT ON ACCOUNT OF THE CONDUCT OF OR BENEFIT TO A THIRD PARTY

We have already explained in Chapter 8 that voidable contracts are those involving mistake, fraud, coercion or exploitation. The injured party may seek restitution and termination as a result of the unlawful conduct (or the mistake) of the other party. Articles 135ff CC stipulate that a contract may also become voidable by acts of third parties. Article 135(1) CC specifically refers to fraudulent misrepresentation whereby the subterfuge (deceit) is attributable to the other contracting party's representative or subordinate; situations involving the broker empowered to conclude the contract, or the party in whose interest the contract was concluded. In such cases the deceived party may seek voidance only if it is established that the other contracting party 'was, or should necessarily have been, aware of the fraudulent misrepresentation'.[44] The same is true in respect of a contract or gift in respect of which consent was procured by means of fraud caused by a third party,[45] equally as regards duress caused by a third party.[46] A vulnerable person who is exploited to conclude a contract in favour of a third party that contains an excessive imbalance of obligations may request the voidance of such contract or the adjustment of obligations.[47]

12.7 TERMINATION BY REASON OF LAWFUL THIRD-PARTY INTERFERENCE

Where a third-party lawfully interferes with the subject matter of a contract, then the parties cannot be expected to fulfil their underlying obligations,

---

[44] Art 135(2) CC.
[45] Art 136 CC.
[46] Arts 138 and 139 CC.
[47] Art 140 CC.

assuming of course that neither party contributed to such interference. Hence, where the government lawfully expropriates property subject to a lease contract, this contract may be terminated.[48]

The sub-tenant is not a party to the contract between the tenant and the landlord. Even so, the sub-tenant's contract with the tenant is dependent on a tenant–landlord lease. As a result, upon termination of the latter, so too the agreement between tenant and sub-tenant must necessarily be terminated.[49]

---

[48] Court of Cassation Judgment 34/2011, relying on Art 12 of Law No. 13 of 1988 regarding the temporary expropriation and seizure of real estate for the public benefit.

[49] Court of Cassation Judgment 138/2010.

13

The Contract Regulations of the Qatar Financial Centre

13.1 INTRODUCTION

The Qatar Financial Centre (QFC) can best be described as a special economic zone (EEZ) and its legal system as a system within a system (the Qatari legal order).[1] It was set up under Law No 7 (2005) [QFC Law], which is both its founding law and its Basic Law (effectively its internal constitution). The aim of the QFC was to attract foreign investment in the financial, banking, asset management and insurance sectors, chiefly through favourable incentives. This was expanded to encompass non-regulated activities that fall outside the broader financial sector. These include holding companies, special purpose companies, trusts, single family offices, professional, corporate and business services, as well as company headquarters. Even though the QFC legal system is distinct from the ordinary Qatari legal system and a variety of regulations regulate all matters related to the QFC, several Qatari laws are applicable, particularly Law No 11 of 2004 establishing the Penal Code[2] and Law No 4 of 2010 Combatting Money Laundering. There are two significant incentives for incorporating in the QFC as opposed in the State of Qatar. Firstly, QFC-regulated entities are not susceptible to the regulation of the Qatar Central Bank. Secondly, QFC entities may have 100 per cent foreign ownership, which is not the case under the Qatari Law No 13 of 2000, establishing the Foreign Capital Investment Law.

[1] The academic literature on the QFC is feeble and most of it focuses on the QFC Court. See Z Al Abdin Sharar, M Al Khulaifi, 'The Courts in Qatar Financial Center and Dubai International Financial Center: A Comparative Analysis', 92016) 46 HKLJ 529; equally, I Bantekas, 'Transplanting the UNIDROIT Contract Principles into the Qatar Financial Center: A Fresh Paradigm for Wholesale Legal Transplants' (2021) 26 Uniform LR 1.

[2] However, in accordance with Art 18(1) of the QFC Law, where the conduct of an entity is consistent with the laws and regulations of the QFC, such conduct shall not constitute a criminal offence under the law of the QFC or the laws of the State of Qatar.

In the remit of their roles and functions, QFC governing entities possess the power to propose regulations (effectively internal QFC law) to the Qatari Minister of Economy and Commerce, which upon approval becomes an integral part of QFC law.[3] The QFC Law sets out in its article 9 this authority of QFC entities to adopt regulations.

For the purposes of this chapter, our focus will be on Regulation No 4 (2005), known as the QFC Contract Regulations. This was one of the first Regulations adopted following the creation of the QFC, which in turn evinces the determination to create a legal system that is distinct from ordinary Qatari law. Because QFC-regulated entities enter into transactions both within the QFC but largely also with companies across the globe, it was important that said agreements be regulated in a way that made sense. Article 18(3) of the QFC Law stipulates as follows:

> The QFC Laws and Regulations shall apply to the contracts, transactions and arrangements conducted by the entities established in, or operating from the QFC, with parties or entities located in the QFC or in the State but outside the QFC, unless the parties agree otherwise.

This is a deceptively simple conflict of laws provision with significant implications for parties that fail to adequately think about the governing clause of their contract. Several judgments of the QFC Court serve to illustrate the point.[4] As will become evident, the Contract Regulations were predicated (almost verbatim) in large part on the UNIDROIT Principles of International Commercial Contracts (PICC).[5] Given that this book assumes at least a basic understanding of contract law, where the Regulations reflect or iterate the provisions of the PICC no further analysis will be provided, other than a reference to the corresponding provisions.

13.2 THE RELATIONSHIP OF THE QFC CONTRACT REGULATIONS WITH THE QATARI CC

Article 2(1) of the Regulations begins with a rather cryptic statement, according to which 'to the fullest extent permitted by the QFC Law, rules and

---

[3] Z Al Abdin Sharar, M Earley, 'The Qatar International Court: Judicial Update', (2018) MENA Bus L Rev 46, 47. The QFC governing entities consist of the QFC Authority, the QFC Regulatory Authority, the Regulatory Tribunal and the Civil and Commercial Court.

[4] See, in particular, *Daman Health Insurance Qatar Ltd v Al Bawakir Co Ltd*, [2017] QIC (F) 2.

[5] See, in particular, S Vogenauer (ed), *Commentary on the UNIDROIT Principles of International Commercial Contracts* (OUP 2015); M J Bonell (ed), *The UNIDROIT Principles in Practice* (Brill 2006).

regulations of the State [of Qatar] concerning the matters dealt with by or under these Regulations shall not apply in the QFC'. This is concerning because the parties to a contract governed by the Regulations may have specifically intended to exclude the application of Qatari law. In the opinion of the authors, it is quite clear that ordinary Qatari private law shall not override the Regulations, unless the parties have expressly so provided. Even so, Qatari international commitments, as these are transposed in ordinary legislative instruments, can override the Regulations, although this will be rare in practice. The QFC Law is subservient to the Qatari Constitution and as a result references in bilateral investment treaties (BITs) or regional and global free trade agreements that have been ratified by the Shura Council override the QFC Law and by extension the Regulations. Qatari public policy, as opposed to a distinct QFC public policy, is embedded in the QFC Law.[6]

In theory, the Qatari CC, including its interpretation by the Court of Appeals and Cassation, could supplement the Regulations where the latter are silent on a particular issue, but such a likelihood seems to have been excluded. There is no indication in the Regulations suggesting such a supplementary role for the CC, whether directly or indirectly. The QFC Court is not expressly directed to exclude judgments by the ordinary Qatari courts and in fact it is not uncommon for the QFC Court to refer to the case law of the higher Qatari courts.[7] This is tune with the QFC Court's practice of considering common law judgments as authority. Nonetheless, the application of most, if not all, QFC regulations, as is the case with the QFC Employment Regulations, entails the exclusion of ordinary Qatari law on the same matter, but not other QFC regulations, including the QFC Contract Regulations.[8]

A possible overlap may arise where the governing law of the parties' contract encompasses the Regulations in addition to other laws, including ordinary Qatari law. In such eventuality, the QFC Court (although the parties may well insert a choice of court or arbitration clause in their contract) may be

---

[6] Art 8 of Schedule 6 to the QFC Law provides that the QFC Court is to apply the QFC Law and pertinent Regulations 'unless the parties have explicitly agreed to apply another law provided that such law is not inconsistent with the public order of the State'.

[7] Several QFC Court judgments refer in substance or in passing to judgments of Qatari courts in order to aid their interpretation of provisions in the QFC Contract Regulations. See *Nasco Qatar LLC v Misr Insurance (Qatar Branch)* [2020] QIC (F) 17, para 32.

[8] Art 2(5) of the QFC Employment Regulations excludes the application of any other labour law. In *Chedid and Associates Qatar LLC v Said Bou Sayad*, QFC Case 02/2013, Judgment (20 April 2014), while the QFC Court determined that the dispute was governed by the QFC Employment Regulations, it had no hesitation directing the respondent to Art 36 of the QFC Contract Regulations, following an allegation of threat against the employer in order to agree to a no-competition clause.

compelled to apply the CC – or other ordinary Qatari law – where a provision in the contract is more closely connected to ordinary Qatari law.

13.3 SCOPE OF APPLICATION OF CONTRACT REGULATIONS

It should be pointed out that the parties to any contract, whether operating within or outside the QFC, may rely on the Regulations as their governing law. No doubt, such reliance on the Regulations is meaningful where there exists a connection to the QFC. Article 2(2) of the Regulations makes a distinction between contracts 'incorporating' the Regulations from those where the Regulations serve as governing law. This is a common-sense observation that does not give rise to any kind of contention. Article 2(3) of the Regulations specifies the entities upon which the Regulations apply in their contractual relationships:

(A) contracts between the QFC Authority, the Regulatory Authority, Appeals Body or QFC Institutions and persons licensed to operate in or from the QFC; and

(B) all contracts between persons licensed to operate in or from the QFC.

The first category listed in item (A) concerns contracts between QFC entities themselves, as well as contracts between QFC entities and persons licensed to operate in or from the QFC. Even so, article 2(4) of the Regulations makes it clear that neither of these two types of contracts are governed by the Regulations absent the consent of the parties. The application of the Regulations is optional on QFC entities and licensed persons. Where QFC entities and QFC licensed persons enter into agreements that provide no reference to their governing law (including 'rules of law'),[9] the Regulations are applicable to such contracts. Paragraph 4(B) of article 2 of the Regulations further sets forth a rule of private international law, by stipulating that where QFC entities and licensed persons have failed to designate a governing law, the Regulations shall apply if 'they are more closely connected with the contract than any other system or rules of law'.[10] This is a matter of contractual construction in accordance with articles 46ff of the Regulations. The absence

---

[9] The notion of 'rules of law' is broader than 'laws' and 'legal systems' and encompasses anything that the parties perceive as their personal, communal, or broader relationships, whether or not such 'rules of law' are perceived by other persons or communities as binding, let alone as 'law'. See I Bantekas, 'Transnational Islamic Finance Disputes: Towards a Convergence with English Contract Law and International Arbitration' (2021) 10 JIDS 1–19.

[10] See the implications of Art 18(3) of the QFC Law in the introduction to this chapter, which encompasses also contracts between QFC and non-QFC entities.

of any further clarification suggests that the drafters of the Regulations were disinclined from making a meal of this and sensibly followed a simple rule that grants significant, yet not unnecessary, discretion to the courts.

13.4 THE COMMON LAW AND UNIDROIT PICC IMPRINT ON THE CONTRACT REGULATIONS

It is important to note that while the Regulations constitute an integral part of the QFC legal architecture they do not serve the same purpose as the Qatari CC. The latter encompasses mandatory provisions (i.e. good faith and public order) and in addition serves as a body of default rules. The Regulations' residual function is only as default rules and no part or provision therein possesses a mandatory character if the parties have expressly chosen to exclude the Regulations from their contract.

In equal measure, one should not conflate the jurisdiction of the QFC Court[11] with the application of the Regulations; the two are independent from each other. The QFC Court is meant to apply QFC laws and regulations, as well as the law set out by the parties in their contractual relationships,[12] albeit in practice the court, in the absence of a contrary agreement, will often rely on common law principles[13] and case law, not only because these are more familiar to the majority of the judges[14] but also because English law

---

[11]   See Art 8(3)(c) of the QFC Law, outlining the jurisdiction of the QFC Court, including the entities that are encompassed under its authority; equally, Art 9 QFC Court Regulations and Procedural Rules, which is based on Art 8(3)(c) of the QFC Law. Jurisdictional dilemmas may arise where a party to a contractual dispute is not a QFC-registered entity. In *Daman Health Insurance Qatar Ltd v Al Bawakir Co Ltd*, [2017] QIC (F) 2, the claimant was a QFC-registered company, whereas the respondent was not. Their insurance agreement was governed by QFC laws and as a result the QFC Court ruled that in the absence of a choice of court agreement, it was compelled to exercise jurisdiction. Iterated in *Badri and Salim Elmeouchi LLP v Data Managers International Ltd*, [2020] QIC (F) 1, paras 15–16.

[12]   Arts 7 and 8, Appendix 6 of the QFC Law. This is also spelt out in Art 11 of the QFC Court's Regulations and Procedural Rules, while Art 4 of the latter enunciates the principle of the 'overriding objective' of the court, which is to 'deal with all cases justly'.

[13]   The QFC website prides itself as being a 'legal system based on the English common law', available at www.qfc.qa/en/business/laws-and-regulations. Even though most scholarly and professional commentaries emphasise this common law dimension, no direct reference to the common law is made in QFC laws and regulations, but is certainly part of the QFC Court's consistent practice. In *Qatar Financial Centre Authority v Silver Leaf Capital Partners LLC*, [2009] QIC (F) 1, the Court emphasised that it gave effect to Qatari and English (contract) law principles, while taking into account international best practices.

[14]   Even where the governing law of a contract is not English law, the QFC Court still relies on English contract law to flesh out general principles. In *Obayashi Qatar LLC v Qatar First Bank LLC* [2020] QIC (F) 5, para 90, Qatari law was the contract's governing law. Yet, the

is predominant in the majority of transnational commercial agreements. By way of illustration, in *Leonardo Spa v Doha Bank Assurance Co LLC*,[15] the QFC Court had to deal with demand guarantees under the Uniform Rules for Demand Guarantees, which were adopted by the International Chamber of Commerce in 1991. Even so, the Court went on to examine the nature of such guarantees by reference to English case law.

Despite the prevalence of transnational contracts in Qatar governed by English and Qatari law, this is irrelevant to the civil law origins of the Contract Regulations and their interpretation by the QFC Court – or other courts or tribunals with jurisdiction. The influence of common law on the Regulations is small (but present).[16] However, the Regulations are wholly predicated on the UNIDROIT Principles of International Commercial Contracts (PICC). Despite the frequent use of common law principles by the Court, it should be emphasised that otherwise fundamental tenets of the common law are missing from the Regulations, notably consideration. Article 31(2) of the Regulations expressly states that 'consideration is not required for a contract to be binding'.

There are some elements of the common law that are poignant in the Regulations. This is true, for example, with respect to good faith and misrepresentation. Unlike good faith in the Qatari CC, whose observance is binding upon conclusion of the contract,[17] there is no similar provision in the Regulations. It must therefore be assumed that good faith is not obligatory upon conclusion of the contract under the Regulations, particularly since article 13(2) of the Regulations makes it clear that a party negotiating or ceasing negotiations in bad faith incurs liability for any losses caused to the other party. No doubt, the drafters of the Regulation felt that since English contract law was predominant in the region, therefore the absence of good faith during the lifetime of the contract would have been an attraction for potential end users of the Contract Regulations. Misrepresentation is equally derived directly from the common law tradition. It is explained in Chapter 8 that misrepresentation during negotiations is not counted as a ground for a valid defect of consent in the civil law tradition and is not counted as such in the Qatari CC.

Court relied predominantly on the English law of demand guarantees, as well as the fraud exception therein, as a condition freeing the debtor from its obligation.

[15] Case 3/2019, unreported, Judgment of 5 September 2019 QFC Court, para 42ff.

[16] In *Chedid and Associates Qatar LLC v Said Bou Sayad*, QFC Case 02/2013, Supplementary Judgment [2014] QIC (F) 3, para 3, the QFC Court made an important statement on the persuasive value of the common law on QFC law. It held that the reasoning in non-QFC judgments, such as common law courts, which concern principles, expressions or concepts similar to those in QFC laws have persuasive value in interpreting and applying QFC laws, including the QFC Contract Regulations.

[17] Art 172(1) Qatari CC.

Overall, it is evident that the drafters of the Contract Regulations wanted to break free from several notions of the Qatari CC, which itself is rather progressive. First and foremost, the Regulations are free from the influence, or the remnants of any influence derived from the Sanhuri tradition[18] and the 1948 Egyptian CC. In this manner, there is also a clear break from past and future case law of the Egyptian Court of Cassation, even if very little of that is evident in the judgments of the Qatari Court of Cassation. Secondly, as already emphasised, the Regulations are very much a verbatim reflection of the UNIDROIT PICC, albeit with notable features of English/common law that have traditionally been viewed as commerce-friendly, including the absence of good faith and misrepresentation. The infusion of sensible common law features is in line with the increased application of English law and business custom[19] as the governing law of contracts in Qatar and the GCC,[20] as well as the choice of judges sitting on the bench of the QFC Court.

13.5 NOTABLE ELEMENTS OF THE CONTRACT REGULATIONS

The remainder of the chapter will focus on some, but not all, of the key features of the Regulations. The Regulations provide a detailed legal framework of the entire gamut of contracts and as such they are more detailed than the contract law provisions of the Qatari CC, albeit less detailed as compared to the PICC.

13.5.1 *Formation of Contracts*

The parties are free to enter any contract and determine its content, including its governing law.[21] That contracts are largely informal is evident not only

---

[18] As noted in Chapter 1, Sanhuri is considered the father of the contemporary civil law tradition in the Arab world and his influence is credited upon the drafters of the Qatari CC, although he himself did not participate in the drafting process. See N Saleh, 'Civil Laws of Arab Countries: The Sanhuri Codes' (1993) 8 Arab LQ 165.

[19] Art 11 Regulations, which renders trade usage binding, unless specifically excluded; see verbatim in Art 1.9 PICC.

[20] I Bantekas, The Globalisation of English Contract Law: Three Salient Illustrations' (2021) 137 LQR 130.

[21] Art 6(1) and 7 Regulations; Arts 1.1 and 1.2 PICC. In *Khaled Hassan Bahr Ahmed v Doha Bank Assurance Co LLC*, [2013] QIC F 1, at 6, the QFC Court was confronted, among other issues, with the absence of any reasons in a dismissal letter. In applying Art 6(1) of the Regulations, it came to the conclusion that the parties could validly agree to exclude the provision of reasons in dismissal notices (i.e. right to determine content). Interestingly, the QFC Court combined Art 6(1) of the Regulations with the QFC Labour Regulations and Labour Law No 4 of 2004 (i.e. the ordinary Qatari labour legislation).

by reference to article 8 of the Regulations, which goes on to say that they do not need to be evidenced in writing only, or any ceremonial form, but also by the variety of means by which to notify the other party, which may include any form of land or electronic dispatch.[22] The QFC has relied on exchange of emails and the parties' conduct in adducing the existence of a contractual relationship, even where the agreement (because of its informality) is not particularly detailed.[23]

Articles 15ff of the Regulations follow almost verbatim the sequence and language of the PICC (articles 2.1.1 to 2.1.14 PICC) as regards offer, acceptance and intention to be bound, as well as the relevant modalities for the formation of contracts. The Qatari CC is not fundamentally different but is a lot less elaborate and, in any event, does not purport to rely on the PICC. There are only slight variations in structure, but not the wording between the PICC and the Regulations.[24] In terms of substance there are only two differences between the PICC and the Regulations. Unlike article 1.1.20 of the PICC which regulates surprising terms, no such provision exists in the Regulations. And as we have already alluded to elsewhere in this chapter, article 31(2) of the Regulations explains that no consideration is required; albeit this is also implicit in the PICC.

13.5.2 *Validity of Consent*

Validity of consent under articles 32 to 44 of the Regulations is generally consistent, and mostly verbatim, with the PICC, but there are notable differences. The Regulations depart from long-standing civil law tradition whereby contracts are voided in the event of serious mistake, coercion, or threats, all of which are encompassed in the Qatari CC. Of these the Regulations only encompass threats and mistakes.[25] The Regulations equally omit any reference to gross disparity[26] or injustice[27] as a ground for avoidance. Instead, article 37 of the Regulations introduces illegality as a ground invalidating consent, as

---

[22] Art 12 Regulations; see Art 1.10 PICC.
[23] *Nasco Qatar LLC v Misr Insurance (Qatar Branch)*, [2020] QIC (F) 17, paras 15–17. The QFC Court relied on *British Steel Corp v Cleveland Bridge & Engineering Co Ltd* [1984] 1 All ER 504.
[24] For example, conflicts between standard and non-standard terms are regulated in two distinct provisions in the PICC (Arts 2.1.19 and 2.1.21), yet they are subsumed within a single provision in the Regulations (Art 30).
[25] Arts 36 and 33, respectively, of the Regulations.
[26] Art 3.2.7 PICC.
[27] Art 143 Qatari CC.

well as misrepresentation, to which we have already alluded.[28] This result is incongruous. While illegality, mistakes and threats apply as grounds for avoiding a contract upon (and not before) the conclusion of the contract under the Regulations,[29] in conformity with general principles of the civil law tradition, illegality is generally not considered as a ground for avoidance;[30] illegality generally serves to render the contract void *ab initio*. The QFC Court has correctly assimilated (in certain cases) illegality with public policy and public order. In *Nasco Qatar LLC v Misr Insurance*, it was noted *obiter dicta* that if it was found that an insurance broker was operating without a valid license, its underlying contract with the insurance company would have been illegal under QFC laws and by extension in violation of the Qatari public order.[31]

Moreover, misrepresentation is peculiar to English law and concerns false statements made prior to the conclusion of the contract.[32] In the opinion of the authors, the conflation of the various grounds is misplaced, creating unnecessary confusion. Given the absence of misrepresentation in the Qatari CC and the common law influence in article 35 of the Regulations, the QFC Court would be well placed to marry misrepresentation in the civil law underpinnings of Part 4 of the Regulations, article 44 of which iterates its mandatory character.

13.5.3 *Contractual Interpretation and Contents of a Contract*

Articles 45 to 51 of the Regulations echo, largely verbatim, Part 4 of the PICC concerning interpretation of contracts, save for article 4.8 of the PICC, which concerns omitted terms. This is covered in Part 6 of the Regulations regarding implied terms. We have already alluded to *Chedid and Associates Qatar LLC v Said Bou Sayad*,[33] where the QFC Court held that the reasoning in non-QFC judgments concerning principles, expression, or concepts similar to those in QFC laws have persuasive value in interpreting the QFC Contract Regulations.

Part 6 of the Regulations concerns unexpressed terms of a contract. Under the civil law tradition this befalls contractual interpretation, while in the common law this issue is dealt by reference to terms implied in law and terms implied in

---

[28] Art 35 Regulations.
[29] See Chapter 8 for a discussion of the position under the Qatari CC.
[30] See Art 3.3.1 PICC.
[31] *Nasco Qatar LLC v Misr Insurance (Qatar Branch)* (n 23), para 20.
[32] Under the leading case of *Smith v Hughes* (1871) LR 6 QB 597, it was famously held that there exists no general duty to disclose information and in principle mere silence is not a ground for avoiding a contract. The English Misrepresentation Act 1967 identifies three types of misrepresentation, namely, fraudulent, negligent and innocent.
[33] *Chedid and Associates Qatar LLC v Said Bou Sayad*, [2014] QIC (F) 3, para 3.

fact.[34] Articles 52 to 60 of the Regulations reflect their counterparts in articles 5.1.1 to 5.1.9 of the PICC, save for the fact that article 53 of the Regulations provided a detailed statement on terms implied in fact in the case of sale of goods contracts. It is important of course to note that the duties of cooperation and best efforts are specifically referred to as drivers of the parties' mutual performance,[35] despite the absence of a good faith provision in the Regulations. The duty of cooperation is narrower than good faith, which is much broader. Moreover, Part 6, unlike Part 4, of the Regulations is not mandatory, which reinforces the notion that there is no general duty of good faith in the Regulations.

13.5.4 *Agency*

The provisions on agency in the Regulations[36] are equally a reflection of articles 2.2.1 to 2.2.10 of the PICC. Interestingly, article 66 of the Regulations adds to the discussion by setting out the duty of the agent towards the principal. These involve: a) duty of care and skill; b) duty of loyalty; c) duty to account for profits; d) duty not to act as adverse party; e) duty not to compete as regards the agency's subject matter; f) duty to avoid all possible conflicts of interest and g) duty against disclosure to a third party.

13.5.5 *Performance*

Part 7 (articles 72–85) of the Regulations effectively iterates articles 6.1.1 to 6.1.13 of PICC, with one notable exception. Paragraphs 2–4 of article 73 of the Regulations make an important contribution to the question of timely performance, by allowing a party to prematurely terminate the contract where a) it is anticipated that the other party will not perform on time and b) time is of the utmost importance (essential) to the terminating party. The Regulations omit any reference to the likelihood of non-performance where the party required to apply for permission by the State is denied such permission. Although this is well entrenched in the PICC,[37] its omission in the Regulations is somewhat baffling. Permissions requested by a QFC entity from the State of Qatar are regulated by the ordinary laws of the State of Qatar, over which QFC laws have no authority. This omission will allow the QFC Court, when dealing with such an issue, to introduce principles arising from the common law, but

---

[34] See R Austen-Baker, 'Implied Terms in English Contract Law: The Long Voyage of the Moorcock' (2009) 38 Comm L World Rev 56.
[35] Arts 54 and 55 Regulations.
[36] Arts 61–72 Regulations.
[37] Arts 6.1.4–6.1.7 PICC.

not the PICC, as it is clear that the latter's regulation was specifically rejected. Other than that, there is no reason as to why the provisions of the PICC, *mutatis mutandis*, should not apply to determine non-performance.

13.5.6 *Non-Performance and* Force Majeure

Part 10 of the Regulations is once again reflective of articles 7.1.1 to 7.1.5 of the PICC. This is not surprising. Even so, there was always going to be controversy about non-performance (generally) and *force majeure* more specifically. This is because of the particularities of *force majeure* across regions, as well as the differences in approach across the civil law and common law traditions.[38]

Article 85 of the Regulations sets out the general rule, whereby performance that becomes onerous for one of the parties does not free that party from performing its obligations. Article 85 makes it clear that where the onerous level of performance reaches the status of *force majeure* the implications are different. Article 94 of the Regulation does not follow the mould of article 7.1.7 of PICC and is in fact far more elaborate and extensive than the PICC in this regard. Paragraph 1 of article 94 of the Regulations defines *force majeure* to mean:

> any circumstances which are not within the reasonable control of the party concerned and which that party could not be reasonably expected to have taken into account at the time of conclusion of the contract, including without limitation strikes, damage to premises, plant and equipment, breach of a contract by an unrelated third party, governmental action, civil commotion, riot or war and natural physical disaster.

While the general definition is consistent with article 7.1.7 PICC the types of incidents that may give rise to *force majeure* are exceptional. There are some types of incidents in the list of paragraph 1 that are clearly reasonably foreseeable, such as damage to premises. Breach of contract by an unrelated third party is baffling, given that a third party cannot possibly breach a contract to which it is not a party; the only possible explanation is that the unforeseen impossibility to perform arose from the unexpected termination or breach of another contract with one of the parties, which (contract) was crucial for that party to perform its obligations in the first contract. The list is evidently favourable to the distressed/affected party, far more than any statutory definitions the present authors are aware of. Be that as it may, paragraph 2 of article 94 of the Regulations stipulates that where *force majeure* exists neither party is in

---

[38] Readers should consult the discussion on unforeseeable circumstances and *force majeure* in the Qatari CC, as set out in Chapter 12.

breach of its contractual obligations nor is it liable for its non-performance. The party not affected by such *force majeure* shall be relieved from any obligation to make payment to the affected party for so long 'as the performance is suspended except in respect of performance which has been actually carried out, and which complies with the terms of the contract'.[39]

A party whose performance is delayed or prevented by *force majeure* must, in accordance with article 94(4) of the Regulations:

(A) forthwith notify the other party of the nature, extent, effect and likely duration of the circumstances constituting the *force majeure*;

(B) use all reasonable endeavours to minimise the effect of the *force majeure* on the performance of its obligations; and

(C) subject to Article 94(5) forthwith after the cessation of the *force majeure* notify the other party thereof and resume full performance of its obligations.

Paragraph 5 of article 94 of the Regulations caters for the likelihood of the extension of the *force majeure* well beyond an initial impossibility. Hence, where it prevents or delays performance for a continuous period in excess of six months, the non-affected party shall be entitled to give notice to the affected party to terminate the contract. This is consistent with the FIDIC Standard Contracts, whereby once an exceptional event takes place, a notification is required. A further notification is required once such an event has ceased so that performance can resume. If, however, the exceptional event continues beyond six months, the innocent party can seek termination of the contract. The FIDIC Rules assume that *force majeure* is temporary in nature and suspends performance only for a limited period of time. Yet, it does not render performance impossible for the future. Therefore, termination is only admissible if the duration of such event exceeds six months. The FIDIC Rules reflect to some extent the notion of frustration under English law,[40] especially given that English Law discharges the parties from future performance only.[41]

13.5.7 *Remedies*

Articles 95–99 of the Regulations correspond verbatim to articles 7.2.1 to 7.2.5 of the PICC. These concern performance generally. Oddly, articles 7.4.2 to

---

[39] Art 94(3) Regulations.
[40] See the rules under term 19 of the FIDIC Red Book 2017.
[41] See Law Reform (Frustrated Contracts) Act 1943; also *BP Exploration Co (Libya) Ltd v Hunt (No 2)* [1979] 1 WLR 783.

7.4.6 of the PICC are omitted from the Regulations. These provisions of the PICC set out the general principles for assessing the right to damages, namely, certainty and foreseeability of harm, as well as damages for non-pecuniary losses. Article 100 of the Regulations addresses the right to damages, stipulating that damages arising from non-performance are available where the loss can 'fairly or reasonably' have been contemplated at the time the contract was made. Although not expressly stated in the PICC,[42] article 101 of the Regulations emphasises that damages for breach of contract effectively translate into such compensation that places the affected party in 'the position it would have been if the contract had been properly performed'. No doubt, this is not the same as restitution. Just like the PICC, the aggrieved/affected party's right to damages is limited where it failed to mitigate harm or partly contributed to the harm.[43] It is not clear why the drafters of the Regulations omitted articles 7.4.2(2) and 7.4.3–7.4.4 of the PICC, but the wording of article 100 of the Regulations effectively renders this question moot. Given the QFC Court's practice in respect of other Regulations, it is not at all clear whether the Regulations recognise, or not, physical suffering and emotional distress as a loss that is susceptible to damages.[44]

The provisions on interest and the manner of payment in the Regulations[45] correspond almost verbatim with their counterparts in the PICC.[46] This is important in order to dispel any doubts as to whether the QFC Court – or other courts and tribunals applying the Regulations – are empowered to award interest. The QFC Court possesses discretion to award pre-judgment interest by taking into account all relevant circumstances. It has held that:

> Interest is generally awarded to compensate a party for being kept out of money rather than for damage done, such as alleged lost investment opportunities, or to punish or to call the defendant to account for his use of the money. The merits of the underlying case are not relevant to the award of interest, but delay in the prosecution of that case may well be.[47]

---

[42] Art 7.4.2(1) PICC.
[43] Arts 102 and 103 Regulations.
[44] In *Khaled Hassan Bahr Ahmed v Doha Bank Assurance Co LLC*, (n 21) at 12, the QFC Court awarded damages to an employee for 'worry and anxiety' arising from the breach of its contract by the employer. In the case at hand, the QFC Court did make reference to the Contract Regulations, in conjunction with applicable labour law, and did not specifically explain the legal basis of such damages. Hence, it may reasonably be adduced that where the Court applies the Contract Regulations in employment cases non-pecuniary damages may be awarded.
[45] Arts 104–106 Regulations.
[46] Arts 7.4.9–7.4.13 PICC.
[47] *Dentons and Co (QFC Branch) v Bin Omran Trading and Consulting LLC*, [2020] QIC (F) 15, para 13.

In applying such discretion, the QFC Court will not uphold contractually agreed rates of interest, if these are found to be excessive and hence not 'in the interests of justice',[48] or are otherwise higher than the interest rates applicable in Qatar.[49]

Article 107 of the Regulations makes a significant innovation that is prevalent in the common law, as indeed the practice of transnational commercial contracts,[50] by allowing the parties to agree in advance in their contract to the so-called liquidated damages. Article 107(1) stipulates that:

> Where the contract provides that a party who does not perform is to pay a specified sum to the aggrieved party for such non-performance, the aggrieved party is entitled to that sum irrespective of its actual harm.

Paragraph 2 of article 107 of the Regulations, in concert with practice limiting the parties' ability to impose any sum in respect of liquidated damages, stops short of penalty-style or grossly excessive liquidated damages. It goes on to say that:

> However, notwithstanding any agreement to the contrary, the specified sum may be reduced to a reasonable amount where it is grossly excessive in relation to the harm resulting from the non- performance and to the other circumstances.

13.5.7.1 Limitation Periods for Damage Claims

Articles 108 and 109 of the Regulations are oddly placed in the Part dealing with remedies (Part 11). The same principles are regulated in a distinct chapter in the PICC (Chapter 11). The Regulations do not discuss limitations in general, but only in respect of damages. Given the importance of limitations in both civil codes and the common law, it is slightly puzzling why the drafters of the Regulations thought this was a good idea. The only reasonable explanation seems to be that the forward-thinking rationale of the Regulations had little place for an extensive set of limitations, which prudent commercial parties can dispense with. Article 108(1) of the Regulations posits the rule that an action for breach of any contract must be commenced within six years[51] after

---

[48] Ibid, para 17.
[49] Ibid, para 17 and *Badri and Salim Elmeouchi LLP v Data Managers International Limited* [2020] QIC (F) 3.
[50] See, for example, *English Hop Growers v Dering*, (1928) 2 KB 174, CA; s 2–718(1) US Uniform Commercial Code; Art 1226 French CC.
[51] The general limitation period in Art 10.2 PICC is three years, or exceptionally a maximum of ten years from the day the right can be exercised.

the cause of action has accrued.[52] This is not a mandatory limitation period and the parties may validly agree to reduce the period of limitation to not less than one year[53] but they are not allowed to extend it.[54]

In *Nasco Qatar LLC v Misr Insurance (Qatar Branch)*, the broker had set up a single account with the insurer on the basis of which all referral fees would be paid as agreed in the claimant's bank account. The respondent claimed that the limitation period prescribed in article 108 of the Regulations commenced from the date of the last payment for each referral, with each referral constituting a distinct contract subject to distinct limitation periods. The QFC Court disagreed. While agreeing that the Contract Regulations did not expressly provide for running accounts in the context of limitation, nor indeed in most statutes such as the English Limitation Act, even so, the courts in England had made such distinction. In particular, the QFC Court referred to English authority, according to which where a customer has a current account with a bank, a cause of action does not accrue to the customer until a demand for payment is made on the bank.[55] Exceptionally, it may accrue earlier if in the meantime the business relationship comes to an end.[56] The QFC Court went on to emphasise that

> For the purposes of Article 108 [of the QFC Contract Regulations] the relevant starting date for any limitation period is the date of the relative breach. Where a claim is made with respect to a sum said to be due under a contract, the date of the breach is not necessarily the date when the claimant became 'entitled' to the sum in question but may be the (possibly later) date when the creditor failed or declined, expressly or implicitly, to make payment.[57]

The Court subsequently noted that under the terms of the single running account (contract) in question, the proper inference is that a breach of

[52] The QFC Court in *Nasco Qatar LLC v Misr Insurance (Qatar Branch)* (n 23), para 23, made a useful distinction between actions arising from breach and those predicated on a simple claim for payment under the contract. It held that Art 108 of the Regulations did not apply to the latter.

[53] Consistent with Art 10.3(2)(a) PICC.

[54] Art 108(2) Regulations explains that a cause of action occurs when the breach occurs, regardless of the aggrieved party's lack of knowledge of the breach.

[55] *Nasco Qatar v Misr Insurance* (n 23), para 28, citing with approval *Joachimson v Swiss Bank Corporation* [1921] 3 KB 110, cited with approval by Lord Reid in *Arab Bank Ltd v Barclays Bank* [1954] A.C. 495 at 531.

[56] Ibid, citing with approval, *In re Russian and Commercial Bank* (1955) 1 Ch. 148, per Wynn-Parry, J at 157.

[57] Ibid, para 30.

contract arose only when the respondent declined to settle the outstanding balance on the single account. That event may have been when the Claimant first demanded payment and the demand was not met.[58] It was not a far leap for the Court to reject the respondent's contention that the limitation period under article 108 of the Regulations had not expired.

As regards the question as to whether the limitation period may be interrupted by a partial payment, the QFC Court referred with approval to article 29(5) of the English Limitation Act 1980, which so provides. The Court conceded that this represents good law in the absence of an express provision in the QFC Contract Regulations and referred to common law authority to this effect, noting its equitable underpinnings.[59] The QFC Court further relied on article 414 Qatari CC to that effect, which in its opinion reflected a general principle of contract law, thereby seeing no reason 'why it should not be recognised judicially as implicit in the Contract Regulations'.[60]

Article 109 of the Regulations is a verbatim reflection of article 10.9 of the PICC, according to which the expiration of the limitation period does not extinguish the right, merely its exercise against the other contracting party. The right itself may be asserted in other contexts (i.e. for tax purposes).

13.5.8 *Termination of Contracts*

Termination under articles 110–115 of the Regulations reflects articles 7.3.1 to 7.3.7 of the PICC, save that the restitution provisions in the PICC are significantly more elaborate than article 115 of the Regulations.

13.5.9 *Transfer of Rights and Obligations*

Articles 116–129 of the Regulations concerning assignment (transfer of a right) constitute a verbatim iteration of articles 9.1.1 to 9.1.15 of PICC. There is a slight variation in the Regulations regarding the assignment of future rights, which the Regulations (following mandatory Islamic law principles)[61] reject in the first instance, but ultimately seem to accept once the right comes into existence.[62]

---

[58] Ibid, para 31.
[59] Ibid, para 33, citing with approval *Surrendra Overseas Ltd v Government of Sri Lanka* [1977] 2 All ER 481, per Kerr J at 487.
[60] Ibid, para 33.
[61] See E Injadat, 'Futures and Forwards Contracts from the Perspective of Islamic Law' (2014) 1 Journal of Economics and Political Economy 241.
[62] Art 119 Regulations.

The transfer of an obligation (novation) is regulated in articles 131 to 134 of the Regulations, which correspond to articles 9.2.1 to 9.2.8 of the PICC, albeit the PICC is a lot more elaborate.

13.5.10 *Third-Party Rights*

These are regulated in articles 135–138 of the Regulations, corresponding to articles 5.2.1 to 5.26 of the PICC.

Index

Milton Keynes UK
Ingram Content Group UK Ltd.
UKHW012327010224
437074UK00024B/327